Journeying with Joseph

Edited by Mary Cresp rsj

Series Editors: Josephite Editorial Committee

The Josephite Series offers contributions on various aspects of:

Theology and spirituality
Historical perspectives
Cultural and life experiences and faith communities

1. *In the Land of Larks and Heroes: Australian Reflections on St Mary MacKillop*, edited by Alan Cadwallader, 2011.
2. *St Joseph's Island: Julian Tenison Woods and the Tasmanian Sisters of St Joseph,* Josephine Margaret Brady rsj, 2012.
3. *God's Good Time: The Journey of the Sisters of St Joseph of the Sacred Heart in the Ministry with Australian Aboriginal and Torres Strait Islander Peoples,* Mary Cresp rsj, 2013.
4. *Never See a Need: The Sisters of St Joseph in South Australia 1866–210,* Marie Therese Foale rsj, 2016.
5. *Mary MacKillop 1873: One Year of an Extra Ordinary Life,* Sheila McCreanor rsj, 2016.
6. *A Priceless Treasure: Sister Teresa McDonald Pioneer Sister of St Joseph 1838–1876,* Marie Crowley, 2016.
7. *Fire in the Red Land: A Two Act Play on the Life of Saint Mary of the Cross MacKillop,* Margaret Therese Cusak rsj, 2017.
8. *A Faith-Filled Family: Mary MacKillop's Sisters & Brothers,* Judith Geddes, 2017.
9. *One Door Closes Another Opens: Mary MacKillop in New South Wales 1880–1090,* Bernadette O'Sullivan rsj, 2018.
10. *Bobs the Dog,* Diane Phillips rsj, 2019.
11. *Watch Out Tommy Tantrum,* Kathleen Mooney rsj, 2019.
12. *Watch Out,* Kathleen Mooney rsj, 2020.
13. *Watch Out Worry Worm,* Kathleen Mooney rsj, 2020.
14. *Go Where the Work is Waiting: The Story of Sisters of Saint Joseph of Goulburn And The Places They Have Worked, 1882–2012,* Laraine Crowe rsj, 2021.

Journeying with Joseph

Josephite Essays for the Year of St Joseph

Edited by Mary Cresp rsj

ATF THEOLOGY

Adelaide

2021

Cover image: Stephen Todd
Cover design: Cyrilla Almeida
Copy editor and indices: Gabriel B Siqueira

ISBN: 978-1-922582-39-3 soft
978-1-922582-40-9 hard
978-1-922582-41-6 epub
978-1-922582-42-3 pdf

Published and edited by

Making a lasting impact

An imprint of the ATF Press Publishing Group
owned by ATF (Australia) Ltd.
PO Box 234
Brompton, SA 5007
Australia
ABN 90 116 359 963
www.atfpress.com

Table of Contents

Indices

Credits and Abbreviations

Painting of St Joseph by **Steve Todd,** 'In St Joseph's Care', presented to the Sisters of St Joseph of the Sacred Heart by the artist, with the original painting hanging at 9 Mount St North Sydney. The painting is used with the artist's permission in this book.

This publication is jointly sponsored by
Sisters of St Joseph, Lochinvar and
Sisters of Saint Joseph of the Sacred Heart

Josephite Companions (formerly called 'Associates') are people who identify with the Spirit of St Mary MacKillop and Julian Tenison Woods and commit themselves to living that spirit in the circumstances of their lives, in informal relationship with the Sisters of St Joseph and supporting each other in furthering the reign of God through friendship, prayer and service. Josephite Companions are drawn from all walks of life.

Covenant Josephites (women and men) express their baptismal consecration in affiliation with the Sisters of St Joseph through participating with them in community and mission according to their lay situation in life. After a period of guided discernment, they draw up an affiliation agreement and commit to ongoing formation and personal growth in ministry while remaining self-supporting and living independently.

Abbreviations

CSJ	Congregation of St Joseph (Sisters of St Joseph)
CSSJ	Congregations of Sisters of St Joseph
RPA	Sisters of Perpetual Adoration, Brisbane
RSJ	Religious of St Joseph (Sisters of St Joseph)
SJC	Sisters of St Joseph of Cluny
SJCA	St Joseph's Congregational Archives, North Sydney
SSJLA	Sisters of St Joseph Lochinvar Archives, Lochinvar

Foreword

'Joseph went from the town of Nazareth in Galilee to Judea, to the city of David called Bethlehem because he was descended from the house of David' (Lk 2:4). And so begins a story of the symbolism of journey in the life of Joseph and those who in their daily lives continue to journey with Joseph's wisdom and humility.

The infancy narratives of the Gospels are full of stories of Joseph on the journey. One finds Joseph setting out on an arduous journey from Nazareth to Bethlehem with his pregnant wife Mary following the decree of Emperor Augustus to register in their own towns. This begins for Joseph a life of entering the unknown, of taking risks in new and strange encounters and situations and of letting no obstacles deter him from acting with courage when this was what required of him. As you read the many and varied reflections on the life of Joseph contained in this book you will meet Joseph the man of justice, humility, obedience, courage, tenderness and silence.

The reader will engage with Joseph, the man who inspired the founding of different groups of Sisters of Saint Joseph around the world. In particular, Fr Julian Tenison Woods and Saint Mary MacKillop found in Joseph one to whom they could entrust the institute they co-founded, placing it under his protection. 'On the 19 March 1866 Saint Joseph was first honoured as Patron of little children and the work of the Sisters of Saint Joseph committed to his care' (Mary MacKillop: *Letter to the Sisters 4 March 1891).* Julian Tenison Woods encouraged the Sisters to live with humility, simplicity and trust in the Providence of God like Joseph their Patron. Mary MacKillop speaks of Joseph's obedience, generosity and protection in the time of difficulty: 'In every difficulty apply to Joseph with confidence and you will never be disappointed' (*Mary MacKillop: Letter to the Sisters, 9 March 1906*).

Statue presented to Mary MacKillop by Pius 1X during her visit to Rome in 1873 and following the declaration of St Joseph as Patron of the Universal Church.

With gratitude to the authors of these reflections you will meet beneath their words Joseph the vulnerable one who will inspire you to be a hopeful, tender and courageous presence in our world. You will encounter his fatherly protection as well as his capacity for deep listening, risk-taking, educating and working. You will experience how his life has influenced the faith in different cultural contexts. You will hear the call to be audacious like Joseph willing to step out and move beyond the familiar as you navigate the journey to the Bethlehems, Egypts and Nazareths of your life. The call to be creatively courageous was his at each phase of the journey. May you, like Joseph, have the determination to choose life and to follow your dreams at each crossroad.

Inspired by these writings, may all who read these reflections continue to walk in the footsteps of Joseph the Patron of the Church Universal.

Sr Monica Cavanagh rsj
Congregational Leader
Sisters of St Joseph of the Sacred Heart.

Introduction

When we were children we were encouraged by our teachers to contribute to a 'Spiritual Bouquet' which would then be gifted to special dignitaries visiting our school. So written in beautiful calligraphy on parchment and presented to a Bishop or Mother-General would be a list of prayers such as '100 Masses, 45 Rosaries, 20 Litanies' and so on.

This practice of former years might be passé, but we could describe this collection of essays as a new form of 'Spiritual Bouquet' in honour of Saint Joseph. A flowering of spiritual reflection and scholarship, the essay topics join the first item on the list—the Apostolic Letter of Pope Francis, *Patris Corde*, written to mark the Year of Saint Joseph. Pope Francis gives us the lead in reflecting on what Saint Joseph has meant to the Church in its journey of faith throughout its history. He notes the virtues and qualities that inspire and give courage. He recognises Saint Joseph as a privileged respondent to God's call in the unfolding of the Good News of salvation.

The shape of this volume of essays is similar to the model given by Pope Francis by taking up the three aspects of our appreciation of Joseph: his significance, guidance and impact.

1. In the section dealing with *Joseph's Foundational Inspiration*, we recall the place Joseph held in the accomplishment of God's mission as described in Scripture and Tradition and in the founding of two Congregations of Sisters of St Joseph. During the tumultuous years following the thirty-years' religious and dynastic war in Europe (1618–1648), a group of women guided by the Jesuit Jean-Pierre Médaille in Le Puy, France, gathered in Saint Joseph's name to minister with the ordinary people in

their daily struggles. In 1853, an English student Julian Woods was impressed by these Sisters of St Joseph, and on coming to Australia and being ordained a priest, co-founded with Mary MacKillop the Sisters of St Joseph of the Sacred Heart according to the spirit he had observed in France.

2. *Joseph's Radiant Influence* is traced in the experience of those who minister in the world of today. They have learnt what Pope Francis tells us of Joseph:

   > Joseph, then, teaches us that faith in God includes believing that he can work even through our fears, our frailties and our weaknesses. He also teaches us that amid the tempests of life, we must never be afraid to let the Lord steer our course.[1]

3. The third section, *Joseph's Cultural Outreach*, reflects on Saint Joseph's presence in a selection of the cultures which make up the Josephite family—Asia, Australia, Aotearoa New Zealand, the Pacific, South America, Timor Leste. The authors illustrate their understanding of the explanation given in *Evangelii Nuntiandi:* 'evangelising means bringing the Good News into all the strata of humanity, and through its influence transforming humanity from within and making it new.'[2] As for the universal church, Saint Joseph has become not only patron but is also identified within these different cultures as type and model of the Christian life.

It is my sincere hope that this work will be of value to readers who are looking for 'enrichment of soul' through articles that are theologically sound, spiritually healthy and historically informative. I thank all contributors who generously gave of their time and scholarship under the pressure of time, since the request for this book came only a few days before Christmas 2020. To Cyrilla Almeida who assisted in the cover-design and to the readers who cross-checked the editing of essays and made comments I owe special thanks—Dr Henry Abramovitch, Sr Laraine Crowe rsj, Dr Janice Garaty, Dr David Hilliard OAM, Dr Lesley Hughes, Sr Carmel Jones rsj, Professor Anne O'Brien, Sr Dianne Phillips rsj, Sr Gen Ryan rsj, Sr Marie White

1. Pope Francis, *Patris Corde* paragraph 2.
2. Pope Paul VI, *Evangelii Nuntiandi*, paragraph 18.

rsj. Thanks, too, to ATF Press Publishing Group publisher Hilary D Regan for his initiative in suggesting that the book be produced and to Gabriel B Siqueira, also of ATF Press, for the copy editing and the index. Together we have plucked from our garden a bouquet that will, I hope, continue to resource families, teachers and ordinary disciples as we join the whole church during this jubilee year in honouring God's favoured one, Saint Joseph.

Mary Cresp, rsj
Adelaide, South Australia
19th of March 2021

Contributors

Marcia Allen is a Sister of St Joseph of Concordia, Kansas USA. Formerly the president of her Congregation and the National Leadership Conference of Women Religious in the USA, she is a staff member of the Manna House of Prayer, a spiritual companion, retreat and conference leader. She has a BA in French and History and a DMin in Spirituality.

Virginia Bourke is a Sister of St Joseph currently living in country New South Wales. She worked in Secondary schools and later in the ministry of Adult Faith Formation in the Maitland-Newcastle Diocese as a resource person in Sacramental ministry, supporting parishes in preparing parents to prepare children within Initiation processes. She has served the ongoing mission of Religious across Australia as facilitator and in Congregational leadership, and now ministers in the areas of general spirituality and the giving of retreats.

Jo Brady is a Sister of St Joseph with many years' experience as a teacher and principal in Tasmanian Catholic schools. She was a senior lecturer at Australian Catholic University in secondary teacher education and foundation Vice Rector at the Jesuit Secondary Teachers' College (ISJB) in Timor Leste. Jo was Head of Mission at Caritas Australia and is currently working for the Plenary Council.

Betty Brown is a Sister of St Joseph of Lochinvar. She taught Infant classes in Maitland-Newcastle, Sydney and Townsville, and served as a Primary School Principal. Appointed Library Consultant at the Catholic Schools Office in Newcastle, she was recipient of the

School Library Association of NSW John Hirst Award for 2003. She established Penola House at Hamilton and later at Mayfield to provide pastoral care to refugees from war torn countries in Africa.

Susan Connelly is a Sister of St Joseph who taught in Catholic and State schools during her ministry in education. She has been involved with the Timorese people since 1994, and is now connected with efforts towards justice in relation to the Australian spying on Timor-Leste. Her forthcoming book to be published by Bloomsbury is *East Timor, René Girard and Neo-colonial Violence: Scapegoating as Australian Policy*.

Michele A Connolly is a Sister of St Joseph of Lochinvar in the Hunter Valley, New South Wales. She is an Associate Professor of Biblical Studies at the Sydney College of Divinity and lectures in Biblical Studies at Catholic Institute of Sydney. In 2018 her doctoral thesis was published by T&T Clark under the title, *Disorderly Women and the Order of God: An Australian Feminist Reading of the Gospel of Mark*.

Mary Cresp is a Sister of St Joseph born in Berri, South Australia. Her ministries have involved her in teaching and pastoral work, leadership for the Congregation and other groups of Religious, ecumenical dialogue, associations of Spiritual Directors, formation of staffs, theological reflection, facilitation and refugee assistance. She has produced a number of books and articles on Spirituality, Theology and Religious History. Her main focus at present is on writing and accompaniment in Spiritual Direction.

Getrudes Da Silva is a Covenant Josephite and Companion, having begun her Josephite journey of commitment in 2013. For eleven years she worked with 'Mary MacKillop Today' on the *Tetun* Literacy Teacher Training Program. She also served as an Early Childhood Music Teacher. She is currently working with Caritas Australia, responsible for Shelters for Victims of Gender-Based Violence and Safeguarding. The spiritual companionship of Saint Mary MacKillop and the friendship of Sisters of St Joseph nourish her Josephite vocation.

Michele Fairbairn, Covenant Josephite, is a naturopath, manual therapist, and transpersonal psychotherapist on the pathway towards registration as a psychologist. Her passion for story-telling and freelance work as a playwright, multimedia artist, and writer, have resulted in produced plays, exhibitions, artist residencies, published short stories and articles.

Nola Goodwin is a Sister of St Joseph. Born in outback Queensland, she has spent most of her life ministering in education in isolated areas. These areas include outback Queensland and Aboriginal communities in the Kimberley, Western Australia and in the Norther Territory. She has also worked in Timor Leste.

Trish Hindmarsh, a retired teacher and educational leader, has worked in Catholic Education in Victoria, New South Wales, Western Australia and Tasmania. She is a member of the Catholic Earthcare Australia Advisory Committee. Present involvements include mentoring and staff formation in Catholic Social Teaching and ecological awareness, and volunteering and engagement with a number of charitable bodies, reform church groups and preparation for the Plenary Council. Grand-parenting and family are constant joys and top priorities.

Sue and Leo Kane are Josephite Companions, whose ministry has included leadership roles in Catholic education. Their focus in recent times has been on spirituality, with an emphasis on Josephite spirituality, as reflected in the four books they have published—*The Little Brown Book, The Little Brown Book Too, The Pocket Contemplative* and *A Daily Cuppa with Mary and Julian.* They enjoy being grandparents.

Lusiana Matai is a Sister of St Joseph of Cluny, living in Suva, Fiji. She has taught in schools in Fiji and the Cook Islands, and is currently Formator for the Sisters of St Joseph of Cluny in the Province of New Zealand and the Philippines.

Catherine Mead is a Sister of St Joseph ministering in Catholic education as a teacher and Principal in South Australia for more than thirty years. Catherine is currently serving in the role of Leader of Catholic Identity in Catholic Education Northern Territory. She was awarded a Doctorate of Education through Notre Dame University Fremantle, Western Australia, on completion of her thesis 'Educational Leadership in the Josephite Tradition'.

Jenny Mori León is Sister of St Joseph from Peru. Having been engaged in education in a number of schools, she now teaches ethics in Antonio Ruiz de Montoya, a Jesuit university in Lima, Peru. She is also in charge of the Pastoral Care office there, and is a tutor of several groups of students.

Carmel Pilcher is a Sister of St Joseph originally from Australia but now serving as lecturer in liturgy and sacraments at the Pacific Regional Seminary in Suva Fiji. Carmel has extensive experience as a liturgical consultant and educator in many dioceses throughout Australia. Her studies include an MA in Religious Education from the Catholic University in Washington DC, and a PhD in Sacramental Theology from the Flinders University of South Australia. Carmel's particular interest is liturgical inculturation, particularly amongst indigenous peoples.

Susan Pollard is a Sister of St Joseph whose psycho-analytical practice, theological and educational administration background have been enriched by living and working in Australia, Africa and Europe. From 1991 to 2000, Susan completed her analytical training at the CG Jung Institute, Zurich and also her Doctorate in Psychoanalysis at the Union Institute & University, Cincinnati. Susan, a Training Analyst with the Australian and New Zealand Society of Jungian Analysts (ANZSJA) and registered Clinical Psychologist, is in private practice.

Makareta Tawaroa, a Sister of St Joseph, helps promote cultural understandings through the celebration of Maori Mass in her European parish; through tutoring Social Analysis in the Maori community and concerning Maori migration; co-ordinating religious knowledge at Hui Aranga, (Easter Festival); and promoting Maori understandings of Te Taiao (Environment) and of racism from a Maori lens. She was formerly the editor of Mana Tangata Maori newspaper and is trustee of a local Maori bank. Currently involved in the local school and garden, she is writing a short history of the Catholic community, but is focussed mainly on being a good 'nan' to many mokopuna.

Jan Tranter is a Sister of St Joseph of Lochinvar. She taught in Josephite Secondary Schools, then gained her MA on a study of the early history of her congregation. This thesis won her the Newcastle City Council 1988 Local History Award. Jan has several published articles on Josephite history, Irish Josephites and Father Julian Tenison Woods. She is a current member of the Conference of Josephite Leaders History Committee.

Rose Vu is a Sister of St Joseph, her original background being Vietnamese. She arrived in Australia as an international student, later became an educator for twelve years in a Catholic secondary school, and was then involved in Pastoral Care and as Sacristan at St Joseph's Aged Care Hostel, Hunters Hill, Sydney. She currently works in the Congregational Archives, North Sydney.

Part 1

Joseph's Foundational Inspiration

Matthew's Joseph: A Man of God for Jesus

Michele A Connolly rsj

Introduction

'Joseph, the husband of Mary of whom was Jesus was born, who is called the Messiah' (Matt 1:16). With this description, the Gospel of Matthew introduces us to the figure of Joseph. Joseph figures strongly in the first two chapters of this Gospel, his name being mentioned nine times in all. In contrast to the Infancy Narrative of the Gospel of Luke in which the focus is on Mary, in Matthew Joseph is the one to whom an angel speaks and who shows us how to hear and respond to the word of God.

Much of what the Christian community has come to revere about Joseph is told in these two opening chapters of Matthew. Benedicta Ward writes that among the early Christians, there was a form of 'spontaneous respect for those most closely associated with Christ in his earthly life . . . [and veneration] . . . for their participation in the life of Christ'.[1] These people were called Saints from very early times. St Joseph as the Gospel of Matthew portrays him is a man who was very closely associated with Jesus but who did much more than simply participate in his life. In the Jewish culture of his day, Joseph gave Jesus a respectable identity in a settled family, and through his descent from King David, the potential to be seen as Judaism's long-awaited Messiah. More than that, Joseph ensured that Jesus survived the terrors of life in a world of violent politics and settled him in a safe place to grow to maturity.

1. Benedicta Ward, 'Saints, Cult of', in *A New Dictionary of Christian Theology*, edited by Alan Richardson and John Stephen Bowden (London: SCM Press, 2002), 518.

Although it is not said plainly, the gospel narrative assumes that Jesus grew up under the fatherly guidance of Joseph. Joseph is portrayed as a conscientious Jewish man, attentive and obedient to the directions of God in his life, ready to do whatever was necessary to enable the intention of God insofar as he understood it, to be realised. The narrative dynamics of the gospel make it natural to see Jesus as a man shaped by Joseph, having learned from him not only a trade but also how to attend to the ways of God and to live with integrity, courageous in the midst of life's turmoil, with respect and compassion for others.

In order to see how Matthew 1–2 suggests this understanding of Joseph, it is necessary as a preliminary step to consider some potential areas of misunderstanding that can rob us of what these two complex chapters have to offer. First, we need to be aware that as twenty-first century people reading this ancient text, we have to make every effort to read the text in the way it tries to communicate with its audience. This may not be according to values we hold today about how narratives should deal with historical persons and events. Second, we need to recognise that our scientific, technology-focused worldview may understand reality in very different ways from the people of Jesus' day. From these two points, a number of consequences flow that will enable us to read Matthew 1–2 in a fruitful way, so as to be spiritually enriched by the figure of Joseph.

Preliminary Clarifications

Dei Verbum (DV), the Dogmatic Constitution on Divine Revelation of Vatican II, explains in paragraph 12 that the Scriptures consist of many different styles of writing which we must respect in order to interpret them fruitfully. It is worth citing some of DV 12, with apologies for the sexist language:

> Seeing that, in sacred Scripture, God speaks through men in human fashion, it follows that the interpreter of sacred Scriptures, if he is to ascertain what God has wished to communicate to us, should carefully search out the meaning which the sacred writers really had in mind . . . In determining the intention of the sacred writers, attention must be paid, *inter alia*, to 'literary forms' for the fact is that truth is differently presented and expressed in the various types of

> historical writing . . . Hence the exegete must look for that meaning which the sacred writer, in a determined situation and given the circumstances of his time and culture, intended to express and did in fact express, through the medium of a contemporary literary form.[2]

To glean what we can about Joseph from the Gospel of Matthew, we have to work with Matthew's intentions and chosen genre of writing, within his historical context. This may expose a clash between us and the worldview, cultural practices and literary practice of the ancient people of the Mediterranean.

First, there is the genre of writing that Matthew 1 – 2 is. Because it is about historical persons and events, we modern people tend to think that it will be like a contemporary biography of a famous person. We expect such a biography to give an absolutely verifiable, rational interpretation of a person's life and achievements. It should be based on exhaustive factual research, with every claim that is made about any person supported by detailed, accurate reference to source material that others can check.

The Gospel of Matthew reads like a biography but it is the genre of ancient biography, profoundly shaped by the belief that its subject, Jesus, is the Son of God raised from the dead. Each New Testament gospel is written primarily to express this belief. They intend to show that in Jesus, God has acted definitively in the world to restore the entire world to reconciled relationship with God. Thus, while the gospels use the style of the ancient genre of historical biography they reshape it to this new, theological purpose. The gospels are thus primarily theological statements, narrating the life, death and resurrection of Jesus in history to make God's action in the world luminously clear to us.

Second, when it comes to narrating the origins of Jesus, we moderns tend to think that Matthew is reporting facts that are verifiable from official documents, such as a Register of Births. But Matthew is writing to the expectations of his time about how to write about the origins of a famous person. Studies of ancient Greek and Roman education curricula show that students were taught to write

2. *Dei Verbum* 12, in *Vatican Council II: The Conciliar and Post Conciliar Documents*, edited by Austin Flannery (Northport, NY: Costello, 1992), 757–758.

in certain ways on the topic of the birth of a famous person.[3] They were to comment on any signs that the child born was favoured by God or the gods. These signs could appear 'on land or in the heavens or on the sea', or in such things as dreams.[4] Warren Carter explains that as well as noting divine favour, 'It was customary in Matthew's world to define an elite hero by associating him with prestigious and virtuous (usually male) ancestors who had wealth, power, and status'.[5]

Third, we would find it helpful if Mary and Joseph were developed as fully fleshed-out characters. To achieve this something of their internal processes, their inner thoughts, feelings and decisions would need to be shown. In a narrative, this inner world is revealed most effectively by the character speaking or expressing himself or herself in private situations. In Matthew 1 – 2, neither Joseph nor Mary ever speaks. It is the narrator who tells us something of Joseph's private decision about Mary, when her pregnancy is discovered (Matt 1:18–19). We may draw a great deal from this, but in Matthew's Gospel it primarily serves the purpose of showing that Joseph only turns away from an honourable course of action because of God's intervention through the message of an angel in a dream. It is really all about providing a way of seeing God, from Abraham onwards, acting in the world to fulfil God's promises.

Fourth, there can be major differences between the way the people of Jesus' time and the way we today in our scientific, technology-focused world understand basic realities. We naturally tend to think that when Matthew writes about 'how the birth of Jesus the Messiah took place' (Matt 1:18) he must be writing against the background of contemporary science, which knows that conception of a male child requires not only twenty-three chromosomes from each parent, but also a Y chromosome from the male parent.

However, Matthew was operating with first century CE biology, not ours. In his world it was believed that God could act in bringing about conception—indeed that if God was acting, a male parent was

3. We must remember that the Gospels were written in everyday (*koiné*) Greek of the first century CE, both by and for people shaped by ancient Greco-Roman culture.

4. Bryan A Nash, 'Birth Stories in the Synoptics', in *Restoration Quarterly*, 56/3 (2014): 167.

5. Warren Carter, 'Matthew 1–2 and Roman Political Power', in *New Perspectives on the Nativity*, edited by Jeremy Corley (London: T&T Clark, 2009), 77.

not strictly necessary. Based on a study of ancient biological theory that prevailed well into the medieval period, Andrew Lincoln explains that ancient writings both Greek and Jewish 'assume the dominant biological understanding that the male seed is implanted in the womb and gives life to the blood, the substance contributed by the mother'.[6] On this basis, it was possible for ancient people to see that in Jesus' conception, 'His mother, Mary, provided his human substance and . . . God, through the agency of the divine Spirit, supplied the animating principle instead of a human father'.[7]

This expresses a worldview that we cannot share; it does not account for Jesus' birth in terms of modern reproductive biology. However, we do not read Matthew to learn science. If we wish to read Matthew for its theological and spiritual message to us, we have to come to terms with the fact that he is operating with a different biological theory than ours. Having recognised the worldview that informed Matthew, we have to ask what Matthew meant by the way he wrote the story of Jesus' origins.

Navigating these challenges to interpretation, we will be able to read Matthew 1–2 more clearly for what it seeks to communicate to us. Thus, we can read in sympathy with the Scripture rather than at cross purposes to it, perhaps influenced more by piety or art than by the word of God.

Matthew's Structures: Clues to Interpretation

Matthew offers many clues to interpreting his meaning. These clues lie in the way he structures the first two chapters of his gospel and in specific statements he makes. Nearly all Matthean scholars agree that the structure of these two chapters consists of four clearly distinguished sections, namely:

1. the genealogy of Jesus (1:1–18),
2. the conception and birth of Jesus (1:81–25),
3. the political terror instituted against Jesus by King Herod (2:1–21) and

6. Andrew Lincoln, 'How Babies Were Made in Jesus' Time', in *Biblical Archaeology Review,* 40/6 (November 2014): 44–45.
7. Lincoln, 'How Babies Were Made in Jesus' Time', 45.

4. the migrations of Joseph, Mary and their infant child from Bethlehem to Egypt and finally back to Israel, to the northern town of Nazareth (2:13–23).[8]

Matthew is a very organised writer: he signals clearly at the beginning of each of these four sections what he is going to tell us. The first two signals point strongly to his theological meaning. Matthew 1:1 opens the gospel with the forthright description, 'an account of the genealogy of Jesus the Messiah'; the next section opens with 'Now the birth of Jesus the Messiah took place in this way' (Matt 1:18). The final two sections, at 2:1 and 2:13, refer to moments in human history that determined what Joseph had to do in order to preserve and foster the life of Jesus.

While the later three sections are narratives, the opening pericope of the gospel is another genre, that of the genealogy or list of the generations that preceded Jesus. This genre looks back to the book of Genesis where similar lists, called '*toledoth*' in Hebrew, named the ancestors of the Jewish people, going back to Adam and including Abraham, Isaac and Jacob (see, for example, Gen 5:1; 11:27; 25:19 and 37:2). In opening his gospel with a similar list, using the Greek word '*geneseōs*' which translates '*toledoth*', Matthew suggests that Jesus' human ancestry is utterly grounded in the Jewish people, starting from Abraham with whom God made the great covenant to bless all people.[9] Joseph is the necessary means for this to be achieved.

A further structure built into this sequence of pericopes is historical, with a focus on the theological meaning of these persons and events. The genealogy situates Jesus within the entire history of God's relationship with the Jewish people; the other three narratives situate Jesus in his own time and place, the eastern Mediterranean dominated by the ascendant Roman Empire. Matthew shows that in Jesus, God is acting in human life, in a specific place and time, bringing God's promises of blessing to all the nations to their fulfillment. Only with the collaboration of Joseph can this happen.

---

8. See for example, the structure of the Matthean Infancy Narrative provided in William David Davies, *A Critical and Exegetical Commentary on the Gospel According to Saint Matthew,* Volume I (Edinburgh: T&T Clark, 1988), xiii; Craig A Evans, *Matthew* (New York, NY: Cambridge University Press, 2012), vii; Daniel Harrington, *The Gospel of Matthew* (Collegeville MN: Liturgical Press, 2007), v.
9. Craig A Evans, *Matthew,* 31–39 discusses this structure and many more within Matt 1:1–7 that cannot be treated here.

Finally, Matthew uses a number of ways to build these two chapters around the word of God. The most obvious way is his formulaic use of quotations from the Hebrew Scriptures. That is, in the three sections other than the genealogy, Matthew introduces a quotation from the Hebrew Scriptures with this or a similar expression, 'This was to fulfil what had been spoken by the Lord through the prophet.' The genealogy is built on references to many books of the Hebrew Scriptures. The other way in which the word of God is present in Matthew 1–2 is through an angelic messenger who brings God's present, living word into the world, to Joseph, who obeys this word, collaborating with God in the work of salvation. Thus, Matthew tells the story of Jesus' ancestry, conception and early growth under the care of Joseph through God's own word, both from the past in the Scriptures of Israel and in the present through God's messenger delivering God's word to Joseph.

These structures combine to make it clear that Matthew is writing a theologically oriented account of the ancestry and birth of Jesus, the Messiah. That is, he sees the birth of Jesus as fulfilling the religious history of Israel as well as speaking to the history of the time of Jesus, dominated by the Roman Empire. Matthew presents Jesus as the Messiah of Israel who realises God's promise to Abraham that he will be a cause of blessing to all peoples (Gen 12:1–3). For Matthew, Joseph and Mary matter insofar as they enable God's will to be achieved. They do this by collaborating with God's intention, acting in the world at times with great bravery, enduring hardship and risk. In each of these stories Joseph contributes something significant to the identity, survival and maturation of Jesus. To see how Mathew conveys his theology we will read each of these pericopes in turn, taking note of the interpretive difficulties explained above, alert to Matthew's intention and focusing particularly on Joseph.

Joseph in Matthew 1–2: Fair-minded, Compassionate, Deeply Thoughtful, a Man of Resolve

When Joseph is introduced as a person in Matthew 1:19–20, the narrator describes him for us with three words in Greek that show the depth of the man. First, Joseph is called δίκαιος (*dikaios*), usually translated 'righteous.' A broader range of meaning includes 'Upright, honest, good and fair'.[10] These words describe a human being rather than a mere stickler for the law. Similarly, Joseph's decision to avoid socially shaming Mary with a public divorce is named with the verb 'ἐβουληθη' (*eboulēthē*), which at root means 'to desire to have or experience something, with the implication of some reasoned planning or will to accomplish the goal.'[11] A further word, 'ἐνθυμηθέντος' (*enthumēthentos*), usually translated 'resolved', means 'to process information by giving consideration to various aspects'.[12] This word contains in it the Greek word 'θυμος' which contains the ancient idea of mind, heart and will working together as the seat of emotion-fused thinking. All of this suggests a fair-minded, emotional and perceptive person, processing in all aspects of his consciousness, how to respond to the news of Mary's strange pregnancy. It is this man we see emerge as we read Matthew 1 – 2.

Reading Matthew 1 – 2

a. Matthew 1:1–17

In this pericope, Matthew's major point is that Jesus is descended from Abraham, through the great ancestral figures of Judaism but above all, through King David, son of Jesse. Matthew 1:1 lists in this order, Jesus, David, and Abraham. He then unpacks the links between these three by beginning with the most ancient, Abraham, and working forward through David to Jesus. A rhetorically powerful list of male names, interrupted by the names of five unconventional women without whom David himself could not have been born, names Joseph in verse 16. Unlike the more than forty fathers of Israel named before him, Joseph is described not as fathering a child but as being 'the husband of Mary of whom Jesus was born, who is called the Messiah' (1:16).

---

10. See *A Greek-English Lexicon of the New Testament and Other Early Christian Literature: A Translation and Adaptation of the Fourth Revised and Augmented Edition of Walter Bauer's Griechisch-Deutsches Wörterbuch Zu Den Schriften Des Neuen Testaments Und Der Übrigen Urchristlichen Literatur,* edited by Walter Bauer, William F Arndt, Frederick W Danker and F Wilbur Gingrich (Chicago: University of Chicago Press, 1979), see 'δίκαιος'.
11. See *Greek-English Lexicon of the New Testament: Based on Semantic Domains,* edited Johannes P Louw and Eugene A Nida (New York: United Bible Societies, 1989), see 25.3, 'βουλομαι'.
12. Louw and Nida, *Greek-English Lexicon*, see 30.1, 'ἐνθυμεομαι'.

The most important point for Matthew is that because Joseph is shown to be a descendant of David, so also is Jesus. This fact matters because David, the anointed King of Israel, was the first 'messiah'.[13] Israel believed that God had promised that David's anointed royal house would last forever (see 2 Sam 7:1–17, especially verses 12–16). However, David's line had been exterminated during the time known as the Exile in the early sixth century, BCE. From that time, instructed by Isaiah the prophet's promise, 'A shoot shall come out from the stump of Jesse, and a branch shall grow out of his roots' (Isa 11:1), the Jewish people had hoped for God to restore David's kingly, messianic line. Matthew declares that Jesus, son of Joseph, son of David, is that long-awaited one, anointed for God's purposes, to bring peace and flourishing life to all peoples (Isa 11:1–16). In the Jewish worldview, this is possible because Joseph provides for Jesus, descent from David.

b. Matthew 1:18–25

This pericope begins 'Now the birth of Jesus the Messiah took place in this way' (Matt 1:18), but its task really is to account in a way satisfying to ancient minds for the significance of the way Jesus was conceived. Matthew's point is that Mary was 'with child from the Holy Spirit' which means that Jesus has unique religious significance (1:18, 20). If we can allow a worldview different to ours in biological science to speak to us about religious matters, this pericope has much to say about Jesus and about Joseph. As Bryan Nash explains, for the ancient mind, 'That Mary was with child of the Holy Spirit would certainly have been viewed as a marvelous [*sic*] occurrence', one that ranked Jesus with other famous men.[14] Another sign of Jesus' significance is that 'an angel of the Lord' comes to instruct Joseph about the cause of Mary's pregnancy and about how Joseph is to respond, particularly what he is to name the child. David Wenkel writes, 'In Second Temple Judaism, dreams were associated with royal persons and expressed God's special concern in human affairs.'[15]

There are layers of meaning to the name Joseph is to give Jesus. First, the fact that Joseph gives this child a name '. . . stresses that, while Joseph was not Jesus' actual human father, he—by naming Jesus

13. 'Messiah' is the anglicised version of the Hebrew verb that means 'anointed.'
14. Nash, 'Birth Stories in the Synoptics', 167.
15. David H Wenkel, 'The Angel of the Lord Aids the Son of David in Matthew 1–2', in *Bibliotheca Sacra*, 177/705 (January 2020): 62.

(Matt 1:21a, 25b)—adopts him as his own and thereby enables the child to inherit his Davidic lineage . . .'[16] Second, the name 'Jesus' has multiple meanings. It is a name bestowed by divine authority both from the angel of the Lord and interpreted through the words of the Prophet Isaiah, which provide a second, beautiful name for Jesus, 'Immanuel', which means 'God is with us' (1:23). The name 'Jesus' also recalls 'Joshua' which means 'the Lord saves'. Warren Carter explains, 'Putting Matt. 1:21 and 1:23 together, [Jesus'] task or commission is to manifest God's saving presence.'[17]

The one who saves is a 'saviour'. Bernard Robinson writes that 'In pagan sources . . . the term "savior" . . . was used with reference not only to the gods but also to Roman emperors such as Augustus and Vespasian.'[18] Thus, Jesus' name presents him as a challenger to the political power of the day, a ludicrously dangerous claim but one which the Gospel of Matthew argues strongly. Joseph is the one entrusted with the task of identifying Jesus with this name that is so saturated with the promise of God's saving presence among us, yet also fraught with political challenge to the dominant world power of the time, the Roman Empire. Only a strong, conscientious man could do all that Joseph does here: trust a messenger from God about the cause of Mary's pregnancy despite his own natural disquiet; put aside his decision to divorce Mary quietly to assume public responsibility for her and her child; and name the child in a way fraught with a significance which he must have feared.

c. Matthew 2:1–12

This pericope does not mention Joseph by name but he is presumed quietly present with his wife as she gives birth to Jesus (2:1, 11). Joseph as head of this family sits in the midst of a power play between two different cultures, each seeking by its own means to deal with a new power figure in their domains. King Herod, the representative of Roman Imperial Power in Palestine, has the Jewish Scriptures searched to discover the identity of a rumoured royal rival (2:2); three wise men from the East use ancient astronomy to locate this new king

16. Lincoln, 'How Babies Were Made in Jesus' Time', 49.

17. Carter, 'Matthew 1-2 and Roman Political Power', 82.

18. Bernard Peter Robinson, 'Matthew's Nativity Stories: Historical and Theological Questions for Today's Readers', in *New Perspectives on the Nativity*, edited by Jeremy Corley (London: T&T Clark, 2009), 110–131, here at 118.

whose star they have seen rising. For Matthew's original audience this star was another sign of Jesus' pre-eminence, since 'The idea of a new star or a comet heralding a birth or a death is extremely common in antiquity . . .'[19] Between Herod and the wise men there is deep political manoeuvring; it was in this context that Joseph had to keep the infant Jesus safe.

If this gospel was written around 85–90 CE as most scholars calculate, it was in the wake of a very destructive war that Rome fought in Palestine against the Jewish nation (66–70 CE), culminating in the Roman capture of Jerusalem and the destruction of the Jewish Temple in the year 70 CE. As Warren Carter sums up, '. . . Roman imperial power pervades the world of Jesus' birth, as well as the world of the folks for whom Matthew's Gospel was written, nearly a hundred years later around 90 C.E.'[20] To survive in this context, subject to the efforts of competing political agents to control Jesus, Joseph had to be wary, astute and politically adept.

d. Matthew 2:13–23

In this final pericope, Joseph takes decisive action under the direction of the angel of the Lord in a way that fulfils the Hebrew Scriptures not once but twice. First, warned about Herod's intention to kill Jesus, Joseph escapes by night with his wife and child to Egypt, the conventional refuge for people oppressed in Israel (2:12–15). Remaining there until Herod died, Joseph had to face the trials of any refugee husband and father, providing a home and living for his family in a foreign country.

Jesus' stalwart protection of his family enabled God's plan to be fulfilled as the prophet's words say, 'Out of Egypt I have called my son' (2:15). For Matthew, Hosea's words come true but saturated with new meaning, because in coming out of Egypt, Jesus is like Moses who led God's people out of slavery in Egypt into new life. This first hint of Jesus' Moses-like character will be developed later in the Gospel, for example in the Sermon on the Mount (Matt 5–7). Here we see the first glimpse of Jesus as '. . . the Israelite par excellence. He embodies Israel and recapitulates her story as he is called out of Egypt.'[21] It is

19. Robinson, 'Matthew's Nativity Stories', 122.

20. Carter, 'Matthew 1–2 and Roman Political Power', 78.

21. Wenkel, 'The Angel of the Lord', 60.

Joseph whose combined receptivity to the word of God and human intelligence in an ever-changing, dangerous world symbolically makes possible this new Exodus.

Conclusion

Vincent Pizzuto argues that Matthew's close structuring of these two chapters shows that '. . . God is properly identified as the protagonist of the narrative.'[22] The genealogy shows that through all of Jewish history, God had been preparing the lineage into which Jesus would be born as David's son, the longed-for Messiah. This is reinforced by the words of the Scripture, available to interpret the circumstances of Jesus' birth and the constant guiding presence of the angel of the Lord to Joseph as he negotiated many difficult decisions. Pizzuto claims that as God is seen constantly to act in Jesus' birth, Jesus himself, 'God with us' is '. . . an occurrence of God.'[23]

An occurrence of God is a mighty act. Joseph is the steady man of faith, fair-minded, compassionate, judicious under pressure and able to act effectively himself, who enables God's act of salvation in Jesus to be realised in human history. Socially, religiously, politically and strategically, Joseph is the truly holy man who guided Jesus to adulthood, ready to take on his mission to proclaim the true, living God to the world. He is a saint not only for the early Christians but for our times also.

22. Vincent A Pizzuto, 'The Structural Elegance of Matthew 1–2: A Chiastic Proposal', in *The Catholic Biblical Quarterly*, 74/4 (October 2012): 730.
23. Pizzuto, 'The Structural Elegance of Matthew 1–2', 729.

The Late, Loved Saint Joseph

Virginia M Bourke rsj

When I mentioned to another Sister that I was writing about St Joseph, she simply said, 'Oh, I love Joseph. It might sound funny, but when I find myself talking to someone across the day, it's usually Joseph.'

It is not surprising that a Sister of St Joseph would express such a sense of ready connection with him. Both the Institute's co-founders, Fr Julian Tenison Woods and Sr Mary of the Cross, saw him not just as their nominal Patron, but as a real companion who shared their enterprise with God, guiding them at every turn. He was one of the 'realest' aspects in their real world, without underplaying their acknowledgement of Christ as the centre of their life and work. Their letters mention Joseph with easy familiarity, whether in reference to him individually or as part of the Holy Family.[1]

In 1867, for example, writing to Mary before she moved from Penola to join him in establishing the Sisters in colonial Adelaide, Julian expressed his sense of the *sine qua non* of having Joseph with them in facing their ongoing challenges: 'Without St Joseph I know what I would expect, but with him and his Divine Foster Son, I am sure of placing the work right amid the Holy Family, and they will do what we cannot.'[2]

1. Thomas Boland in *Quiet Women* (Deception Bay, Qld: Refulgence Publishers, 1974), 249, comments on this point: '[Tenison Woods] lived in the presence of the Holy Family and an appeal to one was an appeal to all. The only reason he found the Family his hope and his happiness was the Son; so there is no question of his relaxed invocations of Mary and Joseph being to the detriment of Christ.'
2. Julian Tenison Woods, Letter to Mary MacKillop, 12 June 1867, St Joseph's Congregational Archives, Mount Street North Sydney (SJCA). Quoted in Isabel Hepburn, *No Ordinary Man* (Whanganui NZ, Sisters of St Joseph, 1979), 126.

Then before Mary left for Rome in 1873 to secure the approval of the Institute, she wrote to the Sisters identifying her 'cause' in Rome as synonymous with 'St Joseph's cause'. As she ended that letter, Joseph's place in the spiritual psyche of the Sisterhood is clear:

> In St Joseph's care I leave you—May you as faithful children advance in the imitation of his hidden virtues. May he watch over and bless you my dear, dear Sisters.[3]

Given the high regard for Joseph by many who have lived, worked or been educated under his name in this country and across the world, and given my earlier personal assumption that Joseph was a highly- rated saint, it has amazed me now to realise that he made a relatively late entry into official acknowledgement in Catholic history. This tardiness has stirred me to cogitate more on why he became, nevertheless, so appreciated by ordinary people.

Joseph is first encountered in the gospel of Matthew 1:18–2:23. Here, he is a person seemingly minding his own business, provoked in his dreams to assume the life of a refugee, 'getting up and going' repeatedly in response to the unfolding dimensions of God's call to him through the events of his life. Matthew portrays Joseph torn, but ultimately choosing to follow that call for the sake of those God entrusts to him, the pregnant Mary and the unborn Jesus. One might speculate that the appeal of this Joseph for ordinary people over the centuries has been because he has been perceived in this scriptural narrative as a family man in real life circumstances, an 'every-person', called to make his way one foot after the other, through unexpected situations. People resonate with him, recognising in him someone who can be imitated, because he is like them, not above or removed from them. We sense he would not have been comfortable on a quick route to a high pedestal.

Matthew 1:19 refers to Joseph as a 'just' man, suggesting he is known for his commitment to God within a life of faithful Jewish practice. Yet Matthew 1:18 – 2:23 also reveals he is moved by respect for Mary to take her and her child into his life. He chooses not to put her aside, as the law could allow, thus saving her from disgrace, harsh judgement and even stoning. Joseph shows he is capable of acting beyond the literal observance of the law for the sake of compassion.

3. Mary MacKillop, Circular to Sisters, 25 March 1873, SJCA.

In this way, he is able to resolve the stretched loyalties in his life, proclaiming loudly by his actions, rather than by any recorded words, that he has moved from being 'of two minds' with regard to Mary, to being 'of one heart' with regard to God. Thus he takes upon himself all that is involved under the law as spouse of Mary and father of Jesus. This text reveals that it is God, in fact, who spurs Joseph to move to compassion as the truest law to follow.

In considering why Joseph comes late to official prominence in Catholic history, it needs to be recognised that the early Church was not without documentary reference to him. Mark alone among the evangelists does not mention him. Even though their descriptions are brief when compared with those of Matthew, Luke 1:27, 2:4 and 16 and John 1:45 name the essentials: Jesus was born into the family and tradition of Joseph and Mary and grew up with them. Besides these, there are other ancient Christian apocryphal writings which witness to a simple honouring of Joseph from early Christian times. The most influential of these is the *Protoevangelium of James* written in the late second Century. Though attractive to people, it was not considered officially normative for faith as the four canonical gospels were. Nonetheless, it is the source of many legendary narratives about Jesus within the Holy Family and characterisations of Joseph. These have sparked devotional practices and artistic depictions of Joseph across the ages. It is, for example, within this *Protoevangelium* that we read of Joseph's death in the company of Mary and Jesus, spurring a still-enduring devotion to him as patron of a happy death. In 'the world within the text' of the *Protoevangelium,* Joseph is an old man with sons from a previous marriage. This document therefore helps protect the tradition's earliest conviction about 'Mary, ever virgin', and helps provide a possible 'explanation' with regard to references to Jesus' 'brothers' in Mark 6:3 and his unnamed sisters in Matthew 13:55–56.

Though these elements of the devotional tradition about Joseph arose in early Christian times, they did not feature in the Church's formal teaching through the creeds proclaimed by the various Councils.[4] These Councils settled doctrinal disputes, carefully countering a series of heresies denying the true identity of Jesus

4. The Councils of Nicea (325 CE), Constantinople (381 CE), Ephesus (431 CE) and Chalcedon (451 CE).

as God's Son, and Mary his mother as *Theotokos*/Mother of God. Those doctrines became the acknowledged 'classical theology' in which there seemed to have been no need to pronounce formally on Joseph or to move to canonise him officially or insert his name into liturgical texts. Almost unbelievably for us today, there was no wide or significant veneration of Joseph in Western Europe till after the Crusades in the eleventh through to the thirteenth centuries.[5] From then on, private devotion spread after the Crusaders' contact with the Eastern Coptic tradition which had a strong tradition of honouring Joseph from its beginnings. One might say that from that period, private devotion to Joseph 'took off' at 'the grassroots' of European communities and beyond, as Christianity moved into the rest of the world through missionary endeavours and colonisation.

In spreading devotion to Joseph, spiritual guides stressed Joseph's humility as a model for holy Christian living. Saints Bernard in the twelfth century, Thomas Aquinas in the thirteenth century, and Gertrude in the fourteenth century were followed by the Franciscans, Dominicans and Carmelites, as they moved amongst ordinary people, influencing monks and nuns and parishioners alike. Yet Joseph was not honoured in the Church's official calendar until Pope Sixtus IV established a universal feast on the 19th of March in 1480. It took three more centuries before Pope Pius IX solemnly declared Joseph official Patron of the Universal Church on 8th December, 1870, and almost another century before John XXIII (whose baptismal name was Giuseppe) declared him patron of the Vatican II Council on the 19th of March 1961 and included him within the Roman Canon of the Mass on the 8th of December 1962. A succession of papal exhortations began to bring Joseph more formally before the minds of Christians. These came from Popes Paul VI and John Paul II. Then in 2013, Pope Francis placed Joseph's name in the other standard Eucharistic prayers, and in 2021 called for a year in honour of Joseph, supporting this with his recent letter *Patris Corde* ('With a Father's Heart') for the universal Church.

While formal pronouncements on Joseph came gradually, the passage of simple devotion to him showed that Christians were not

5. Francis Xavier Weiser, *Traditions Related to Saint Joseph* (New York: Harcourt, Brace and Company, 1956). At https://www.catholicculture.org/culture/liturgicalyear/activities/view.cfm?id=1050. Accessed 24 February 2021.

content to leave him in quiet shadow. Rather, people seeking to be followers of Jesus found in Joseph a champion, a holy man worth emulating, someone who did not 'go out on a white charger' to find and deal with the will of God, but one who met and walked with that will face to face in his life, someone who did not avert his gaze from God as he experienced Love's pull in his life from many directions. Across the generations, it seems, people have used their inner compass to sense what is good and true in others and have found the humble, willing Joseph to their liking.

So Joseph gradually became a person 'for all seasons', patron of many nations and multiple causes: of families, fathers, parents, expectant mothers, unborn children, travellers, immigrants, house sellers and buyers, craftsmen, engineers, workers, carpenters, those in doubt and hesitation, the persecuted, Christian families and homes, purity and interior life, engaged couples, people in temporal distress, the poor, aged, and dying. In fact, the list of those who have claimed his patronage is too long to include. He has also been patron of many nations including Canada, Croatia, Korea, China, Mexico, Austria, Belgium, Peru, the Philippines, Vietnam, and the Americas.

And so it could come to pass in 1851 in a Religious community in Aston Hall, England, a nineteen year old Passionist novice, Julian Tenison Woods, found himself inspired when he heard the life of St Teresa of Avila, a sixteenth-century Carmelite and one of St Joseph's greatest European devotees, being read in community. Many years later in his memoirs, Julian wrote of this experience:

> What [St Teresa] said about St Joseph so took possession of me that I resolved in a special manner henceforth to choose him as my patron and protector.[6]

6. In Chapter 6 of St Teresa's autobiography, for example, Julian would have heard her words, 'I wish I could persuade everyone to be devoted to this glorious saint, for I have great experience of the blessings which he can obtain from God. I have never known anyone to be truly devoted to him and render him particular services who did not notably advance in virtue, for he gives very real help to souls who commend themselves to him. For some years now, I think, I have made some request of him every year on his festival and I have always had it granted. If my petition is in any way ill directed, he directs it aright for my greater good' in 'Carmelites' at <http://carmelourladyscovecote.wordpress.com/ 2012/07/13/ st-teresas-devotion-to-st-joseph/>. Accessed 12 March 2021.

As mentioned at the outset of this paper, St Joseph 'meant everything' to both Fr Julian and Mother Mary. He accompanied their journey: Julian reached his first parish of Penola in South Australia on St Joseph's day, the 19th of March 1857, and built St Joseph's church there. It was consecrated on St Joseph's Day, 1859, and on the same date in 1866 Mary MacKillop donned a simple black dress and became known as Sr Mary, the day Sisters know now as Foundation Day.

The earliest official document on the Institute of the Sisters of St Joseph, written by Fr Julian in co-operation with Sr Mary, was approved by Bishop Sheil of Adelaide in October 1867.[7] It is not surprising then to find that in the first few sentences of its first chapter the document draws an immediate connection between the virtues of St Joseph and the way the Sisters were to live and minister.

> [The Sisters] must be poor, humble, and consider themselves the least among all religious orders, studying to keep their lives hidden in God as the life of St Joseph was.[8]

To these named qualities of St Joseph that were familiar in the devotional tradition, was added a unique quality of personalism to the spirituality of the document. The Sisters were encouraged pointedly to imitate Joseph in their humanly-friendly and happy manner with the children they were to teach:

> In honour of their glorious patron, they shall recognise in the children committed to their charge the person of the Infant Jesus, and try to discharge the same holy office towards them which St Joseph did.[9]

> [Let them] remember that the conversation of St Joseph and Jesus is to be their model . . . They are to make themselves the companions of the children, and not assume the authority of superiors except in the gentlest manner . . . They are to be moderately grave, yet cheerful, making their children happy

7. Julian Tenison Woods, 'Rules of the Institute of St Joseph for the Catholic Education of Poor Children, 1867', in *Resource Material from the Archives of the Sisters of St Joseph of the Sacred Heart*, Issue number 3, Sesquicentenary Edition, 2016, SJCA.
8. 'Rules of the Institute' I. 'Objects of the Institute'.
9. 'Rules of the Institute' VI 'Of the Daily Duties'.

> by the way in which they show in practice that the service of the Lord is sweet.[10]

A similarly gentle type of praxis is recommended to the 'Little Sister' (that is, the 'community leader'), with regard to her mode of treating other Sisters, especially those in training:

> No exercise shall be made which would be likely to wound charity. If the Little Sister sees that any command gives pain, or causes distress, she should withdraw it until a more favourable occasion, for like the Holy Family, they must love and cherish each other, and bear with one another's weaknesses.[11]

This attention to the Holy Family in the new Institute's ideals is consistent with what has been mentioned already on Fr Julian's familial approach to Mary, Jesus and Joseph. As Fr Tom Boland wrote in his work on the Sisters of Perpetual Adoration, also founded by Fr Julian:

> Life [for Julian] was a family relationship in which Christ was their brother, Mary their mother and alternately, The Father and St Joseph their father . . . There is no doubt that Julian entered into the family as one of them.[12]

This insistence on 'companioning' also lies below the founding document's reference to the monogram which each professed Sister was to wear on her habit. This displayed three Js for 'Jesus, Joseph and John the Baptist' within the letters A + M for *Ave Maria*. The world of the Holy Family was pointedly extended in this instance to include the child John the Baptist, suggesting that Jesus, like all children, would need a companion. The monogram was intended as a visible reminder to the Sisters that their way of relating must be like that of Joseph and the other members of the Holy Family:

> They shall also speak much to [the children] of devotion to the glorious Mother of God, to St Joseph and to St John the Baptist, the companions of our dear Lord's infancy, and the members of the Holy Family.[13]

10. 'Rules of the Institute' VI 'Of the Daily Duties'.
11. 'Rules of the Institute' V 'Of Employments'.
12. Boland, *Quiet Women*, 237.
13. 'Rules of the Institute' VI 'Of the Daily Duties'.

It is worth remembering that this founding document of the Sisters was written and approved in 1867, three years before Pope Pius IX's solemn declaration in 1870 that Joseph was to be honoured officially as Patron of the Universal Church. Furthermore, the founding document drew on those simple scriptural understandings about Joseph which predated by at least seven decades the 1943 encyclical of Pope Pius XII, *Divino Afflante Spiritu,* which opened Catholics to new insights into biblical writings, based on original translations and modern scholarship. Therefore, the characteristics of St Joseph which the earliest Sisters were encouraged to imitate rose from approaches to scripture prevalent at the time, from pious devotions that had grown up over many centuries and from emphases within the personal spirituality of their co-founders.

Since Vatican II in the 1960s, Catholicism has integrated its approaches to biblical scholarship, theology and spirituality. Naturally this has influenced viewpoints on not only God and Jesus, but also Joseph. With the advent of such scholarship, scriptural texts about Joseph are approached with an awareness that first century gospels cannot simply be read literally as if they were intended as that type of 'historical' recording with which people are familiar twenty-one centuries later. The gospels are seen as *Heilsgeshichte* ['heaven-history'] texts written primarily to focus on God's saving grace operating in human lives. In the main they address the question of theology and spirituality: 'What does this narrative tell us about God and about people's relating with God?'[14]

Joseph has typically been written, sung and prayed about as 'humble', 'hidden' and 'silent'. Even though these qualities are still mined for spiritual significance, in the light of renewal we come to them with an awareness that they arose simply from the fact that scripture does not record Joseph's side of any conversations with anyone, let alone with God's angel-agents in his dreams. Matthew's gospel is deliberately designed to evoke an appreciation of Joseph as a person caught up in willing co-operation with the God who grounds his life. He is less focused on recording historical details about Joseph

14. Pontifical Biblical Commission, *The Interpretation of the Bible in the Church* (Boston: St Paul's Publications, 1993), 72–75. This work points to the danger of literalistic, fundamentalistic readings of scripture that assume texts can simply be taken as history.

or what he said than in highlighting God's 'Mystery' in his life.[15] In the world beyond this text Joseph may have had plenty to say as he struggled to respond to what was asked of him, but that lies beyond the concern of Matthew's writing.

In the task of passing on the whole world of Christian faith known as Sacred Tradition—and this includes the movement of devotional beliefs over the centuries—one Church document offers particular wisdom. This is the Vatican II 'Dogmatic Constitution on Divine Revelation', *Dei Verbum*. It explains how the ongoing transmission of faith is a 'living voice':[16]

> [T]here is a growth in insight into the realities and words that are being passed on. This happens through the contemplation and study by believers, who treasure these things in their hearts (*cf* Luke 2:19, 51) . . . As the centuries go by, the Church is always advancing towards the plenitude of divine truth, until eventually the words of God are fulfilled in her. The words of the holy Fathers [sic] witness to the presence of this living tradition, whose wealth is poured into the practice and life of the believing and praying Church.[17]

It was Vatican II's commitment to affirming the goodness of 'human-being-hood' and the revelatory nature of human experience which led to a landmark movement in incarnational Christology.[18] Since then there has been more readiness to recover a more balanced appreciation of the humanity as well as the divinity of Jesus. Though

15. Yet that does not mean the gospels ignore history totally, for the saving presence and action of God amongst human beings does happen on planet Earth in human history. They are not fairy stories of a world ungrounded in real life. In his book *Responses to 101 Questions on the Bible* (New York: Paulist Press, 1990), 54, Raymond Brown cautions against both assuming gospel accounts are primarily intended as historically accurate, and cancelling altogether a sense of historicity in biblical accounts.
16. 'Dogmatic Constitution on Divine Revelation', *Dei Verbum*, in *The Documents of Vatican II*, edited by Walter M Abbott (London: Geoffrey Chapman, 1967), 117, 8.
17. Vatican II, *Dei Verbum*: 29, 12.
18. For example, Vatican II's Pastoral Constitution on the Church in the Modern World, *Gaudium et Spes*, in *The Documents of Vatican II*, edited by Walter M Abbott (Geoffrey Chapman, London, 1967); Vatican II's Declaration on Religious Freedom, *Dignitatis Humanae*, in *The Documents of Vatican II*, edited by Abbott (London: Geoffrey Chapman, 1967).

the Council of Chalcedon of 451 CE had been at pains to declare Jesus 'fully human and fully divine without separation of these two natures within his one person', there had grown up over the centuries such an emphasis on his divinity that it often downplayed, or even seemed to ignore his humanity. Some of this sprang from gnostic heresies in the early Church. These taught that created 'matter' was evil—certainly not something God would have taken on for Godself in Christ. In that type of imbalance it is easy to understand how Joseph's role stayed in shadow, God being the only real Father of Jesus who counted.

Belgian Dominican theologian, Edward Schillebeeckx, having given theological support at the Vatican Council, went on to develop seminal scholarship on Jesus. In his work, *Jesus: An Experiment in Christology*, he drew attention to the significance of the special relationship Jesus claimed to have with the God in his use of the tender, familial, reverential term *Abba*. Schillebeeckx maintained that 'the secret and source of [Jesus'] being, message and manner of life was his unique experience of God as *Abba*.'[19]

Years later, in his book *Jesus and the Cosmos*, South Australian theologian, Denis Edwards, echoed Schillebeeckx:

> If God can be addressed familiarly as *Abba*, then everything else in life is different. This mystical core of Jesus' life is directly connected to his identity and his mission.[20]

American theologian Elizabeth Johnson concurs: 'Jesus' *Abba* experience is the heart of the matter, the dynamism behind his teaching the reign of God and of his typical way of acting. God *Abba* was the passion of his life.'[21]

In a further work, Elizabeth Johnson showed some of the fruit of developing cultural and linguistic studies of scripture which helped transform a sense of who God is for Jesus as *Abba*. His use of that term is more than just one word; it revealed a whole world of meaning:

---

19. Edward Schillebeeckx, *Jesus: An Experiment in Christology* (New York: Seabury Press, 1979) quoted in Denis Edwards, *Jesus and the Cosmos* (Homebush: St Paul's Publications 1991), 59.
20. Edwards. *Jesus and the Cosmos*, 59.
21. Elizabeth Johnson, *Consider Jesus: Waves of Renewal in Christology* (London: Crossroad, 1990), 57.

> The Aramaic *Abba* connotes an intimacy of relation between Jesus and God, along with a sense of God's compassion over suffering, willing good in the midst of evil. Made concrete in Jesus . . . [this *Abba* sense of God] is subversive of any form of domination . . . Jesus' *Abba* . . . is a God of the oppressed, a God of community and celebration. Everyone related to the one *Abba* stands in a relation of mutuality with one another.[22]

Brazilian theologian Leonardo Boff also wrote that Jesus' 'root experience' of God was as *Abba*. What is now significant for the purpose of this paper is that Boff proceeds from that to draw out a significantly transformed sense of the role of Joseph in the world of God's Mystery. He writes,

> In one person in human history, in Joseph, the Father projected someone who could express the character of Mystery and of worker in his creation. This person does not speak or say words; he speaks through hands that work. He only dreams. Dream is the dimension of depth and of the inaccessible. That is where Mystery has its home . . .
>
> [This person] is Joseph, Joseph of Nazareth. He lives his mission as father so deeply that he experiences God as the great and mysterious Father. With the Father he enjoys such intimacy that he then passes it on to his son, Jesus, who later begins to call God *Abba*-Papa. Jesus can only call God Abba because Joseph lived this intimate dimension of a kind and tender faith.[23]

Boff's sense of Joseph is certainly not of someone who became useful, simply because he was readily available, as if Joseph was made to 'cover the tracks' of a divine intervention in Mary's life. For Boff it is Joseph himself who is the focus of God's deliberate choice because of the calibre of his own fidelity and *fiat*, and because of God's recognition of the divine Mystery working in him. Reading Boff's reflective, contemplative writing I find in myself the sense of a Joseph who is himself 'pregnant' with the Christ, who is aching to be born into the world of humanity's awareness to reveal God's ever-present Mystery there.

22. Elizabeth A Johnson, *She Who Is* (New York: Crossroad, 1995), 81.
23. Leonardo Boff, *Christianity in a Nutshell* (New York: Maryknoll, 2013), 28–9.

Whereas the early Church spoke of Joseph as 'Foster Father' and Guardian, more recent writings, including various papal pronouncements since 1870, have paid serious attention to the significance of the human 'fathering' and influence of Joseph in guiding Jesus' human and spiritual maturing within the Mystery of the Incarnation. One example of this is in 'The Apostolic Exhortation on St Joseph', *Redemptoris Custos*, in which Pope John Paul II wrote:

> The growth of Jesus 'in wisdom and in stature, and in favour with God and man' (Lk 2:52) took place within the Holy Family under the eyes of St Joseph, who had the important task of 'raising' Jesus, that is, feeding, clothing, and educating him in the Law and in a trade, in keeping with the duties of a father.[24]

Pope Francis' recent Apostolic letter on Joseph also warmly communicates recognition of the human fathering of Jesus. The title and first sentence of his letter carry the heart of its message: '*Patris Corde* ('With a Father's Heart'): that is how Joseph loved Jesus.' Seven section-headings in the letter are devoted to Joseph's life as 'father'. He is described as 'beloved', 'tender and loving', 'obedient', 'accepting', 'creatively courageous', as a 'working father' and a 'father in the shadows'. But Pope Francis is not simply saying pious things about Joseph. The heart of the letter is that through Joseph's fathering 'Jesus saw the tender love of God'[25] so that 'in his relationship to Jesus, Joseph was the earthly shadow of the heavenly Father'.[26]

Furthermore, the Pope's image of Joseph being an incarnational mirror of God illustrates what the Constitution of Divine Revelation (*Verbum Dei*) maintained—'the Church constantly moves forward toward the fullness of divine truth until the words of God reach their complete fulfillment'.[27] In our time *Patris Corde* is a 'living voice' illustrating that the tradition of Joseph has deepened. Through Pope Francis, the Church is now declaring as part of its formal teaching that 'Saint Joseph was called by God to serve the person and mission of Jesus directly through the exercise of his fatherhood' and that in

24. Pope John Paul II, *Redemptoris Custos,* 15 August 1989, 16.
25. Pope Francis, *Patris Corde*, 2.
26. Pope Francis, *Patris Corde*, 7.
27. Vatican II, *Dei Verbum*, 8.

this way, 'he cooperated in the fullness of time in the great mystery of salvation and is truly a minister of salvation'.[28]

The Pope reflects also on terms such as 'humble' and 'silent' used for centuries in devotion to Joseph, but he does not allow us to rest with any sense of weakness or reserve in Joseph: 'Joseph is certainly not passively resigned, but courageously and firmly proactive.'[29]

This Pope has expressed his love of St Joseph several times, including at his installation as Pope on St Joseph's Day in 2013. Then in Manila in 2015 he spoke of his personal trust and practical devotion to Joseph:

> I have a great love for St Joseph, because he is a man of silence and strength. On my table, I have an image of St Joseph sleeping. Even when he is asleep, he is taking care of the Church! Yes! We know that he can do that. So when I have a problem, a difficulty, I write a little note and I put it underneath St Joseph, so that he can dream about it! In other words, I tell him: 'Pray for this problem![30]

Like their co-founders Fr Julian Tenison Woods and St Mary of the Cross MacKillop, Sisters of St Joseph have maintained across their years an active devotion to the Holy Family: Mary the Mother of Jesus, the Sacred Heart and St Joseph. In most tangible ways they have felt St Joseph accompanying them wherever they have experienced a practical need in their lives. They have, for example, put his statue out in times of drought to encourage rain, and then they have put it out again to ward off flooding. In the Upper Hunter River town of Denman in the flood of 1955, the resident community of Sisters put the statue out on their verandah as they went to bed with the news the river was rising. They awoke to check on Joseph and saw him bobbing away on the flood waters. I do not know if they retrieved the statue but I do know they never felt Joseph had, or ever would, forsake them.

---

28. Pope Francis, *Patris Corde*, 3.
29. Pope Francis, *Patris Corde*, 4.
30. Pope Francis, 'Discourse to families in Manila', 16 January, 2015 at <https://www.vaticannews.va/enpope/news/2018-03/pope-francis-st-joseph-5-anniversary-pontificate.html>. Accessed 4 January 2021.

Jean-Pierre Médaille
Founder, Sisters of St Joseph, Le Puy, 1610–1689

Joseph, the Cordial Servant

Marcia Allen csj

Introduction

The prayer, 'Go to Joseph', was like a second skin in the early days of most CSSJ devotions.[1] We said it. We sang it. We meant it. We went to Joseph for just about everything. What did it mean then? What does it mean now? In the early days it meant what any petitionary prayer meant. Would the saint work a miracle, just this once? Over and over again. Did he? Who knows? And now? Now it is a different story altogether—maybe.

Historical Context

Following late 1960s research of our earliest known documents authored by our founder, Jean-Pierre Médaille, SJ, we learned a much different aspect of Saint Joseph. He was no longer the mysterious figure sketched into the dim background of old holy cards.

Médaille was born in Carcassonne, France in 1610, and entered the Jesuits in Toulouse, France in 1626. As a Jesuit, it was said that he was 'born for the missions' with a 'gift for spiritual direction'.[2] While assigned to many internal responsibilities in various local Jesuit communities, he also moved from town to town as a confessor and preacher of missions in small rural parishes.

Médaille, from what we can tell from very sketchy records, encountered devout women in his missionary travels throughout

1. The acronym CCSJ stands for 'Congregations of Sisters of St Joseph'.
2. Marguerite Vacher, *Nuns Without Cloister: Sisters of St. Joseph in the Seventeenth and Eighteenth Centuries*, translated by Patricia Byrne, CSJ (New York: University Press of America, 2010), 111.

the region of France known as the Massif Central.[3] These women were part of a cultural movement that consisted of an inner spiritual dynamic that slowly evolved into many women's communities which began to make themselves visible during the first half of the seventeenth century in France.

Known as *filles séculières* (secular daughters), these women engaged in the spiritual and corporal works of mercy. Elizabeth Rapley describes this as 'feminist activism', a movement which had its origins in the collapsed infrastructure of the French culture and in women's desire to create a new social soul not only for their families but also for church and society.[4] The original communities of Saint Joseph were clearly part of that devout movement sweeping through France.

The times were desperate. In the shorthand of historians who analysed that era, it was a time of 'war, plague and famine'.[5] In the Massif Central region of France, armies advancing the Thirty Years War (1618–48) marched back and forth through this area, confiscating and pillaging, raping and spreading disease. Men of the family were conscripted into the army or left for cities to find work; women were left to manage at home. Rural villages were enclaves of people who lived from hand to mouth, worked from dawn to dusk, starved because of malnutrition and died untimely deaths. There were few competent pastors in the local churches who could provide for the care of souls. It was a time and place of profound poverty of body and spirit.[6]

Historians also agree that both civil society and the Church marginalised women, excluding them in matters of religion, politics, the law, medical practice, literature, business, and marital and family relationships.[7] In short, women had two choices, the cloister or marriage. In either case they were not free agents and were subject to men's authority.

---

3. Vacher, *Nuns Without Cloister*, 7.
4. Elizabeth Rapley, *The Dévotes: Women and Church in Seventeenth-Century France* (Ontario: McGill-Queen's Press, 1993), 254.
5. Anne B Hennessy, *The Social History of Seventeenth-Century France*, quoting David Maland, *Culture and Society in Seventeenth-Century France* (London: Ratsford, 1970), 72, (Orange, CA: Sisters of St Joseph), 23.
6. Hennessy, *The Social History*, 23.
7. Rapley, *The Dévotes*, 4.

Truth be told, seventeenth century France, especially the first half of that century, held little promise for anyone, poor or rich, male or female. And yet, the twentieth century historian, Carlo M Cipolla, concluded from his study that in spite of external circumstances that indicated total collapse, there seemed to be an 'incredible amount of robust human energy . . . fermenting under the troubled surface'.[8] This energy was demonstrated particularly in the 'mysticism' of devout persons. Mysticism, in whatever way mystical experiences were judged, was the product of a time when the extreme suffering created by the collapse of the culture, produced questions about God and the meaning of being human. Traditional answers failed; new language had to be invented. Poets and mystics represented the attempts at new images for God and identity for the human. Documents produced by Médaille reflect his 'felt sense' of God as an outcome of his own mystical prayer and his effort to create a new language of meaning and purpose.[9]

The founding of the *Filles de Saint Joseph* and its Rules are proof of that. Like many devout groups of women, they asked their spiritual director for rules. Ordinarily they received adaptations of rules from already-established traditions: Franciscan or Dominican Orders, Ursulines or Carmelites. For the most part groups who adopted these rules were eventually cloistered. A notable exception was the Daughters of Charity which did not claim the category of 'real religious' because the members made their vows for only one year at a time.

Research shows that, by the mid-1640s, Médaille had provided rules adapted from his Ignatian tradition for some women living singly or in twos and at most threes in rural areas, and for a group of six women, some of whom were in charge of an orphanage in the Montferrand Quarter in Le Puy-en-Velay. Although rules provided by a board of directors governed their work, they wanted rules that would enable them to live a religious life. Bishop de Maupas approved Médaille's rules for the six living at the orphanage in 1650.

8. Carlo M Cipolla, *Clocks and Culture: 1300–1700* (New York: WW Norton & Company, 1978, 1967), 74.
9. Jean-Pierre Médaille, *Eucharistic Letter*, translated by Intercongregational Research Team, USA (Erie, PA: Villa Maria College, 1975), 1.

The same rules appear to have been given to the women living in the surrounding rural areas.[10]

These tiny communities were placed under the patronage of Saint Joseph. Why, has always been a question. Marguerite Vacher suggests that it might have been because of Bishop de Maupas's devotion to that saint.[11] Other than this fact, the reason for the naming is only guesswork. The most important thing here at the origins is that Médaille included Joseph in his rules for a specific reason. It is through his description of Saint Joseph that Médaille's own deeply-rooted Ignatian spirituality is revealed. It also implies his complete confidence in the mature spirituality of the women whom he directed.

While the women looked and worked like every other devout group of women of the time, they were evidently searching for a deeper intimacy with God. Médaille's response to their desire for a more profound and fulfilling inner life was an invitation to enter into a contemplative life, a mystical life that would transform their vision of reality. In fact, when they asked for rules, he would give them an outline, not for how to meet the needs of the neighbour, but for how to lure the neighbour as well as themselves into closer union with God.

The Mystical Movement in the Rules–*Acatamiento*

The original *Règlements* (Rules) *of the Daughters of Saint Joseph Grouped in Honour of the Holy Uncreated Trinity of God the Father, Son, and Holy Spirit and the Created Jesus, Mary, and Joseph* are filled with the devotions common at the time. Hidden within them is a consecration to two trinities: the Uncreated Trinity and the Created Jesus, Mary and Joseph.[12] A close look at this section reveals the mystical nature of a foundational rule within the Rules. In fact, this section is revolutionary in meaning and practice. It was not just a set of rules, similar in appearance to most other rules of the time for devout groups of women, but rather, a single Rule, illuminating the nature of a profound relational dynamic within God and all others.

10. Vacher, *Nuns Without Cloister*, 57.
11. Vacher, *Nuns Without Cloister*, 37.
12. Jean-Pierre Médaille, *The Règlements*, translated by Intercongregational Research Team for the Federation of the Sisters of Saint Joseph, USA, (Erie, PA: Villa Maria College, 1975), 3.

Bartolomé Esteban Murillo, 1617–1682, 'The Two Trinities'

The Consecration to the Two Trinities is described as the 'goal and purpose of the association'.[13] The text, deferential and non-committal in tone, describes the goal of the association and its purpose as a humble and lowly one, inconsequential in human eyes, but indicated by six points, one point for each of the six persons comprising the two trinities. The six points, however, present an astonishing goal and purpose, not inconsequential by any means.

Comprehension of the language of the Consecration is critical to the life required for Communities of Saint Joseph. Each point begins with the phrase 'in honour of'. This phrase introduces the assumption that each of the six persons are to be honoured by imitation. Their 'virtue' is something to which members and the institute are to aspire. Thus, there is nothing unusual here; it appears to be a devotional exhortation. This in itself would be a worthy life work, indeed, if it did not miss the mark entirely. Médaille, however, was not prescribing more devotions for women who desired something more substantial.

Research provided by the Jesuit, Charles E O'Neill, assists in the understanding of the true vocation of Communities of Saint Joseph. In delving into Ignatius' frequent use of the word 'reverence', O'Neill found another word that begins to reveal the true nature of the goal and purpose.[14] 'Reverence', he says, devolved over the century after

13. Médaille, *The Règlements*, 4.
14. Charles E O'Neill, SJ, *Acatamiento: Ignatian Reverence in History and in Contemporary Culture* (St Louis: American Assistancy Seminar on Jesuit Spirituality, January 1978), 2.

Ignatius' direct influence from a much more powerful word with a much more robust meaning: *acatamiento*. Frequently translated as awe or reverence, this Spanish word from the fifteenth century Spanish culture derived from the verb *acatar*, with its root meaning 'to be caught up in'. *Acatamiento* contains a sense of being caught up in or carried more deeply into the transcendent.[15]

O'Neill's research suggests additional synonyms: communing presence, pregnant with, stimulating communion. Latin versions, says O'Neill, had to be content with 'anemic honor'.[16] Ignatius, as he described his relationship with God and what he wished for those to whom he wrote, meant to communicate the seizing love of God, 'a happy consciousness of divine presence' that grasped the person and sent him or her into God's work.[17] Rather than acquiring a virtue, the person is filled with a sense of God who is in all things and, in communion with God, is moved to action. *Acatamiento*, suggests O'Neill, is an ecstatic movement of the communing presence of God. Médaille understood this and outlined its presence as the dynamism out of which the women of the Communities of Saint Joseph would live and work. This consecration is not a list of virtues, rather it is a description of the one Rule. That one Rule flowed from their felt experience of God which impelled them into the world to find God in every kind of neighbour.

Joseph, Servant of Cordial Charity

It is in this context that we find the sixth point:

> In honour of Saint Joseph their Patriarch, they will be one in the service of each other, and one in the service of the neighbour without distinction for whom they will try to have cordial charity, as Saint Joseph had for his dear spouse and for the Savior Jesus.[18]

15. O'Neill, *Acatamiento*, 3.
16. O'Neill, *Acatamiento*, 3.
17. O'Neill, *Acatamiento*, 3.
18. Médaille, *The Règlements*, 5.

To achieve the goal and purpose, we live in stimulating, communing presence with Saint Joseph, servant to neighbour without distinction, servant of cordial charity.

There's a sleeper in the sixth point, a word that is easily overlooked because of our assumption that we know what it means. That word is 'cordial'. Cordiality is related to hospitality. It is certainly a virtue to imitate. It implies an amicable demeanor, a pleasant and warm friendliness, what one offers as openness when one welcomes another. Médaille, however, creates a new meaning for us. It was probably no surprise to the seventeenth-century women for whom he wrote the Rules. He likens Joseph's charity to a cordial.

Cordials originated in Europe and were refined for medicinal uses during the fifteenth and sixteenth centuries. Basically, a cordial was a mixture of herbs, spices and alcohol and sometimes included other substances reputed for healing. It was given as a medicine to anyone who demonstrated indifferent health, a malaise of spirit, impotency, or a disorder of heart or stomach. A cordial was meant to invigorate, stimulate, stir up, animate, activate or enliven in some way whatever appeared as a physical malfunction.[19] With this single word, Joseph moves from passive by-stander to model of the active and dynamic stirring of divine energy in the world that the earliest communities occupied.

Joseph, the agent and activist in the sixth point, sums up the whole of the Consecration. Joseph symbolises the stimulating presence of the Uncreated Trinity and the communing actions of Jesus and Mary in the Created Trinity. He is the symbol for the all-inclusive love of God the Father of the first point (Matt 5:48), the servant's self-givenness of God the Son in the second point (Phil 2:1–11), and love's dimensionless nexus of God the Holy Spirit in the third point (Eph 3:18). At the same time, he is the reflection of Jesus' zeal in the fourth point: human finitude in God's infinite capacity for self-giving and Mary's obedience as faithful and discerning abandonment to God's desire in the fifth point. And, in the sixth point, there is Joseph, who with the service of cordiality offered and delivered in 'pure and perfect love', wraps it all into a single reality: Love incarnate and all that Love is and does.[20] With Joseph, Médaille presents the full portrait of a *Fille de Saint Joseph*.

19. Wikipedia, Cordial (Medicine) at <https://en.wikipedia.org/wikiCordial_(medicine)>. Accessed 3 March 2021.

20. Médaille, *Eucharistic Letter*, 20.

This was their Rule: to live the communing presence of these two trinities so as to be the 'Congregation of the Great Love of God'.[21] O'Neill would suggest 'pregnant with' God who is all inclusive, all self-giving, all uniting. It is out of this divine dynamic that the Sister of Saint Joseph lives and works. She is filled with, pregnant with, stimulated by the communing presence of the triune God. In this Consecration she is not trying to imitate God who is perfect, self-given or pure and perfect love; rather, she is so filled with this communing love that she is carried into the world as the same love incarnate. Her sole reason for being is to be the God-presence among those with whom she lives and works. She is the dynamic of communing presence in her world that abides and stirs within her. It is deeply personal and yet always sending her into the world in whatever way she can use her gifts to effectively communicate God's desire for others' fulfillment.

Her response to the triune God is characterised by the communing presence of Jesus, Mary and Joseph. In Jesus, she is pregnant, always expecting, ever filled with and caught up by her zeal. Zeal in the Ignatian sense is the simultaneous activity of humility and magnanimity, that is, honest acknowledgment of one's finite limitations and absolute dependence on God's infinite capacity for love. The humble person readily lives with realistic self-knowledge and at the same time with large-hearted courage. She does not hesitate to act in the service of God and others. She believes in the trinitarian dynamic which will manifest itself in the exigencies of life if one dares to trust.

At the same time, actions are not rash or unconsidered, the result of idealism or momentary enthusiasm. Rather they are the result of loving consideration, the application of rational assessment and fierce faith in God's providence accompanied by the courage to say 'yes', as Mary did in accepting the pregnancy God offered.

Then there is Joseph. Joseph, servant of God, faithful guardian, hidden one, silent one, dreamer and the provider for the family whom God gave him. We can only guess that Médaille offered Saint Joseph as a patron growing out of Joseph's growing popularity of the time. The Rules include a litany to Saint Joseph and the young communities probably had other prayers to Saint Joseph although there is no evidence for that. In fact, there is more evidence that

21. Médaille, *Constitutions for the Little Congregation of the Daughters of St. Joseph*, translated by the Intercongregational Research Team USA (Erie, PA: Villa Maria College, 1967), 12.

they were devoted to the Blessed Sacrament, a common devotion during those post-Protestant Reformation times. In the first Rules, however, Médaille is more interested in Joseph as the summary of the Consecration. Joseph becomes the synthesis of his concept for this new community of non-cloistered religious.

Joseph, Model and Symbol for a Community of Saint Joseph

We regard Saint Joseph, then, as all that a member of a Community of Saint Joseph can be as well as what the Institute itself can be. Referring back to the original Rules of the late 1640s, we find further evidence of the active Saint Joseph. In his summary of the goal and purpose, Médaille says that the sisters are to live the six points within their homes. In addition, they are to lead their neighbour to do the same, that is, to live the communing presence, the Divine Energy already within them, so as to do as the sisters do: create among themselves union with God, self and all others. And finally, they are to enter into their world through the 'tools' offered in the spiritual and corporal works of mercy in any way they are capable. In his day, Médaille added 'in keeping with their rank and activities' particular to women.[22] In our day we would say according to her talents, gifts, education and training. This summary underscores the subtlety of Médaille's notion of Joseph. Joseph was not only a symbol of the two trinities but he was also a model for the sisters themselves. This was a daring departure from the culture's expectation for women.

In addition to the summary, Médaille says elsewhere that the sisters, besides the spiritual and corporal works of mercy, will also 'take care to give spiritual formation and direction of life to all persons of their sex, conformable to their station, age, and occupation in life-formation and direction that they will have well prepared so that nothing is done that is not first discussed with prudent and virtuous persons.'[23] Mary Ward's English Ladies were suppressed in 1631 for arrogating to themselves the 'power to speak of spiritual things' and otherwise undertake the work reserved for clergy.[24] Mary Ward's sally into the world deemed proper only to males all but extinguished any effort to establish non-cloistered communities for women. Médaille

22. Médaille, *The Règlements*, 6.
23. Médaille, *The Règlements*, 'Exercises Pertaining to the Neighbor', 11.
24. Rapley, *The Dévotes*, 31–32.

and the earliest communities succeeded, however, because on the surface the description of their Rules seemed ordinary. But beneath the surface was the mystical impetus of *acatamiento*.

Médaille also built into the Rules a regular practice with sustaining power. In the 'Exercises Pertaining to Their Own Religious Life', Médaille lists prayers and practices that should be performed yearly, monthly, weekly and daily. These practices describe the usual devotions that would be found in any monastery for women. Tucked into the weekly list that regulates reception of Holy Communion and confessing there is the rule to 'consult for a half hour on the state of their Congregation and the works of zeal ordinarily done'.[25]

This consultation implied deliberation and taking counsel from others. This weekly meeting was an opportunity to talk with 'prudent and virtuous persons' the way the six points of the consecration had been lived in their own lives. This communal deliberation about the 'works of zeal ordinarily done' was not only the discernment about how they were living their own consecration, but it prepared them to engage in the 'formation of life' with others. Weekly then, they examined the ways in which their very finite selves courageously lived in God's magnanimity had enabled them to be the Trinity's communing presence through their presence and works of service. Thus they were continually discerning how to live the consecration in the world. For further emphasis, Médaille also mandated that they renew their consecration on the first day of the year and every three months thereafter.[26]

Acatamiento Today

The *Règlements* (Rules) as given by Médaille incarnates as a single rule the Great Love of God. This Rule and its practices are as timely today as they were yesterday. We live in a world that is as tumultuous as that of our seventeenth-century ancestors. And we, like they, are the ones for this moment. The charism and its mission are key to the health and healing of creation. So, how do we go about it? Where do we find ourselves as communing presence? Effective presence; effective love?

Communities of Saint Joseph thrive throughout the world. We are the charism of 'inclusive and active love' incarnate wherever we live

25. Médaille, *The Règlements*, 8.
26. Médaille, *The Règlements*, 7.

and work.[27] This charism is deeply rooted in our relationship with all others. Our goal and purpose is the same as that of our founders. In participation and co-operation with the Triune dynamic that is ceaselessly creating, loving and keeping all things in creation, we willingly give ourselves over to this same process: the art of living in such a way that the world and earth around us flourishes. We collaborate with God's desire for creation through our presence that affects harmony, balance, good order and right relationship. We enable others to do and be the same.

Acatamiento is a realisation of God's presence that grasps us in a loving embrace, fills us and then releases us into our world with the dynamism of the Great Love for which and in which the Community is founded. It is the felt comprehension and the faith conviction of God's communing presence within us. *Acatamiento* is a dynamic that achieves what it is. It is an active and effective love that manifests itself in relations with all others. It is the realisation of a love that unifies, reconciles, heals, stimulates, challenges, connects, animates and stirs up love in others. It conveys meaning and purpose where there is only despair and indifference. It gives itself unselfishly and unselfconsciously to others in a movement that is always offering what it is: the gracious, fecund Love that is God in all things.

To live *acatamiento* is our vocation, its aim and purpose and its outcome and effect. It is the art of always expecting God's presence wherever we are and in whatever circumstances, adverse or consoling. It is being alert in every event, experience and encounter to the potential of realising God's capacity for loving in it. It is the awareness of God's desire within us to be always that capacity for loving with openness to the cordiality required. We live a mystery of relationality, a 'mysticism of relationship'.[28] We incarnate the fundamental existence and vocation of all creatures: we are all one in the One whose creatures we are and in whose household we live.

Who knows who Joseph was? Who can know? But in Médaille's imagination, Joseph was an elixir and balm, and the nexus of his family of Nazareth with their very chaotic first-century world. And so today, he is our symbol for that in our twenty-first century world. And so, we still go to Joseph!

---

27. Bette Moslander to USA Federation Leadership Meeting in Holyoke, MA, 6 November 1992, Archives of the Sisters of St Joseph, Concordia, KS.
28. Bette Moslander, Lecture for 'Bearers of the Tradition', Concordia KS, June 2003, Archives of the Sisters of St. Joseph, Concordia, KS.

Julian Tenison Woods, 1832–1889
Co-founder, Sisters of St Joseph
Penola, South Australia

Julian and Joseph

Jan Tranter rsj

> *To Father J E Tenison Woods is due the honour of arousing devotion to the 'most hidden though the greatest Saint' by placing this new family which he trusted would do so much good in the Church under the protection of him, to whom the Incarnate God was subject.*[1]

In these words Mary MacKillop concludes the chapter of her book on the life of Julian Woods referring to the months leading to the inauguration of St Joseph's Institute in Adelaide.

The chapter narrative begins in February 1867 with Julian in Melbourne writing to Mary in Penola. Keen to get to Adelaide to launch his Catholic education plan and the Institute of St Joseph, but working temporarily in Melbourne as arranged by Bishops Sheil and Goold, he gave daily instructions there on St Joseph. Brimming with plans and with the person of St Joseph before his mind, he reached Adelaide in early April, a few weeks before Sheil left for Rome. Four weeks later, Julian wrote to Sheil about what he had done in organising 'the grand school movement'. It was a remarkably full list of activities for a month. He concluded, 'I leave you in the care of my ever watchful Guardian and Protector, St Joseph'.[2]

The '*my* ever watchful Guardian and Protector' shows the source of Julian's confidence for his plan and the energy to put it into action. Joseph was in the detail. Going into the cathedral to pray for help, he met Miss McMullen, a teacher at a private school, lighting and replacing

1. Mother Mary of the Cross MacKillop, *Julian Tenison Woods: A Life*, edited by Margaret Press (Strathfield, NSW: St Paul's Publications, 2010), 93.
2. MacKillop, *Woods*, 88–91.

oil in the sanctuary lamp. He said, writes Mary, that 'he considered her presence as a promise of aid from our glorious Patriarch, St Joseph'.[3] Hearing from Julian of his needs with the planned institute, Miss McMullen offered all possible help. On 12 June, in his last letter to Mary before she left Penola for Adelaide, he wrote,

> Human resources are so weak and what we aim at so high; and then, everybody says, 'What can you expect from colonial girls without any knowledge of a religious life, and no one to train them?' Without St Joseph, I should know what I should expect, but with him and his Divine Foster Son, I am sure of placing the work right amid the Holy Family, and they will do what we cannot.[4]

Just before the end of the chapter, Mary points to the 'Joseph' manner of the institute's formal beginning in Adelaide. As arranged by Julian with the permission of Fr Smyth, Vicar General,[5] on the Feast of the Assumption, 15 August, she made her Religious Profession and two postulants were received. Mary continued, 'In a quiet little room for Oratory, few visitors, no music, no Benediction or Presence of the Blessed Sacrament—in St Joseph's own silent way the new institute was inaugurated.' Julian presided, entrusting the venture to St Joseph. Joseph was Julian's inspiration and model.

Origin of Julian's Devotion to St Joseph

What was the origin of Julian's love for and confidence in St Joseph? How did this love shape the spirit of the Rule and Instructions which he gave to the Sisters of St Joseph, and later to the Sisters of Perpetual Adoration?

Julian grew up in England, and in his mid-teen years showed a vital interest in religious life. Aged eighteen, in the first of his two years as a Passionist, Julian spent six weeks at Aston Hall where Fr Ignatius Spencer was Superior. Here Julian heard Teresa of Avila's words on St Joseph. Two years before his death, aged fifty-four, he told of the experience:

---

3. MacKillop, *Woods*, 87.
4. MacKillop, *Woods*, 92.
5. Margaret Press, *Julian Tenison Woods: 'Father Founder'* (Blackburn, Victoria: CollinsDove, 2004), 91.

> What she says about St Joseph so took possession of me that I resolved in an especial manner henceforth, to choose him as my patron and protector. I had always a special devotion to the Glorious Spouse of my Mother, but after this I tried to honour him in a particular manner and thenceforth experienced in many ways what I may truly term the richest return in the way of his favours.[6]

Weighing his impulse, he wrote to his novice master for permission for this special commitment. The novice master was pleased.[7] From then on, Julian's entrusting himself to Joseph and his honour was a constant in his life.

What words from the sixteenth-century Saint Teresa so possessed him? At one stage she had contracted malaria and almost died. After recovering from her illness she had written:

> I took for my advocate and lord the glorious St Joseph and earnestly recommended myself to him. I saw clearly that as in this need [illness] so in other greater ones . . . this father and lord of mine came to my rescue in better ways than I knew how to ask for. I don't recall up to this day ever having petitioned him for anything that he failed to grant . . . I have not known anyone truly devoted to him and rendering him special services who has not advanced more in virtue. For in a powerful way he benefits souls who recommend themselves to him.[8]

Another factor strengthening Julian's love of Joseph was the Passionist community spirit of living with the Holy Family. As well, his spiritual sensibilities were heightened in the community with Fr Ignatius where Julian felt 'that I was living with a saint'.[9]

---

6. Julian Tenison Woods, *Memoirs* 1 (dictated), 1887, typescript copy, Sisters of St Joseph Lochinvar Archives, (SSJLA), 79.
7. Julian Woods, 'Conference to Sisters of Perpetual Adoration', 29 February 1887, Archives, Sisters of Perpetual Adoration, Brisbane (RPA).
8. *Life*, 6: 6–7 in 'St Joseph and St Teresa', Leaflet for Fifth Centenary (2015), Carmelite Nuns, Varroville NSW.
9. Woods, *Memoirs*, 1, 65. Julian said in 1887, 'no one doubts now that he was a saint of God'. Fr Ignatius' cause has recently advanced. On 20 February 2021 Pope Francis declared Father Ignatius 'Venerable'.

Julian's words, however, that he 'had always a special devotion to the Glorious Spouse of my Mother' must not be overlooked.[10] He had felt an attraction to Joseph, an affinity with Joseph, from childhood.

Julian's year with the Marist Fathers was a further catalyst to his love for Joseph.[11] A constant Marist instruction was to live with and like the Holy Family. Another particular influence was residing in community for a month with 'an old priest, a great servant of St Joseph, a very holy man'. He gave Julian the book, *The Month of St Joseph,* which Julian brought to Australia, lending it to many. Julian himself speaks of having spread awareness of the church's dedication of March to St Joseph when he was parish priest in Penola in 1866. Twenty-one years later, preparing for March, he gave a talk in Brisbane to the Sisters of Perpetual Adoration on 'The Month of St Joseph'.[12]

Julian's love of Joseph was no formality. It was personal, lifelong, as friend to friend. He said, referring to St Joseph, 'I always used say a prayer and give him a friendly look.' At the end of his active life, after ten years in Penola, four in Adelaide, eleven in the eastern Australian colonies and three in Asia, he made an emphatic, categorical statement of Joseph's role in his life. He said, 'It is he [Joseph] who has helped me in all I have ever done'.[13]

Penola–Adelaide Years: Special 'Joseph' Events

There were three special 'Joseph' events in Julian's ten years in Penola Parish, encompassing his life there. They were all in the little town at the centre of the parish. The first was his arrival. 'It was on the feast of St Joseph', he said, 'that I went to my first parish'. Arriving on this day in 1857 was for Julian a sign of Joseph's protection. Julian had not planned it.[14] The second was Easter Sunday, 1859, just over two

10. Julian's words expressed with Victorian emotional fullness are not always in our contemporary style. The challenge is to discern the inclination of the heart.
11. With his illness causing his leaving the Passionists, he joined the Marists. After a year with them in France, illness and local events led to his return to London.
12. Woods, 'Conference, 29 February 1887'.
13. Woods, 'Conference, 29 February 1887'.
14. Julian Tenison Woods, 'Ten Years in the Bush', in *The Australasian Catholic Record*, lxvi/3 (1989): 261. Also Woods, *Memoirs,* 11, 13, 20. The journey from Adelaide was longer than planned, with storms driving the boat to sea. After reaching Guichen Bay, there was a 120 km two-day ride to Penola.

years later: the opening and blessing of St Joseph's church. Julian said 'the first church I built I dedicated to him', fulfilling his promise to dedicate his first church to St Joseph.[15] And it was on his last feast of St Joseph as Parish Priest of Penola that he launched with Mary MacKillop the Institute of St Joseph. The following February he left for Melbourne, en route to Adelaide, as directed by his Bishop.

In Adelaide with Joseph as his model and protector, Julian set about his tasks. Along with planning and creating a system of Catholic education and attending to large pastoral duties, he gave time and effort to forming the hearts of the growing number of Sisters in the spirit of Joseph. He did this by his own example and by the Rule and Instructions he gave them.[16]

As well as the profound, humble inauguration of the Institute of St Joseph in Adelaide on 15 August 1867 when Mary MacKillop made her religious profession as described above, there were other special 'Joseph' days in Adelaide.

Despite being exhausted to near breaking point by January 1871, Julian did not let a 'Joseph' opportunity pass. In his monthly publication, *The Chaplet*, the 28th of January 1871, he wrote that the Bishops of the world were presenting to the assembled Council in Rome a petition that Joseph be named Patron of the Universal Church. In the February edition he reported 'the joyful news', quoting the 8 December declaration from Rome.[17]

Steering through the barely disguised hostility to him and the Sisters mounted by his avowed enemy, Fr Horan, Julian persevered with his many tasks. No opposition would destroy his confidence in Joseph's protection, nor his commitment to honour Joseph. On the feast of St Joseph, 1871, almost four years after Julian had arrived from Melbourne, a milestone was reached: the opening and blessing

---

15. Woods, 'Memoirs' 11, 40. St Joseph's was opened on 24 April 1859. Press, *Woods*, 72. (Print error has 1865). In 1859 he also began churches at Mt Gambier (St Teresa's) and Robe (Our Lady Star of the Sea). Anne Player, 'Julian Tenison Woods, 1832–1889: The Interaction of Science and Religion', unpublished MA thesis, Australian National University, Canberra, 1990, 151.
16. Julian Tenison Woods, *Rules for the Institute of St Joseph*. Julian wrote the Rule in May 1867, sent it to Mary, edited it in October and had it printed after Sheil approved it on 17 December 1868.
17. The delay in reporting the declaration is due to the time it took for overseas news to arrive in Australia. Pope Pius IX declared St Joseph as patron of the universal church on 8 December 1870.

of the Chapel of the Sisters of St Joseph in Franklin Street, Adelaide. The Chapel was dedicated to St Joseph, Patron of the Universal Church. Julian reported the event in the March *Chaplet*. His friend Fr Hinteroecker SJ had preached the occasional homily, noting that it was 'of no common significance' that this day was the first festival by which Joseph was 'invocated as Patron of the Universal Church' and that this was 'the first church in Australia of that title and perhaps the first in the Church.'

Fr Hinteroecker's words resonate today, 2021. 'It is of no common significance' in this Year of Joseph that one hundred and fifty years ago, Julian honoured Joseph with the new universal recognition. The Sisters whom he and Mary founded continue to honour Joseph, seek to live with his spirit and work for God under Joseph's protection.

Rule of St Joseph's Institute: Forming the Hearts of the Sisters in the Spirit of Joseph

Foundational to the way of life of the Sisters of St Joseph is the Rule that Julian composed for them in May 1867. The Rule opens in the name of Joseph: 'In the name of the glorious patriarch St Joseph, this institute has been erected for the pious education of children whose parents are in humble circumstances.' The first paragraph states:

> In honour of their glorious patron they [the Sisters] shall recognise in the children in their charge the person of the Infant Jesus, and try to discharge the same holy office towards them which St Joseph did to his charge.

Julian set Joseph before the Sisters as their model. To be as Joseph was to Jesus was the Sisters' call and identity.

Mary MacKillop tells how Julian himself loved children, saw Jesus in the children and called teachers to do the same. She quotes him saying, 'Think you see in the children our Lord as a Child and you will never do to them what you would not do to that Divine Infant had He been committed to your care.'[18]

Julian's image of Joseph as a father was one of tenderness. During a profession ceremony at Perthville on 8 April 1877, Julian described how the Sisters were to live:

---

18. MacKillop, *Woods*, 96.

> Their lives were to be like that of St Joseph, the poor man, the hidden man, the man upon whom the child Jesus loved to rest, and while carried in his arms, sought love and sympathy from his humble and generous heart.[19]

He went on to say that he 'firmly believed' that this work in the spirit of Joseph, in particular for children in circumstances of poverty, remote from religious education, was the way in which 'the mystery and the sacrifice of the life of Our Lord was to be reproduced in our days to meet the wants of our adopted country.'[20] Today, Julian's words could read that he 'firmly believed' that a Joseph-like manner and approach, with priority for the poor, for children and those remote from Christian instruction, was the way to renew the church in our country, Australia, and wherever the Sisters feel called to serve those who live in poverty.

The Rule continues: 'They [Sisters] must be poor, humble and consider themselves the least among all religious orders, studying to keep themselves and their lives hidden in God as St Joseph was.' Julian saw Joseph not as an isolate nor in the limelight, but hidden, loving and loved in the Holy Family. Joseph, in loving companionship with Mary and Jesus, was faithful to his tasks, unnoticed by the world.

Julian called for this loving companionship of the Holy Family to be mirrored in the founding Sisters, and the same call is made today. Julian encapsulated this relationship in the drawing of the monogram which he included in the text of the Rule. The monogram, to be worn on Sisters' habits, indicates a unity of interrelated persons. It shows Joseph with Mary and John the Baptist as companions of Jesus in His early childhood.[21] Joseph does not stand out. He is inconspicuous in the very pattern of the monogram. In Julian's words, Joseph, the 'representative of the Blessed Trinity itself in the guardianship of

19. 'From Our Correspondent: Bathurst—Religious Profession', in *Freemans Journal* (14 April 1877).
20. *Freemans Journal* (14 April 1877).
21. The Marist emblems showing Jesus, Mary and Joseph and which inspired Julian, never include John the Baptist. In personal correspondence with the writer, the 13th of April 1995, Gaston Lessard, Marist author then living in Rome, said, 'John the Baptist has no special place in Marist tradition.' Julian's inclusion of John is part of Julian's legacy: his awareness of John, known to Joseph, close to Jesus and courageous precursor of Jesus.

the Incarnate Word',[22] was neither dominant nor dominating. His role was humble. This was the Joseph model Julian gave the Sisters for their communal living and presence and work with the children and in any mission. The Sisters were to live and work as in the Holy Family where Joseph, the humble man, was the faithful provider and loving father.

Julian wrote in the Rule:

> They [the Sisters] are to make themselves the companions of the children, and not assume the authority of superiors except in the most gentle manner. They are to be moderately grave, yet cheerful, making their children happy by the way in which they show in practice that the service of the Lord is sweet . . . They should talk cheerfully to their charges, so as to gain their young hearts.

Through the Sisters' Joseph-like teaching and example, the future of the church would be nourished:

> They should also speak much to them of devotion to the glorious Mother of God, to St Joseph and St John the Baptist, the companions of our dear Lord's infancy, and the members of the Holy Family. They should do their utmost to make the little ones of the Church the means of drawing God's blessings upon all and the seeds of the future perfection of their generation.

What standard of teaching were the Sisters to offer? The Rule states:

> In teaching they should take every pain, leaving nothing untried as a matter of justice to the parents, that the children may progress in worldly learning . . . They must patiently use every effort to make the children learn and see that they understand what they learn . . . They . . . must ask St Joseph to assist them . . . that even dull children will learn better under the Sisters than elsewhere.

---

22. Woods, *Memoirs* 1, 90.

Again, Julian's Rule conveyed the sense that Joseph's primary care for family opened him to embrace others. So, while the children in the schools were their first care, the Sisters were to extend their concern to all in need:

> [Sisters are] to do all the good they can and never see an evil without trying how they may remedy it . . . Though the Institute has its peculiar duties . . . the religious must do any good that they can and make their charity all-embracing.

To help the Church 'hold against the wicked secular instruction of the world', the Sisters' 'mission' was to offer' 'a superior education'. The image of Joseph's loving, happy and thorough education of Jesus was to be reflected in the happiness and energy of the Sisters. Similarly, in community sharing the heavy tasks, the Sisters 'shall be ready to help each other in all charity, as in the Holy Family'.

Julian expanded on the Rule in another document, 'Instructions on the Rule' which, with Sheil's approval, he had printed in 1870. They were the fruits of Julian's daily hour of prayer which he had then shared with the Sisters before Mass at the convent during these embryonic years of the Institute.[23]

This *Book of Instructions for the Use of the Sisters of St Joseph of the Sacred Heart* continued to be a formative Joseph experience for the Sisters. It opens with a section on prayer: 'It all depends on prayer. They should begin with it and end with it.' The next section describes 'The Spirit of St Joseph':

> The spirit of the Sisters of St Joseph is a spirit of poverty, and the love that the Sisters have for their Order should make them most earnest in pursuing it. Poverty and humility go hand in hand. If our poverty is not a humble poverty, it will not last.

The Instructions go on to name and define characteristics of the Joseph spirit. They include notions of 'courage that rises with difficulties' and 'candour and simplicity'.

The Instructions speak of drawing the children to Joseph, the humble and great man with a father's heart:

23. Press, *'Father Founder'*, 91.

> It will enlist the love of children for St Joseph, if we tell them of all his love for children who remind him of the charge he had in the Infant Jesus. How he watches them and shields them from danger, taking them up in his arms to repose upon his heart, as he did his foster Son. We should also insist much upon the great power St Joseph's prayers have, and how there is nothing he asks that he does not obtain, so they should pray to him with utmost confidence.

Julian's Rule was grounded in Joseph. For the first seven years of the Institute it was lived out by the Sisters before adoption of the Roman revisions at the Chapter of 1875. With Perthville and later offshoots then coming under diocesan governance, Julian re-wrote essentially the same Rule adapted to their new circumstance.[24] By his founding impetus and example in Adelaide, then at Perthville, and the Rules and the Instructions he gave the Sisters, he left the imprint of Joseph on the whole sisterhood of St Joseph.

Joseph was involved only in the formative period of Jesus' life. Julian was involved only in the formative period of the Josephite life. Anne Player named Julian's role 'the paramount involvement of his life.'[25]

In All, Julian Guided by Joseph

In 1867 Julian directed the hearts of the founding Sisters to the humility and poverty of St Joseph. Twenty years later, he continued to point towards the power of St Joseph. He told the Sisters of Perpetual Adoration, 'Ask St Joseph to make you humble', he said. 'He can and will do wonders for you if you only ask him.'[26] Julian's founding of the Sisters of Perpetual Adoration was like an echo of his previous founding of the Sisters of St Joseph, another dimension of living in the Holy Family, led by Joseph.

---

24. In 1878 at Bathurst, under Bishop Quinn's direction, Julian completed a two-section Rule. The 'Roman style' twelve and a half pages is followed by twenty pages headed 'Explanation of the Rules'. This is the substance of the 1867 Rules as far as the spirit of the Sisters was involved. He wrote 'no change whatever has been made in its spirit'. The quotations of the Rule in this article are in the both the 1867 Rule and the 'Explanation' Julian included at Bathurst. Quinn gave his approval to the Rules and the Explanation as one document, enabling the spirit and most of the 1867 text to be maintained.
25. Player, 'Julian Tenison Woods, 1832–1889', 205.
26. Conference, the 29th of February 1887.

Along with and between the founding of the Sisters of St Joseph and the Sisters of Perpetual Adoration, Julian preached to countless people in South Australia and eastern Australia. In Penola and after he left Adelaide, he undertook scientific endeavour as a foremost observer of God's creation, becoming a leading natural scientist of his time, loving God in His creation, our common home. Julian had placed his missionary endeavours, his scientific work and his whole life under the protection of Joseph.

The last word goes to Julian, this great lover of St Joseph. On 14 September 1887, in his second-last circular to Sisters of St Joseph, he wrote:

> May Jesus Mary and Joseph reign over our hearts. St Joseph will surely share our love when we love Mother & Her Son. For Who was ever loved by them as St Joseph was? & who was ever such a lover of Mary & Jesus as the faithful & fond, the meek and hidden St Joseph?[27]

---

27. *Letters from Father Julian Tenison Woods to Sr M Joseph Dirkin & Sisters at Lochinvar 1883–1887,* edited by Jan Tranter and Marie Hughes (Sisters of St Joseph Lochinvar, 2012), 43. The circulars are held also in the archives of the Sisters of St Joseph of the Sacred Heart, North Sydney.

Mary MacKillop 1871. Her statue of St Joseph is on the desk.

Mary MacKillop and St Joseph: A Love Story

Mary Cresp rsj

Could we be bold enough to describe the relationship of Mary MacKillop and St Joseph as a 'love story'? Newly-weds are frequently asked, 'Where did you two meet?' We all enjoy the tale of relationships that develop into love. In her letter to the Sisters on 19th of March 1893, Mary MacKillop unfolds the story of her relationship with Joseph and how it affected her situation and purpose in life.[1]

So what was the relationship of Mary MacKillop and St Joseph? Where did they first 'meet'?

A story that appeals to me is one that took place during the time Mary was a young teacher in Portland, Victoria. One night, while carrying out some duties in the church, she was inadvertently locked in and, as Paul Gardiner relates, 'spent an unplanned vigil of prayer' there.[2] Local legend has it that she spent the night sitting beside the statue of St Joseph. I like to think that that may have been a reassuring comfort for her as the hours passed by.

Of course, we do not have evidence of how and when Mary's devotion to St Joseph burst into flame. She would have been familiar with him all her life, as devotion to the Holy Family of Jesus, Mary and Joseph was a part of the Catholic tradition in which she grew up. When Mary first came to Penola in 1860 she met Father Julian

1. Mary MacKillop, Circular to Sisters, the 19th of March 1893, St Joseph's Congregational Archives, North Sydney (SJCA). Mary asks the Sisters to consider their relationship to St Joseph under three statements and then shares her own responses to them: '*Who we are; what we are doing here; in what relation we stand towards this great Saint*'.
2. Paul Gardiner, *Mary MacKillop: An Extraordinary Australian* (Sydney: E J Dwyer, 1993), 47.

Woods who had arrived in the town on St Joseph's feastday, 19th of March 1857, and had named the church he built there, 'St Joseph's'. Moreover, he had told her about the Sisters of St Joseph he had met in France. It was therefore assumed that the enterprise she and Julian were proposing would be under St Joseph's patronage. Years later, in May 1867, Mary wrote to her mother:

> I have such an earnest longing for the Order of St Joseph and know well how hard it will be to get it established here . . . none other is so fitted for the want of this Colony . . . but unless Sisters come from France, it will be long before there are enough of us for the work that is to be done.[3]

Lack of funds precluded any thought of Sisters coming from France, and Julian and Mary therefore embarked on the foundation of their own variant of the Sisters of St Joseph. Mary was convinced that 'our good and gracious God' placed them in this venture 'under the direct protection of the glorious Foster Father of His Divine Son'.[4]

In following the call to dedicate her life as a Sister of St Joseph, Mary's ultimate aim was to live in total union with God, Love of all loves. But having been given St Joseph to show her the way, she developed a relationship with the saint that we can identify as love. American artist and novelist, William Wharton, observed that 'Love is a combination of admiration, respect and passion'.[5] In the letters Mary wrote to her Sisters, and especially that of March 1893, we can see all three of these elements at work. This essay will use these elements as cues to explore Mary's relationship with St Joseph as described in her writings.

Admiration

Admiration receives the other with veneration and warm approval. Mary admired Joseph for how he conducted himself in life as

3. *Mary MacKillop & Flora: Correspondence between Mary MacKillop and her mother, Flora McDonald MacKillop*, edited by Sheila McCreanor (Sydney: Trustees of the Sisters of St Joseph, 2004), 15.
4. MacKillop, Circular to Sisters, the 19th of March 1893.
5. William Wharton, *Ever After: A Father's True Story* (New York: William Morrow, 1995), 3.

described by the evangelists Matthew and Luke. They portray his actions as those of a man full of faith; it was as though he achieved in life those virtues to which Mary herself aspired.

Humility:

'First of all,' says Mary, 'and as the sure foundation of his other virtues, we must admire [Joseph's] wondrous humility.'[6] Mary knew of Joseph, through the Gospel stories, as being a man in the background who listens to God's word and acts on it without demur. Because he does not push himself forward God works through him and, 'hidden in the shadows', he plays, as Pope Francis says, 'an incomparable role in the history of salvation.'[7] It was this aspect of Joseph that impressed Mary. 'Who . . . was so highly honoured as St Joseph?' she asks. 'Yet . . . the more the Eternal Father exalted him . . . so much more did the humble heart of our revered Patron . . . place itself in spirit beneath the mercy of its God'. This 'quiet humility' endeared Joseph to her: 'the humility of our glorious father is something wonderfully beautiful in itself... It was a humility of heart, not of words', something basic to his character.[8]

The shape that a 'humble and hidden presence' takes is avoiding centre-stage and, instead, giving of self so that others can shine. Pope Francis says of Joseph: 'He did not think of himself, but focussed instead on the lives of Mary and Jesus.'[9] In a circular written in 1880, Mary MacKillop likewise urged the Sisters to keep their ultimate goal in mind and so avoid self-absorption: 'Like our glorious Father and patron, may we ever seek to work for God, hidden as much as possible in the love of His Sacred Heart.'[10] Her retreat notes of 1882 record her prayer, 'St Joseph, sweet patron of the hidden life, obtain for me that I may walk in thy footsteps, and that in these moments given to recollection and prayer, I may discover and know my own nothingness.'[11]

However, the picture of a humble person being one who grovels in 'nothingness' is not what Mary had in mind. 'Nothingness' is truth, in

6. MacKillop, Circular to Sisters, 19 March 1893.
7. Pope Francis, *Patris Corde*, Introduction.
8. MacKillop, Circular to Sisters, 19 March 1893.
9. Pope Francis, *Patris Corde*, 7.
10. Mary MacKillop, Circular to Sisters, 11 December 1880, SJCA.
11. Mary MacKillop, Retreat Notes, Kensington 10–19 March 1882, SJCA.

that our existence depends on the source of all life, God: 'In [God] we live and move and have our being' (Acts 17:28). Given this premise, Mary received her life as gift and responded to what she believed her God-given potential was asking of her. She sees in Joseph one who did the same, calling upon the legend of the nuptials of Mary and Joseph to describe her appreciation of Joseph's humility being lived in truth. She refers to the assembled suitors, 'the youngest and richest among the children of Israel', vying for the hand of the 'beauteous Virgin' Mary in marriage and wondering how 'the poor, hardworking carpenter', Joseph, could dare to put himself forward for this honour. But it was because of his humility, she says, that he could hear 'the voice of God (which whispered in his heart)' and ignore the scorn of those who would judge him, in order to obey God's promptings.[12]

Indeed, on hearing that Julian Woods was feeling oppressed by fellow-priests in Adelaide, Mary wrote to him from Brisbane, urging him to have courage and to believe in the 'sacred duty' to which he was called. 'At any cost', she said, he was to guard against 'false humility' that would shrink away before criticism and discouragement.[13] With her understanding of 'true humility', Mary urges Sisters who are called upon to take up positions of responsibility for the sake of God's mission to do so: 'In imitation, then, of our great Patron, let our words be few, let us avoid excusing ourselves from any office on the plea of our unworthiness, let us carefully avoid talking of ourselves either in terms of praise or censure'.[14] In other words, true humility does not pretend to be more or less than we are. In her retreat notes of 1882 we find the prayer, 'Dear Father St Joseph help me to become what I should be'.[15]

Obedience to God's Will:

For Mary, God's will was 'a dear book which I am never tired of reading'.[16] She measured life-decisions by what she saw as God's will for her, confident that it was there that she would find what her heart desired. So she wrote to her Sisters:

12. MacKillop, Circular to Sisters, the 19th of March 1893.
13. Mary MacKillop to Julian Woods, the 10th of July 1870, SJCA.
14. MacKillop, Circular to Sisters, 19 March 1893.
15. MacKillop, Retreat Notes 1882.
16. Mary MacKillop to Monsignor Kirby, 22 May 1873, SJCA.

> We have come here at the call of our God … to live only in doing God's ever-blessed will. It is not that God required us, but He gave us the grace to require Him.[17]

On the journey towards union with God, Mary admired Joseph as a companion and model whose focus was doing God's will. In her letter anticipating the Sisters' first Chapter in 1875, Mary prayed: 'May God grant that in questions of conformity to His holy Will, as also in matters of obedience, the example of St Joseph may ever be before your eyes, my dearly loved Sisters wherever you are.'[18] She amplified this instruction in her letter of March 1907:

> We see in our holy Patron a perfect mirror of confidence in God and submission to His adorable Will. … How perfect, my dear Sisters, do we not find he always was in the submission of his heart and will to the mysterious designs of the same great God. His noble heart never faltered, never was deterred by the most trying obstacles from proceeding at once to the accomplishment of the Divine commands.[19]

It is unfortunate that in describing 'obedience to God's will', negative expressions such as 'submission' and 'conforming' give the impression that that God's will is other than what human nature desires. Certainly, discipline is involved. The word 'obey' comes from the Latin *oboedire*—'because of hearing'.[20] Hearing or listening to God requires that we be in touch with our inner selves, the place, according to St Paul, where the Spirit of God dwells (Eph 3:16). While Mary MacKillop may not have been concerned with the etymology of the term, she certainly knew its reality. She admired in Joseph his ability to hear the inner voice and to recognise it as the 'command' of God. As this letter was written only eighteen months before her

---

17. MacKillop, Circular to Sisters, 19 March 1893. Mary's theology of grace is classically Thomistic. Aquinas teaches that even the desire for union with God is the gift of God – existence itself is grace and its God-given goal is union with the divine.
18. Letter to Sisters, 16 January 1875, SJCA. This letter was written from the newly-established Mother House at Kensington, South Australia. The Chapter commenced on St Joseph's Day, 1875.
19. Mary MacKillop, Circular to Sisters, 10 March 1907, SJCA.
20. '*ob*' meaning 'in the direction of' or 'on account of' and '*audire*' 'to hear'.

death, Mary obviously projects on to Joseph, too, her life-experience of having come through 'glaring difficulties' to leave her rejoicing in 'the mysterious ways' of God as, encouraged by the example of her patron, she sought to do God's will.

Dependence on Divine Providence:
In her living with the reality of poverty, Mary found inspiration from reflection on what tradition had taught her of the situation of Joseph in his time.[21] She could appreciate the hardships associated especially with the stories of the Bethlehem stable and the refugee experience in Egypt. However, she does not dwell on Joseph's example in coping with supposed physical poverty so much as apply it to the interior attitudes of detachment and single-heartedness. 'May we, his children, like him, strive to be truly poor in heart', she prayed: 'Let us see whether, like the heart of our glorious Father, they are truly empty, stripped of all things, detached from all, even the smallest things, and like his, centred on God alone.'[22]

Mary deduced that it was because of Joseph's poverty of heart and spirit that he could with confidence and freedom rely on the Providence of God, trusting that, despite difficulties, all would be well. Her own experience verified this. Especially in times of hardship she was constantly reminded of God's care shown through the intercession of St Joseph. As she wrote to Father Woods during the months of the excommunication: 'I have a little purse which St Joseph guards well and never permits to be empty at the needful moment.'[23]

---

21. Tradition has deduced that Mary and Joseph were poor from the reference in Lk 2:22–24 that when they presented Jesus in the temple, they offered a sacrifice of 'a pair of turtledoves or two young pigeons' as prescribed by Lev 12:7–8 for those who could not afford a lamb. Also, 2 Cor 8:9 says of Jesus, 'Though he was rich, yet for your sake he became poor, so that through his poverty you might become rich.' However, we cannot presume too much from this statement, as it refers to the heavenly state of the Son who assumed the comparative poverty of humanity. The Gospels do not describe the social or financial standing of Joseph—that is not the point of the Gospels. We can say Joseph practised a respectable trade, and, from what Matthew tells us, that he was obviously educated and well-versed in the Scriptures. Therefore he was not a peasant, if by that we mean someone unlettered and a social outcast. At the time when Israel was under Roman occupation, life was naturally full of hardship for the country's citizens, especially those whose work after taxes left them little to live on.
22. MacKillop, Circular to Sisters, the 19th of March 1893.
23. Mary MacKillop to Julian Woods, the 19th of February 1872, SJCA.

From life-experience, too, Mary knew that an inner attitude of poverty brings freedom from the need for status, recognition and control. In her letter for St Joseph's Day 1900, she urged the Sisters to apply that same attitude in choosing to serve those without power or prestige:

> Let us be true to the beautiful spirit of our Institute. Let others seek the better more remarkable places, but let St Joseph's true children remember their mission and seek first the poorest, most neglected parts of God's vineyard.[24]

Just as Jesus had come 'to bring good news to the poor' (Lk 4:18), Sisters were to embody that good news in their everyday lives, allowing God's presence with those in difficult circumstances to be seen and experienced through them. Indeed, in being 'with the poor', she and her Sisters did suffer physical poverty, as they often lacked the basic necessities of life. Even in these circumstances, the virtue of 'inner poverty' sustained them. Joseph, with his heart in 'total forgetfulness of self' and centred on God, was their inspiration.

Respect

Respect holds a person in esteem, according them a position of honour because of their qualities and achievements. Mary MacKillop revered St Joseph as one she could look up to. His closeness to Jesus gave him a special place in that assembly we call 'The Communion of Saints'—the bond that exists between all those, living and dead, who share the life of Christ.

Joseph as Patron:

Mary was conscious of owing everything to God, since of herself she was 'nothing'. Nevertheless, God had 'condescended' to give her St Joseph 'as an especial Protector and Advocate', so that she and the Sisters could become instruments through whom others would know and love God.[25] Consequently she could count on Joseph for support and help. As patron, he would hold the interests of the Congregation in his heart and stand by her in times of difficulty.

---

24. Mary MacKillop, Circular to Sisters, the 6th of March 1900, SJCA.
25. MacKillop, Circular to Sisters, the 19th of March 1893.

In her reflection on the history of the Congregation, Mary gave some examples of what she saw as this 'special mark of St Joseph's care for his children'.[26] For example, she cited an incident when Sisters called in to another convent where they met a young woman who showed great emotion upon seeing them. They subsequently learned that the woman had dreamt of Sisters dressed as they were, even though she never knew they existed. She had prayed a novena through the intercession of St Joseph to know God's will, and its end had culminated in the Sisters' visit. Mary comments: 'That child continued the journey with the Sisters as a Postulant', while her confessor 'would never have consented had it not been that he firmly believed St Joseph had a hand in it'.[27]

In arguing against pressure to accept government funding for schools administered by the Sisters which would compromise teaching methods that integrated religion with other subjects, Mary declared that it was 'through their glorious patron St Joseph' that they could take refuge:

> Should our poor schools be taken from us, should our institute even be suppressed, ah no—our courage, our calm trust in the Sacred Heart would only grow stronger, for we would know that when the storm had passed away St Joseph would again assemble his children to work once more and more sweetly than ever in the cause of the Sacred Heart.[28]

With St Joseph as patron, it was necessary, Mary believed, that all works carried out in his name be scrupulously true to his spirit.

Joseph as Advocate:

Right from the beginning, Mary regarded St Joseph as friend and advocate, and entrusted the ministry to which the Sisters were called into his care. From Penola in January 1867 Mary wrote to Rose Cunningham, later Sister Rose:

26. Mary MacKillop, 'The History of the Congregation (1866–1900)', in *Resource Material from the Archives of the Sisters of St Joseph of the Sacred Heart*, Issue No 3 (August 1984): 9.
27. MacKillop, 'The History of the Congregation', 11.
28. Mary MacKillop, 'Rationale Against State Aid, Queensland', June 1870, SJCA.

> Our dear Patron St Joseph has done so much for the schools already that it is evident our Blessed Lord is pleased with the work, so we need not fear what obstacles may be thrown in our way.[29]

In Adelaide, the Sisters conducted a house called 'The Providence' for homeless women and children, but, as they had no reliable income and had to beg, they were often in want. They therefore placed these and other ventures under St Joseph's care and frequently sought his intercession. In April 1872, Mary explained to Father Woods, then in New South Wales:

> I spoke to Father Reynolds about getting a cheaper house for The Providence, and he was quite pleased that we should do whatever was best in the matter, so Sister Teresa will go for a few days to Sister Elizabeth, and between them, St Joseph might find them a suitable place.[30]

In a similar situation ten years later, she wrote to Bishop Reynolds of Adelaide: 'I am hoping that St Joseph will inspire some generous soul to give us a house in some suburb not too far from town.'[31] In Brisbane, a school dedicated to St Joseph and located in 'The Swamp', was so popular that the 'poor crowded little building' was overflowing. Despite this, its reputation was spreading, because 'St Joseph does it all in his own quiet way'.[32]

Mary recognised Joseph's advocacy in the practical response of others. For example, in 1872 when she had to give testimony in court in a libel case, she felt supported by the skill of her attorney, Mr Brooks, in defending the Sisters' cause: 'If our enemies tried to condemn us for our ignorance, I think St Joseph will speak through this man.'[33]

---

29. Mary MacKillop to Rose Cunningham, the 30th of January 1867, SJCA.
30. Mary MacKillop to Julian Woods, the 2nd of April 1871, SJCA. Father Reynolds was then the administrator of the diocese, after the death of Bishop Sheil, and therefore property matters had to be referred to him. He was consecrated as bishop of Adelaide on the 2nd of November, 1873.
31. Mary MacKillop to Bishop Reynolds, the 5th of April 1881, SJCA.
32. Mary MacKillop to Julian Woods, the 17th of October 1870, SJCA.
33. Mary MacKillop to Julian Woods, the 13th of May, 1872, SJCA. The Sisters had been attacked in a newspaper, *The Protestant Advocate* in early April, 1872. The libel case had gone to court and the publisher was found guilty of 'publishing a false, malicious and defamatory libel on the nuns'. (Gardiner, *Mary MacKillop*, 112).

Sometimes St Joseph actually took the place of those who could not fulfil required roles. When Mary was told in Brisbane that there was no priest available to direct the Sisters' retreat, the little community followed the meditations in a book outlining the *Spiritual Exercises* of St Ignatius Loyola. 'We did this all together', Mary wrote to Father Woods, 'but in some way since the Retreat has commenced I seem to feel as if St Joseph is invisibly near and supplying the place of our Director.'[34]

Earlier that year Mary had written to her mother about how, dependant entirely on alms and living in an unhealthy area, they felt St Joseph was looking after them:

> We have a kind good Doctor in our glorious Father, St Joseph. You would smile were you to hear how he has obtained strength and health for some of our Sisters when they were ailing.[35]

Such was her faith in him as her advocate that Mary could assert with confidence: 'St Joseph is quietly waiting, ready to come to our assistance in the moment of need.'[36]

Joseph as Model for life:

The ultimate compliment we can give a person is to hold them up as a model for our lives. For Mary, Joseph was such a model. She urged her Sisters, 'Let us love our Heavenly Father as St Joseph did'.[37] When congratulating the Sisters in New Zealand on students' success in public exams, she attributed the results to the intercession of St Joseph on their behalf and urged them to continue working according to his spirit so that 'his works in our unworthy hands will bring credit to the Church and cause we love so much'.[38]

The way shown by St Joseph was, for Mary, a sure way to total union with God, both in her inner spiritual life and in active love of neighbour. The focus was never on Joseph himself but rather on God: Joseph was a loved friend and companion on the journey. 'We

---

34. Mary MacKillop to Julian Woods, the 3rd of January 1871, SJCA.
35. Mary MacKillop to Flora MacKillop, the 6th of June, 1870, SJCA.
36. Mary MacKillop to Julian Woods, the 7th of November 1871, SJCA.
37. MacKillop, Circular to Sisters, the 19th of March 1893.
38. Mary MacKillop to New Zealand Sisters, the 14th of December 1901, SJCA.

must not forget with how much deep meaning he has been given to us as our model in the discharge of our external duties towards the children of our schools, the poor over whom we have charge, or in our separate relations towards one another in the religious community of which we are members', she maintained in her March 1907 letter to the Sisters.[39] To be given Joseph 'as a Guide and Protector'—the same guide as was given to Mary and to Jesus—was, she considered, a wondrous sign of 'the mercy and goodness of our God' and one for which she was 'humbly thankful'.[40]

Passion

Love involves feelings, and these influence commitment, closeness and trust. The heart of Mary's treatise on St Joseph in the 1893 letter reveals her personal relationship with the saint. It is one that is strong, trusting and affectionate.

Joseph as Father-figure:
For Mary, St Joseph is a father-figure. She imagines Jesus pointing her and others out to Joseph from the time of infancy 'as his future children—as those whom in the course of years, he would place in this Institute, under the care of his own dear Foster Father'. In other words, Joseph loves us, as Pope Francis says, 'with a father's heart'.[41]

Mary was especially grateful for what she experienced as the fatherly care of St Joseph in times when she suffered trauma. The excommunication was, of course, one of those dreadful periods. She described to Father Woods the kindness of the Jesuits and others towards her and the young Sisters who were suffering banishment with her. 'All are in such good spirits', she wrote. 'St Joseph is daily giving fresh proofs of his fatherly love in providing for the wants of his children.'[42]

In 1873, after the excommunication was lifted and the Sisterhood restored, Mary announced to the Sisters that she was travelling to Rome to seek approval for the Rule. Again, it was the month of

39. MacKillop, Circular to Sisters, the 10th of March 1907.
40. MacKillop, Circular to Sisters, the 19th of March 1893.
41. Pope Francis declared 2021 as the Year of St Joseph on the 8th of December 2020 in his Apostolic Letter, *Patris Corde-With a Father's Heart*.
42. Mary MacKillop to Julian Woods, the 12th of December 1871, SJCA.

March—the month traditionally dedicated to St Joseph. 'Our dear Father St Joseph has not been idle this month', she wrote: 'nor will he ever be so whilst he sees his children suffering and in need of his powerful help.'[43]

Joseph's Tenderness:
Associated with Joseph's fatherhood is tenderness—another aspect of Mary's relationship with him that Pope Francis also stresses: 'In Joseph, Jesus saw the tender love of God'.[44] Mary challenges popular stereotypes of men in the Victorian age as stern and authoritarian when she describes a father's tenderness:

> We know what a good and tender earthly father is to a devoted child; we know how all the warm ardent affections of such a child centre in the love of such a father; we know how he delights in being with him, near him; how, when he feels his infant steps tottering, he looks to his father for help; and how, in his turn, the good father raises him in his arms and nestles him to his bosom. But any picture we can draw of an earthly father's or child's love falls far short of giving a just expression to the wonderful love which St Joseph felt for the Divine Child, so mysteriously confided to his care by His Eternal Father.[45]

Romantic the picture may be. But in that vignette Mary touches on the profound truth that Pope Francis constantly reminds us of—that Joseph mirrors the tenderness God has for us, calling us to place our trust in God's compassion and mercy. We don't have to ensure we are 'good' for God to work in and through us—'most of [God's] plans are realised in and despite our frailty', says Francis.[46] Therefore, Mary encourages us, 'What confidence then should we not have in the unfailing intercession of him whom our good and merciful God has given us as a Father and Protector'.[47]

43. Mary MacKillop, Circular to Sisters, the 25th of March 1873, SJCA.
44. Pope Francis, *Patris Corde*, 2.
45. MacKillop, Circular to Sisters, the 19*th* of March 1893.
46. Pope Francis, *Patris Corde*, 2.
47. MacKillop, Circular to Sisters, the 19th of March 1893.

Joseph's Love:

From childhood Mary MacKillop would have been familiar with books of piety such as St Francis de Sales' *Introduction to the Devout Life* and Thomas à Kempis' *The Imitation of Christ* which she often referred to.[48] These and other writings supplemented the Gospels in a way, since their meditations led devotees to picture biblical scenes in a domestic setting and to express emotions appropriate to them. Thus Mary does not hesitate to speak of Joseph's 'tender solicitude' for the 'comfort and welfare' of his beloved spouse Mary, the mother of Jesus. 'How deep was the love which filled his heart for the Mother and Child', she writes. She invites her Sisters to see Joseph, having returned from his day's work, 'now tenderly turn to that loved ***One***, and with deep emotion, receive Him into his arms'.[49] In turn, Sisters are urged to learn how to love from Joseph:

> Sweet charity and love for Jesus consumed his heart. Let then sweet charity and love for Jesus and those He loves consume ours, and thus render us worthy children of the most humble, generous and charitable of men—worthy children of the most constant heart which for so many weary years and under so many trying circumstances was always faithful to its noble offices of watchful guardian and spouse of our sweet Mother Mary, and tender devoted earthly father of her beloved Child, Jesus.[50]

> Let us ask him to obtain for us a generous devoted love for his Jesus, a love that will make us, like him, faithful to His interests, a love that, true to the spirit and object of our Institute, will make us delight in serving Him in His poor, and in His little neglected ones, that will teach us patience with their faults, and how in loving charity help them overcome these.[51]

---

48. Francis de Sales' books on devotional life, written in the early seventeenth century, had a huge influence on French spirituality which, especially during the nineteenth century, became influential in Australia. *The Imitation of Christ* was written by Thomas à Kempis in the Netherlands in the early fifteenth century, and its English translation might likewise be regarded as a 'handbook for the spiritual life' for Catholics in Mary MacKillop's time.
49. MacKillop, Circular to Sisters, the 19th of March 1893.
50. MacKillop, Circular to Sisters, the 19th of March 1893.
51. MacKillop, Circular to Sisters, the 10th of March 1907.

Mary takes delight in picturing Joseph bending in love to the child Jesus, She herself was able to 'bend down' to children, as she did in a letter to the pupils in Rangiora, New Zealand: 'Besides being good and attentive at school as well as regular in your attendance', she wrote, 'you should often ask St Joseph, your Patron, to help you'.[52] Similarly, she was able to show empathy with those who were going through difficult times. When the Sisters of St Joseph of the Wilcannia diocese were applying to amalgamate with the Sisters at Mount Street, North Sydney, Mary could appreciate the emotional struggle involved. She encouraged them to take heart, adding: 'Indeed, I shall hail with joy the day when I may receive you all as my dear children—St Joseph's most tried ones.'[53]

Mary's love for Joseph expressed in admiration, respect and passion gave her a sense of direction that enabled her to keep her eyes on God as Joseph did. Almost all of the circulars Mary MacKillop wrote to the Sisters contain some form of reminder to 'work, act and live as a true child of St Joseph should'.[54] After her stroke, Mary learnt to type, and on the 27th of September 1904 sent the Sisters 'my first typewritten letter', praying 'most earnestly' 'that St Joseph's humble and hidden spirit may be seen in all'.[55]

Soon after her election as Mother General in 1918, Mother Laurence O'Brien made steps to introduce proceedings towards the Cause of Beatification of Mary MacKillop. The tribunal established by church authorities requested that witness about Mary's holiness of

52. Mary MacKillop, to the children of St Joseph's School, Rangiora, New Zealand, the 27th of September 1895, SJCA.
53. Mary MacKillop, to Sister Mary Aquin, the 2nd of July 1901. When the diocese of Wilcannia in New South Wales was formed in 1887, it included areas previously in the diocese of Bathurst. The Sisters of St Joseph who served there had been members of the Perthville community, and were now established as the Wilcannia Sisters of St Joseph with their Mother House in Hillston. In 1888, the Decree of Pope Leo XIII established the Sisters of St Joseph with their Mother House in Mount Street North Sydney as a Regular Congregation. Diocesan groups of Sisters of St Joseph were to be given the option of joining with them, or otherwise distinguished from them. However, the Wilcannia Sisters of St Joseph did not learn of this until over ten years later. Sister Mary Aquin had then written to Mary MacKillop on behalf of their Guardian General, Sr Helena O'Sullivan, to apply for amalgamation. After many obstacles, the amalgamation was officially recorded on the 2nd of December, 1902.
54. Mary MacKillop, Circular to Sisters, the 12th of September, 1884, SJCA.
55. Mary MacKillop, Circular to Sisters, the 27th of September, 1904, SJCA.

life should be given by Sisters who had known her. Among these was Sister Josephine Carolan. Her evidence includes the following:

> [Mary's] devotion to St Joseph was shown by her instructions, actions, and the prayers she prescribed to be said in his honour, and her confidence in his intercession. Her devotion to our Lord in the Blessed Sacrament, to our Lady and St Joseph ran like little veins through her life.[56]

Those 'little veins' conducted life not only to Mary but to the thousands of people who, over the years, have been led by her to find in St Joseph one who loves with a true father's heart, inspiring us to tenderness, humility, courage, trust, hope and expansive love of God and neighbour. Like Pope Francis, Mary MacKillop loved St Joseph—'the man who goes unnoticed, a daily, discreet and hidden presence—an intercessor, a support and a guide in times of trouble'.[57] 'When we remember all God has done for us', wrote Mary, 'we surely cannot but turn gratefully to our Glorious Patron and thank him for such marks of his watchful care.'[58]

56. Evidence of Sr Josephine Carolan, 'Mother Mary's Cause', SJCA.
57. Pope Francis, *Patris Corde*, Introduction.
58. Mary MacKillop, Circular to Sisters, the 11th of March, 1901, SJCA.

Part 2

Joseph's Radiant Influence

Joseph's Four Dreams, Another Great Conjunction and Invitation to Transformation

Susan Pollard rsj

> The dream is the small hidden door in the deepest and most intimate sanctum of the soul, which opens into that primeval cosmic night that was soul long before there was a conscious ego and will be soul far beyond what a conscious ego could ever reach.[1]

An 'alter-ego' speaks: According to the ancient philosopher, Cicero, an 'alter-ego' is a second personality, a trusted friend. From my perspective as a Jungian Analyst, that 'helpful other' might also be a 'doppelgänger' or 'shadow self'. In this article, I imagine and have called the positive shadow, 'Naomi.' Like her namesake, I envisage that Naomi's family has lived in Israel for as long as anyone remembers. However this story is not specifically about Naomi nor about her family history, although some of those roots may be revisited. Rather my intention is to plumb the strange dreams had by a carpenter from Nazareth, Joseph by name, and whose dreams changed and continue to challenge people's lives. For instance, this man was named 'Guardian of the Mystery of God' in Pope John Paul's letter, *Guardian of the Redeemer.*[2] In contrast to Joseph's silence, his actions speak eloquently about the importance of attending to dreams that come nightly from psyche through the deep layer of the unconscious.

1. Carl Gustav Jung, 'The Meaning of Psychology for Modern Man', in *Collected Works. 10*, edited by G Adler translated by RFC Hull (Princeton, NJ: Princeton University Press, 1933), 304.
2. John Paul II, Encyclical Letter *Redemptoris Custos* (Vaticana: Libreria Editrice, 1989), 1.

> We call the unconscious 'nothing', and yet it is in reality *in potentia*. The thought we shall think, the deed we shall do, even the fate we shall lament tomorrow, all lie unconscious in our today. The unknown . . . we must always reckon with the presence of things not yet discovered.[3]

As well as focusing on the uncanny world of dreams, I want to turn up the volume on the female voice through the person of Naomi. In my fantasy, Naomi is listening to her uncle Matthew relating these dreams at the traditional family gathering of Hanukkah. Through and in this hypothetical remembrance of a Festival of Lights, may we find ourselves animated.

I realise you may already be familiar with the events recounted by Mattai, better known as Matthew, and you may also have come across their different renditions from the pen of Luke, John and Mark. What's more you could also be aware of other versions from the suppressed gospels of Mary and Thomas. Even though these evangelists are long dead, the power of their words persist, leaving indelible marks on one's soul and niggling questions in one's heart and mind about mystery, the unknown and about grace.

Disarming grace shining through the wisdom of the dream prompts this exploration as well as the delight of collaborating in a work about Joseph with other Josephite women. However, I am mindful that alluding to dreams and visions is dubious because they have a kind of chequered notoriety in the collective memory of the Australian Sisters of St Joseph. I am referring to a scandal surrounding a little group of pioneering Josephite Sisters who feigned spirituality by asserting strange dreams and claiming false visions. It happened early in the history of our Religious Congregation in South Australia. It seems timely to challenge the shadow that has resulted from that event and hung around dreams and their potential contribution to personal and collective well-being in our tradition. For I suggest that this scandal abruptly closed the door on delving into the dreaming aspect of the unconscious and seemed to quash 'the glory and the freshness of a dream'.[4]

---

3. Carl Gustav Jung, 'Conscious, unconscious and individuation', in *Collected Works. 9i*, edited by G Adler, translated by RFC Hull (Princeton, NJ: Princeton University Press, 1939), 498.
4. William Wordsworth, 'Intimations of Immortality from Recollections of Early Childhood', *The Oxford Book of English Verse: 1250–1900* (UK: Oxford University Press, 1919), 536.

Fast Forward: In sharing Naomi's anecdotal reveries to Joseph's dream and to our current reality, I encourage you to drop into your imagination as our world faces another Great Conjunction not seen for 800 years. That conjunction is not only of planets but of paradigms spurred on by climate change, pandemics, and economic hardship for Earth and her inhabitants. I am hopeful that Joseph's dreams can help us to be more open to unexpected Grace . . . as it was then, and as we desperately need now, on 'this endangered earth as it is in heaven'.

In this dream work, I have called on another mentor, as well as my imaginary companion, Naomi. He also belongs to that other time which Christians call the Communion of Saints and Jungians describe as the Collective Unconscious. I am referring to Swiss depth- psychologist, Carl Gustav Jung, who, in his approach to dreams, advises a way of allowing space for something new to enter consciousness. How? By way of unknowing and a process of dreaming 'with eyes wide open' or, what Jung called, Active Imagination:

> I have made it a rule, when someone tells me a dream and asks for my opinion, to say first of all to myself: 'I have no idea what this dream means'. After that I can begin to examine the dream.[5]

So in the company of Naomi, who I might name as 'alter ego' and 'shadow sister', and with Jung who for me is an animus figure, could I invite you to enter into Joseph's dream series? Through an Active Imagination process, or actively paying attention, which the German word, '*betrachen*', conveys, I anticipate that our careful listening might become 'pregnant' with new possibility as well as encouraging us to become more attuned to our dreaming selves.

As mentioned, the primary source I take for considering Joseph's dreams is the Gospel according to Saint Matthew. In my reverie, the author is privy to the dream events because Mary welcomed her son's friends not only into their home but into her heart. Hence because she did so, I propose, these enigmatic happenings found a way into sacred scripture. Matthew/Mattai, the story teller, was initially a tax-collector and despised because of working for the Romans. However chosen and called by Christ, Matthew became an Apostle of Jesus of

5. Carl Gustav Jung, 'On the Nature of Dreams', in *Collected Works. 8*, edited by G Adler, translated by RFC Hull (Princeton, NJ: Princeton University Press, 1960), 304.

Nazareth. When Naomi asked her uncle about his experiences as ‹a follower of an-Nāṣirī', I picture Mattai taking a breath and saying 'Ah! I remember . . . ' and in this vein, let us go to the dream series.

The First Dream is as Follows:[6]

> Now the birth of Jesus Christ was as follows. When His mother Mary had been betrothed to Joseph, before they came together she was found to be with child by the Holy Spirit. And Joseph her husband, being a righteous man, and not wanting to disgrace her, desired to put her away secretly. But when he had considered this, behold, an angel of the Lord appeared to him in a dream, saying, 'Joseph, son of David, do not be afraid to take Mary as your wife; for that which has been conceived in her is of the Holy Spirit'. 'And she will bear a Son; and you shall call His name Jesus, for it is He who will save His people from their sins.' Now all this took place that what was spoken by the Lord through the prophet might be fulfilled, saying, 'Behold, the virgin shall be with child, and shall bear a Son, and they shall call His name Immanuel', which translated means, 'God with us'. And Joseph arose from his sleep, and did as the angel of the Lord commanded him, and took her as his wife, and kept her a virgin until she gave birth to a Son; and he called His name Jesus (Matt 1:18–25).[7]

In Jungian circles, it is important to enter into the context of a dream. So let us visualise the location as Nazareth, a non-descript town in Galilee, around the time of the Roman occupation. Matthew cuts quickly to the chase. Mary, while engaged to Joseph, is pregnant and offers no rational explanation for her condition. What is meant by being pregnant through the Holy Spirit? The point that Matthew implies, and that I hear Naomi, my shadow sister, emphasising, is that regardless of who the father is, the outcome is the work of the Holy Spirit . . . in Mary, her unborn child and in the ensuing events. Initially, 'this unknown' is too shocking for Joseph (and for many others) to accept. Mary's fiancé decides to quietly divorce her. Joseph knows too well the stigma, blame and damning judgments

---

6. Ian Roberts, *Feather* (Blyth: Medika Gallery 2014). Used with permission.
7. All Scripture quotes are taken from *The Inclusive Bible* (Lanham: Sheed & Ward, 2007).

that an unmarried mother would face. So while Joseph settles on his path, a dream presents him with another way through the perilous circumstance! However, before we get to the turning point, other clarifications need to be made around the dreamer.

Concerning Joseph, we know from Matthew's description that Joseph is an upright man who can trace his lineage to King David and to father Abraham. I imagine my alter-ego, Naomi, might be interrupting at this point and reiterating that while Joseph is a respected person and carpenter in the village, for all his practicality, Joseph is receptive to dreams. Like his ancestor, Joseph of old, the younger Joseph has dreams and premonitions which impact the wider community. Such dreams may be considered as 'history-changers'.

Quoting esteemed Jewish analyst, Dr Henri Abramovitch:

> Biblical dreams can . . . be understood in terms of Jung's distinction between personal dreams and big dreams.[8] Personal dreams deal with the dreamer's own psychological issues, while big dreams come from a deeper level and have a broader, collective significance.[9]

Just to be clear, I consider Joseph's dreams take us in to the big dream arena with ramifications that go beyond a particular time and space and so can be called 'archetypal' or dreams that hold significance even today.

The Climax: Joseph's dream and the angel's words address his doubts:

> Joseph, son of David, do not be afraid to take Mary as your wife; for that which has been conceived in her is of the Holy Spirit . . . [the child] will save His people from their sins (Matt 1:20).

I can sense Joseph's awe rising and his anguish dissipating. As Naomi reminds me, in many religions and mythologies, supernatural beings or archetypal intermediaries often appear to show a way through the most difficult points in life's journey. In the Hebrew scriptures, some of the names and reputations of these divine tie-breakers are

8. Jung, 'On the nature of dreams'.
9. Henry Abramovitch, 'Daniel: Psychological Development of a Master Biblical Dream Interpreter', in *Journal of Analytical Psychology* (2021): 66, 94.

identified. For example, Archangels Michael, Raphael and Gabriel are known to be particularly 'close to the Creator'.[10]

In our time, Pope Francis has described these mythological or actual messengers as 'gateways to transcendence'.[11] The angel who I am identifying as the transcendent function in Joseph's dream allows Joseph to cross over from his fears and suspicions and see a bigger picture that cuts through his dilemma. Nevertheless it takes a leap of faith. Yet by listening to this inner voice, Joseph finds freedom from a patriarchal view that would have him abandon the vulnerable feminine and the new life she is carrying. Through connecting to his deeper Self, Joseph, there and then, becomes the husband of Mary and father of Jesus. Joseph also exemplifies the poet's words, 'The child is father of the man'.[12]

Dénoument: Matthew steps in, and assists us in and through the sharing, to be brought into this particular event. We have another insight into our being at one with God and with all creation and that bridges time and space. I imagine that shadow sister, Naomi, being more familiar with the Hebrew Scriptures, is reminding us about this allusion to Isaiah and that Immanuel has been, and is always, God with us (Isa 7:14).

When I ask my alter ego why Matthew emphasises that the 'virgin is with child' and hones in on Mary's consenting rather than just submitting to her fate, Naomi replies that here is the timeless message to everyone. Namely to recognise that virginal, incorruptible part in each of us and whose spark can never be tainted, extinguished or lost. At this point, I envisage Naomi turning to me and adding, 'in your work as a therapist you need to draw attention to that inviolable spark in everyone'. And she adds, 'that spark summons us to consent to whatever is our particular destiny. It comes to birth in our consenting to whatever is our vocation.' And in this incident, I see Joseph recognising his call, and in giving his consent, showing himself 'a righteous man':

10. Moses Maimonides, *A Guide for the Perplexed,* translated from original Arabic by M Friedlaender (New York: E P Dutton, 1904), 4.
11. Pope Francis, 'Guardian angels. Our daily gate to the Father', Homily in Santa Marta, on the 2nd of October, 2018 at <https://www.vaticannews.va/en/pope-francis/mass-casa-santa-marta/2018-10/pope-francis-homily-daily-mass-guardian-angels-transcendence.html>. Accessed 24 February 2021.
12. William Wordsworth, 'The rainbow', Public Domain Poetry.

> Even the enlightened person remains what he is and is never more than his own limited ego before the One who dwells within him, whose form has no knowable boundaries, who encompasses him on all sides, fathomless as the abyss of the earth and vast as the sky.[13]

To further appreciate Joseph's openness and integrity, Naomi urges me to attend to the next dream in the quartet according to Matthew.

The Second Dream—The Escape to Egypt

> When they (the Magi) had gone, an angel of the Lord appeared to Joseph in a dream 'Get up', he said, 'take the child and his mother and escape to Egypt. Stay there until I tell you, for Herod is going to search for the child to kill him'. So he got up, took the child and his mother during the night and left for Egypt where he stayed until the death of Herod. And so was fulfilled what the Lord had said through the prophet: 'Out of Egypt I called my son' (Matt 2:13).

A different context: In the ancient world, and in some contemporary circles, people point to geographical portals for crossing over into that time and place which the Irish call the ‹thin space'. You might agree that significant places carry particular potent energies, like Newgrange,[14] Machu Picchu,[15] and, closer to my home in Australia, the Flinders Ranges.[16]

Does it mean we have to find our way to such places? Or can a 'crossing over' to that deeper dimension of the Collective Unconscious, into a world outside time and space, occur wherever

13. Barbara Hannah, *Jung: His life and Work, a Biographical Memoir* (USA: Capricorn Books, 1976), 218.
14. Newgrange is a prehistoric monument in County Meath, Ireland, and is a place of astrological, spiritual, religious and ceremonial importance, best known for the illumination of its chamber by the winter-solstice sun.
15. Macchu Piccu, high up in the Andes Mountains outside of Cuzco, Peru, is a site of pre-Columbian ruins and a symbol of the ancient Incan Empire. This citadel built in the fifteenth century is one of the new Seven Wonders of the World and a UNESCO World Heritage Site.
16. Flinders Ranges is an ancient and iconic mountain range in South Australia. Cave and rock paintings and other cultural artefacts indicate that Aboriginal people have lived here for tens of thousands of years.

we might be? While I think 'yes', Naomi points to two meaningful places that Matthew identifies in the Nativity story as 'the thin space'; namely, Bethlehem and Egypt.

It is Bethlehem, in Judaea, that Matthew identifies as the physical location for Jesus' birth and Joseph's second dreaming encounter with an angelic presence. At this point, I hear Jung advising me to refer to what he called 'synchronicity', a concept best described as meaningful coincidence. For there are echoes of synchronicity in this brief dream. Bethlehem held mythological significance because of Isaiah's prophecy that the Messiah would be born there. Secondly, Joseph is directed in the dream to seek refuge in Egypt. The latter had also provided a safe haven for Joseph of old as well as for Jacob and sons to survive hard times.

Back to Joseph, husband of Mary, father of Jesus: Like others in the Roman Empire, Joseph was obligated to respond to Caesar Augustus' decree. This census meant that Joseph should travel with a very pregnant wife to register the family in his hometown of Bethlehem. Listening to Matthew's story, Joseph comes across as highly intuitive. Attentive to his inner voice, Joseph could foresee the violence that Herod, a narcissistic ruler, was preparing to unleash. I wonder how Joseph broached his fears and this disturbing dream with Mary and Jesus? In my fantasy, Naomi responds with the following passage from the Talmud. I hear her saying, 'Joseph respected its counsel and Mary, knew from her own experience, how important it was to attend to the meaning of the dream'.

> If one has a dream which makes him sad . . . he should have it turned into good in the presence of three. Let him bring three and say to them: 'I have seen a good dream'. And they should say to him, 'Good it is and good may it be. May the All-Merciful turn it to good.'[17]

Climax: As we see with Herod, not everyone welcomes a successor and competition. In contrast to Herod, the dream shows the Persian astrologers who are receptive to the breaking in of the new. These Magi recognise the Spirit alive in nature. They follow the heavenly signs and portents which lead them to an unlikely Messiah in outback

17. Isidore Epstein, *Hebrew-English Edition of the Babylonian Talmud* (London: The Soncino Press, 1989), 55b.

Bethlehem. Then after their visit, the angel revisits Joseph in a dream urging him to get going to Egypt with mother and child. Surely fear and a heaviness impinge on Joseph. Something again unplanned, out of 'left field' intruding. What will happen to them if they become travellers, pilgrims and refugees in a foreign land? The words of the poet capture the perspective of such a journey and the paradox of life and death, personal and collective transformation:

> All this was a long time ago, I remember,
> And I would do it again, but set down
> This set down
> This: were we led all that way for
> Birth or Death? There was a Birth, certainly
> We had evidence and no doubt. I had seen birth and death,
> But had thought they were different; this Birth was
> Hard and bitter agony for us, like Death, our death.
> We returned to our places, these Kingdoms,
> But no longer at ease here, in the old dispensation,
> With an alien people clutching their gods.
> I should be glad of another death.[18]

I can hear Jung commenting that the Magi are undergoing an individuation experience which poet, TS Eliot, expresses as a gradual coming to consciousness. From this epiphany and in our unique journey of seeking for meaning, we learn that any awakening is hard won, at personal cost and often gradual. In our time, there is an urgency for waking up to natural phenomena which render us freer to recognise the Sacred that is both within us and impregnating all creation.

The Third Dream—The Return

After Herod died, an angel of the Lord appeared in a dream to Joseph in Egypt and said, 'Get up, take the child and his mother and go to the land of Israel, for those who were trying to take the child's life are dead' (Matt 2: 19–20).

---

18. TS Eliot, 'Journey of the Magi', *Collected Poems 1909–1962* by permission of the publisher, (London: Faber & Faber, 1974).

Another momentous dream! Joseph learns that Herod has died while the angel urges him to take the family, leave Egypt and return home. As Naomi, points out, Mattai gives no more information about the context for this divine intervention. We simply hear that Joseph has this dream somewhere in Egypt. We don't know how long Mary, Joseph and Jesus have lived in this foreign country, nor details of their exile. It could have been for years. What is clear is that Joseph has this apparition and acts on the messenger's orders to leave with his family for the 'land of Israel'.

I imagine Naomi's commentary now as she fills in some of the unrecorded backstory that she has learnt from Uncle Mattai. She relates how Joseph and Mary were both upset and excited at this prospect of returning home. They have already learnt much about displacement, uprooting and resettling. Secure child that he is, Jesus views the coming trek as another adventure. For Mary and her husband, it has been hard to be immigrants in Egypt and now it is difficult to face that long journey home already knowing its challenges. Namely adjusting to a different culture, making a living, learning another language, even while the journey had opened them to a wider world. Fast forward to 2021: It's much the same for travellers now caught somewhere overseas in the Covid crisis and who are trying to get back to their home country. Whatever the reason, going home can be difficult, precarious and even disillusioning.

Climax and Unfolding: The angel's message declares then and today that even demagogues die! For all his arrogance, Herod, cannot escape his mortality—nor can we. The global pandemic seriously reminds us of finiteness, our fragile earth and human vulnerability. As I reflect further on Mattai's brief narrative, I imagine Naomi exclaiming: 'Can't you see? Uncle is indicating a new Exodus!' Again Israel is leaving Egypt. Joseph's vision arrests him and he obeys its call, much like Moses when confronted by the burning bush. Yet the only certainty that is given Moses and Joseph is that 'I AM' is with them. Similarly that is the only certainty that we have. What difference does that sense of the Other make for our lives?

Re-enter Jung. At this point and on the subject of Joseph's dreams, I envisage Jung drawing attention to the repetition of a well-known archetype that not only crosses time and cultures but appears here. The wise old Swiss points to the archetype or the motif of the journey through the dream series. I hear him commenting that archetypes are actually felt by their numinous quality or charged affect. Writer, Maud Bodkin, describes archetypes or archetypal patterns as 'that within us which leaps in response'.[19]

In this instance, I can sense that the significance of this archetypal pattern in and for our lives becomes clearer with two simple questions. 'When have you felt called to leave home and how did that experience change you'? Secondly, 'what did you bring back to your community because of your journeying'? No doubt, Joseph and his family were inexorably changed by all that has happened. Like them, we may also realise that the journey of life changes us for better or worse and that is a treasure we bring to those who share our lives. I am intimating what Jung identified as the fruit of our life's work: the process of Individuation or Interior Transformation.

Fourth Dream—Galilee Instead of Judea

> But when he (Joseph) heard that Archelaus was reigning in Judea in place of his father Herod, he was afraid to go there. Having been warned in a dream, he withdrew to the district of Galilee (Matt 2:19–20).

Another crisis and transition: In this dream snippet, we learn that Archelaus' reputation for 'reigning' with cruelty exceeded that of his father, Herod the Great. At this point in the narrative, my shadow sister, Naomi, interjects with a proverb from the prophet, Ezekiel: *'Like mother like daughter . . . like father like son'* (Ezek 16:44). Hearing the strange call now urging Joseph to return from exile, Joseph recognises the shadow of the negative father embodied in Archelaus. As a result, the family sets out for Galilee instead of Bethlehem. The journey is coming full circle back to Nazareth; and surely with deep interior changes for Joseph, Mary and their child.

> We shall not cease from exploration
> And the end of all our exploring
> Will be to arrive where we started
> And know the place for the first time.[20]

19. Maud Bodkin, *Archetypal Patterns in Poetry: Psychological Studies of Imagination* (London: Oxford University Press, 1971), 4.

20. Eliot, 'Four Quartets', *Collected Poems* 1909–1962.

Emotional intelligence can be a trendy 'catch phrase'. However, now more than ever, it is important that we grow in this way of knowing. In working with our dreams, CG Jung encouraged people to identify and name their feeling response. One's reaction may be comforting or disturbing. You could call it, 'the voice of the hidden waterfall'.[21]

As we learn in this fourth dream piece, Joseph was able to own his disquiet. His fear of Archelaus is an appropriate response to a dictator who acted out his name 'master of the people'. It is a fact that negative feeling can overwhelm and keep us stuck. So as to find a way forward, anxiety needs to transform in to fear. How can this happen? The act of naming one's fear makes it possible to get a handle on whatever is a particular threat. In this situation, Joseph expresses his rightful distress. It follows then that instead of being overpowered, frozen or engulfed by the grey cloud of anxiety, Joseph is able to listen to, make a decision and act in accord with the Voice of the 'Other'.

This dream scene offers an insight into the potential of the positive and negative father in shaping one's responses. Experience supports psychological research that children often assume the attitudes, behaviors of parental figures. The good news is that the Shadow of the unknown, as in the negative father or mother, can not only prevent but can motivate us to take necessary action. Joseph's capacity for awareness, sometimes called mindfulness, frees him to respond with courage from his essential self rather than to react out of fear. Marie-Louise Von Franz says it well:

> . . . the secret of the psyche . . . is its opening to the divine. One of the greatest contributions of C G Jung's work is that he taught us to keep the door open to the unknown visitor within, which he named, the Shadow.[22]

In encouraging an openness to the unknown even when it feels threatening, I want to hearken back to Henry Abramovitch, a contemporary Joseph figure. Henry referred to Leonard Cohen's song, 'You Want It Darker', written just before the poet-musician's death.[23]

---

21. Eliot, 'Four Quarters'.
22. Marie-Louise von Franz, *Archetypal Dimensions of the Psyche* (Boston & London: Shambhala, 2014), 73
23. Leonard Cohen and Patrick Leonard, *You Want It Darker* (Columbia Records, 2016).

In this particular music track, Cohen suddenly sings in Hebrew, 'Hineni, hineni'. To which I want to add a gem of wisdom from Henry Abramovitch who writes, 'Hineni means "Here I am. Ready!"'

In Scripture, it is the spirit in which a person called by the Voice to be a prophet responds . . . not from ego but from the Self. Joseph could and did respond with 'Hineni . . . Here I am. Ready!' May I wish for you, as Henry Abramovitch wished for me:

> 'Hineni!' (Let us all hope to be ready as was Joseph.) 'Now in living and later when it is time to know'. (Wherever you are . . .) 'Seeing sparkle in your eyes'.

Creative Space:

- Journal any dreams or memorable experiences of the unconscious breaking through to you. As Jung advised 'let the symbol work', to which you might choose to give 'body' by drawing or creating in some visible way.

Joseph and Family Life

Sue and Leo Kane (Josephite Companions)

It is quite fascinating to examine the various ways St Joseph has been portrayed in art. One of my personal favourites is an image from the Book of Hours from Besancon, dating from the fifteenth century, and held by the Fitzwilliam Museum in Cambridge. In this very endearing and novel portrayal, Joseph is shown on the floor nursing the infant Jesus, while Mary sits up in bed, reading. Moreover, in an intentionally revealing touch, the ass, whose breath is meant to keep him warm, cannot resist having a little nibble of Joseph's halo. This is not the patriarchal, somewhat removed figure that conventional art has often given us, but rather an active, helpful, solicitous husband who shares in the care of the Holy Infant, allowing the exhausted Mary to take a little time for herself.

Typical depictions of Joseph had, for a very long time, represented him as a rather static, often elderly figure, sometimes asleep (after all, he was a dreamer). However, gradually, especially in art from Germany and the Netherlands in the fourteenth and fifteenth centuries, artists chose to show Joseph as being engaged in a variety of domestic tasks. These included 'warming swaddling clothes, cooking food, blowing a fire into life', helping to 'prepare the Child's bath' and even 'cutting up his hose to make swaddling bands for the Child' as well as other parental duties.[1] This tradition continued in later centuries, and especially in our own time, when many artists have sought to capture Joseph as a strong, active, loving, and spiritually intuitive man, one who was especially well suited to become the husband of Mary and reputed father of Jesus.

---

1. Pamela Tudor-Craig & Nicholas Rogers, 'Illuminating Christmas with the Friars', in *Church Times*, 21 (December 2012): 4.

Armed with the Scriptures, and with a good dose of intuition and common sense, it seems only right to align ourselves with such interpretations of one who was, first and foremost, a family man. Indeed, we might ask how the old fellow with missing teeth and clutching a pair of spectacles, as portrayed by Joos van Cleve, could possibly have coped with events such as the Flight into Egypt? Rather, a 1470's woodcut showing Joseph leading the Christ-child by the hand, perhaps returning from Egypt, is more consistent with our modern understanding of who Joseph was, as the leader of the holy family.[2]

We know that the portrayal of Joseph given by the evangelists Matthew and Luke was not of a Pharisee, or a teacher, a cleric, or member of a religious order, not a monk, nor an apostle nor martyr. He was not versed in theology, he never wrote a book or preached a sermon, he didn't even leave us any sayings to ponder. He was Joseph, a 'just' man, above all, a family man, one who led a life of quiet service in relative anonymity. Leonardo Boff reminds us that in the gospels Joseph 'always appears within the context of the family, because it is within the family, as a husband and father, that he finds his natural place.'[3] To this observation we might add that it was in the context of the family that Joseph attained a depth of holiness which made him so suitable to be declared patron of the universal Church. For Jewish people, as in our Christian tradition, marriage has always been viewed as a holy state, and one that aids in the sanctification of people.[4] It was in his marriage to Mary, in the spiritual bonding of these two people, in their love and care for one another, that Joseph eventually came to shine a great light into this world. The rather wonderful reality is that Jesus was shaped and formed, and grew in wisdom and understanding of God in the care and nurturing of two married people.

Throughout the centuries, especially since devotion to him was promoted in medieval times, the common people have consistently taken Joseph to their hearts, finding in him the inspiration for their own family life, and recognising some of their personal struggles and dilemmas reflected in his. He has been viewed as an eminently

2. Tudor-Craig & Rogers, 'Illuminating Christmas with the Friars', 4.
3. Leonardo Boff, *Saint Joseph* (Eugene, OR: Wipf and Stock, 2009), 25.
4. Lisa Katz, 'Marriage and Weddings in Judaism' at <www.learnreligions.com>. Accessed 8 March, 2021.

relatable figure because, like most of humankind, he lived his life in anonymity and obscurity, 'hidden from the world, but visible to God', according to Henri Nouwen.[5] All of us live in families at some time, and we know from experience not only the joys, but also the pressures they can face. The messiness and complexity of a real life, with the anguish and confusion it can engender, would not have been unknown to Joseph. Indeed, for those of us familiar with the challenges of parenting and surviving in a difficult world, Joseph is that loving and tender friend with whom we can seriously engage in our search for direction and meaning.

It goes without saying that he was blessed beyond our wildest imagining in the people who were to make up his family, namely Jesus and Mary. Nevertheless, the events of Joseph's life as portrayed in the gospels reveal deep and demanding challenges to his faith and his personhood, ones which would not have been imaginable to him when he first met Mary and came to love her. He would have taken the initial steps towards marriage unaware, as we all are, of what was going to be asked of him. Indeed, his entry into married life was to be unexpectedly dramatic.

No doubt, as a young Jewish man, Joseph would have cherished the hope of natural fatherhood. This would have been central to his identity. It is hard to imagine the depth of the pain he endured when, having become engaged to Mary, 'She was found to be pregnant through the Holy Spirit' (Matt 1:18). So many reactions would have come to the fore in the wake of this revelation. Given typical responses in small communities, some in the village would have wondered if Joseph was the culprit, and would probably have despised and slandered him. For him, there would have been a mixture of shame and hurt, along with confusion and worry. How could this be happening to him? We married people must be able to trust the one we love; it is the very foundation of the relationship. To say 'I trust you' is, in fact, the greatest honour a person can bestow on another, and Joseph's trust was deeply and sorely tested. He had to negotiate this most difficult, awkward and fairly public situation involving the woman with whom he hoped to share his life, not really understanding what had happened. Moreover, in company with

---

5. Mosaieksa Posts, 9 August 2020 at <www.facebook.com>. Accessed 8 March 2021.

many other people throughout the ages, he was asked to abandon his dream of physical parenthood, and bring up a Child who was not his. On any count, this was a rugged introduction to family life.

It must be said that the gospel stories depict him coming through, in the end, with flying colours. Initially, he went for the simple, straightforward solution, the one endorsed by the Law. 'Joseph, her husband, an upright person unwilling to disgrace her, decided to divorce her quietly' (Matt 1:19). There was no trace of ego or anger hinted at in Matthew's description of Joseph's reaction. Also, it has to be said that Joseph arrived at this decision in darkness, not grasping initially the significance of the events of which he was part. Like many believers who would follow in his footsteps, he made his decision from the depths of his confusion, and glimpsing only scattered pieces of the mosaic. He misunderstood Mary's situation. So easily can we see ourselves reflected in all of this, when we recall those times in our own family life where we have rushed to judgement without knowing all the facts.

We can imagine Joseph, being a man of insight, knowing deep down that his inner struggle was not yet fully resolved. Something was gnawing away at him, urging him to reflect more deeply on what he had made up his mind to do. Further discernment was required. Perhaps he had decided too hastily? We can imagine him challenging himself to '*sleep on it*'. It's so interesting to see that Pope Francis has had a statue of a sleeping Joseph on his desk for decades. He states 'Joseph's rest revealed God's will to him. In this moment of rest in the Lord, as we pause from our many daily obligations and activities, God is also speaking to us'. Florian Romero supports the Pope's message: 'St Joseph is a model father for the Christian family. He overcame the difficulties of life because he rested with God.'[6]

There is much to be said for '*resting with God.*' One is reminded of the line from the Song of Songs, 'I slept, but my heart was awake' (Song of Songs 5:2). A heart that is awake is one that is listening, exploring, pondering, considering and assessing. It is a heart that is open to the wisdom of love. Joseph the family man showed that he possessed such a heart. So when Matthew tells us that '. . . suddenly the angel of God appeared in a dream and said . . . don't be afraid to

6. Valerie Schmalz, 'Pope Francis Popularises Devotion to a Sleeping St Joseph', citing interviewee Florian Romero in *Catholic San Francisco* (12 June 2015).

wed Mary: it is by the Holy Spirit that she has conceived this child' (Matt 1:20), the subtext is that Joseph has come to a deeper level of understanding, and has found enough faith to trust in God, whose ways are mysterious. He has arrived at a new level of maturity. John A Walsh writes that Joseph's initial decision had been 'no decision at all', leading him to experience an 'inner struggle', which allowed at last his 'authentic self' to emerge, and a more enlightened position to be arrived at. Walsh goes on to say that the dream was really 'a call to deepen and expand (Joseph's) love for Mary'.[7] For Joseph, as for most of us, his best insights came to him when he was still, and able to listen to a deeper voice within. Another powerful depiction of him is the mosaic which portrays Joseph with his hand up to his ear, in an attitude of listening. The artist clearly sensed that it was the ability to listen that defined so much about this man, who was able to show considered judgement and even go against accepted norms in order to care for his family. A husband and father who knows how to listen—that's precious and much to be desired.

In deciding to go ahead with the marriage, Joseph stepped into the unknown. His newly honed intuition enabled him to take a risk, go beyond the law's prescriptions, and learn to live with ambiguity. While still partly in the dark, he was brave enough to go with a higher law, making his love for Mary his highest priority. Little wonder that Jesus, brought up by such a father figure, would later say, in his sermon on the mount: 'Therefore, treat others as you would have them treat you. This is the whole meaning of the Law and the prophets' (Matt 7:12).

While Joseph has often been rightly described as a man of dreams, as a husband and father he showed himself to be equally a man of action. ('Like St Joseph, once we have heard God's voice, we must get up and act').[8] As soon as he had stepped into the unknown, much more was required of him, and his faith would be profoundly and repeatedly tested. Luke's gospel tells us that at the time of the census, Joseph set off to go and register in Bethlehem with Mary, his espoused wife, who was pregnant. When her labour pains began, it must have been a huge worry for Joseph, unable to find accommodation at such a crucial time. Like many unknown and anonymous people in similar

7. John A Walsh, 'The Dream of Joseph: A Jungian Interpretation', in *Journal of Psychology and Theology*, (March 1983).
8. Schmalz, 'Pope Francis Popularises Devotion to a Sleeping St Joseph'.

circumstances, after assisting with the birth, Joseph had to 'make do', improvising a spot to place the baby and keep him warm. His family, like many others throughout history, faced enormous pressures which required action and leadership from him.

We are then presented with another vignette where, consumed with the challenges of caring for a new infant, Joseph nevertheless stayed true to the interior life, lived, in his case, within the family. We know this to be correct because Matthew's gospel tells us, in the metaphorical language of Scripture, that he had another 'dream', or moment of enlightenment, and yet again, he listened. Love's insight told Joseph that he would have to do that most difficult of things, namely uproot his family and flee to another country. He would have been aware of the danger that King Herod, a despotic monarch, posed to them, especially after Herod ordered the killing of children in the area where they lived. No doubt a scenario of fear and anguish would have ensued for the family, somewhat understated by Matthew when he writes, 'Joseph got up, awakened Jesus and Mary, and they left that night for Egypt' (Matt 2:14). True to form, Joseph showed grace under pressure, and great courage in taking measures to safeguard his family with, as usual, a minimum of fuss.

Nowadays we have some sense of how displaced people and refugees must suffer greatly through feeling out of place in both of their worlds, that is, the one they must leave behind, as well as the one to which they flee. Joseph's family, exiled in Egypt, would have faced all sorts of problems. Would they be welcomed? Would they need to depend on the kindness of strangers? Where might they find food and shelter? Would Joseph be able to make a living in this strange, unknown place? When might they be able to return home? Pope Francis assures us that Joseph did not have 'his head in the clouds',[9] and just as well, because here he found himself having to start over again, in order to keep his loved ones safe. Boff comments on the worries of caring for the young child and the traumatised mother:

> They could fall ill during the voyage, they must eat and drink and have a place to stay overnight guaranteed. All these tasks (were) duties of the father Joseph, which he certainly assumed with courage and determination.[10]

9. Pope Francis, homily, 'St Joseph Raises Jesus in Silence', at Mass in Casa Santa Marta, *Vatican News* (18 December 2018).
10. Boff, *Saint Joseph*, 45.

Caring for his loved ones, and keeping them together and safe in those hard times would have required much of Joseph. No doubt it was the blessing and privilege of being a parent and a husband, and the unconditional love he felt for his family, which kept him going. This quiet, accepting man of rectitude and honour was all too familiar with the beauty, sadness and complexity of everyday family life, and the unexpected challenges that could turn up unannounced. He had a strong sense of duty and was prepared to make difficult decisions. Joseph's determination to keep his family safe resonates still today with people everywhere, especially those who are poor and underprivileged. We all experience the reality that 'Herods' can appear in many guises, for example, when unjust leaders cause havoc in the lives of their people. As well, there may be other 'Herods'—the many temptations and dangers which threaten family life. People need large doses of Joseph's courage, faith and good judgement in order to stay safe. Sometimes one is even required to remove the family from a dangerous and difficult situation, just as Joseph was called to do.

It can be tempting to idealise the life led by the Holy Family, but that would involve glossing over the words of Scripture. Luke's account of the time when Jesus was presented in the temple is a case in point. 'The couple took Jesus up to Jerusalem and presented him to God' (Lk 2:22). As Joseph and Mary were performing the customary rituals, no doubt with happy hearts, Luke introduces Simeon, who predicted a future which would involve misunderstanding, sorrow and rejection. Graham Schmitzer writes, 'The whole event of this day is actually harrowing.'[11] Without realising it at the time, Joseph and his family are shown to have lived, sometimes bewildered but always accepting, in the shadow of the cross that was to come.

That shadow is pictured accompanying them during their enforced exile in a foreign land, and in the aftermath. Matthew tells us that after Herod died, Joseph was prompted to return to Israel, but for fear of the new ruler, Archelaus, he decided to hide the family in Nazareth, a small town in the north (Matt 2:22). Again the language of 'dreaming' surrounded this decision, intimating that Joseph's mystical heart was turned consistently towards the Great Mystery shaping his life, despite his awareness of the shadow. Dreaming, as we know, often

11. Graham Schmitzer, 'Presentation in the Temple', in *Adore: Advent & Christmas Daily Reflections* (2020): 66.

occurs in darkness or semi-darkness, hinting at the notion that Joseph's enlightenment about all of these events was incomplete. So often he was asked to do something he didn't fully comprehend; for example, in this instance he had to start once again from scratch to establish his family. Ordinary folk like ourselves, searching the great Mysteries and seeking to fathom difficult life events, can find a friend and advocate in Joseph, the sincere and humble family man.

He walked a quiet path in Nazareth. Boff writes about the reality of 'callused hands, sweaty faces, daily tiredness and quietness' that characterised the hidden life Joseph lived as a worker.[12] Sometimes, however, what seems apparently insignificant can be fraught with meaning. When people later said 'Isn't this the carpenter's son?' (Matt 13:55) they implicitly recognised the central role Joseph, as a parent, had played in shaping and nurturing Jesus, and contributing to his understanding of life. James Martin SJ makes the point that Joseph, by his manner of living, taught Jesus the importance of quiet service and unrecorded acts of love.[13] Jesus may well have been echoing Joseph when he spoke later about the importance of not drawing attention to one's virtuous acts (Matt 6:4–6). That was the essence of Joseph. His role as the silent figure of the New Testament actually speaks volumes. It has been said that he 'remained always in silence to better express the Mystery without a name' and in doing so he placed before us the eloquence of a peaceful and well-lived family life.[14]

Much of Joseph's popularity with the everyday people in the Church has come from his apparent ordinariness—working in an everyday profession, and living with his family in a small, insignificant town. He was never a 'somebody' in his society. Yet his seemingly unremarkable life has the power to open our hearts to the unseen, showing us that life is larger than the events that fill our days. Ironically, Joseph managed so successfully to remain unobtrusive that Boff informs us that he 'did not feature in any homilies from the Fathers of the Church'.[15] Such a telling oversight! It sums up part of the ambiguity that surrounds Joseph. As a husband and father, he was viewed as being quiet and of little account, and yet he was entrusted by God with the care of Jesus

12. Boff, *Saint Joseph*, 27.
13. James Martin SJ, 'St Joseph is the Patron Saint we Need in this Pandemic', in *America: The Jesuit Review* (13 December 2020).
14. Boff, *Saint Joseph*, 96.
15. Boff, *Saint Joseph*, 84.

and Mary. He was a faithful Jewish man who kept the law, and yet his life experiences taught him that sometimes we are called to go outside the confines of religious regulations to do what is right. As family people, we find such dilemmas to be so familiar. We know only too well those times when love must overtake rules and expectations. In Joseph we find one who shows us that in silence and reflection we can learn to trust the small light we are given, and find our way through to solutions.

Not that it's always so simple. We are told that when Joseph and Mary took Jesus, aged twelve, to Jerusalem, as they did yearly for the Passover, the jagged edges of life were to intervene once again. Any parent knows that the seeming disappearance of a child is possibly the worst scenario one could imagine. We can picture the frantic searching for Jesus among their friends and relatives, then the rushed trip back to Jerusalem, hoping to find him there. Luke recounts that it was only on the 'third day' that he was discovered, 'sitting in the midst of the teachers' (Lk 2:47). Both Mary and Joseph were 'astonished' by this turn of events, and we hear the stress in Mary's reproach, 'Why have you done this to us? You see that your father and I have been so worried, looking for you' (Lk 2:49). Jesus' ironic response, 'Why were you looking for me?' leaves them completely baffled. Luke underlines this with his comment that 'they didn't understand what he told them', and in this state of unknowing and uncertainty Joseph and Mary returned with Jesus to their home (Lk 2:50). As parents we can find some solace and comfort in realising that our own inability to 'have all the answers' is reflected in Joseph's life too. As he went about his daily chores as an artisan, showing Jesus the tricks of the trade, he must have had a head full of questions, many of which probably were to remain unanswered. No doubt he would have 'kept all these things in his heart', as Mary did (Lk 2:51).

For many of us becoming grandparents as we move further into this twenty-first century, there is a wholesome and wonderful joy in seeing our sons develop into hands-on, caring and fully-involved dads, young men who mirror Joseph in their own families. They seem to have Joseph's capacity to be able to 'dream' about their families and children, and the faith to follow through. However, running parallel to this is the reality that in many parts of our world, we see a weakening of the father's role. One thinks of fractured families, high divorce rates, fathers who must work away from home, family violence, even, at times, the impact of social media. Many suffer the effects of having an absent father, whereas the Joseph portrayed in the gospels fits the traditional mould of a nurturing, present figure, adaptable, able to make decisions, to lead, to show courage, and to impose boundaries on a child. 'Jesus went down to Nazareth and was obedient to them' (Lk 2:51).

Boff explains that many modern fathers, who live in a time which is profoundly different from the one in which Joseph lived, 'are in search of a kind of identity that is appropriate for our times'.[16] It's perhaps more difficult to be a good father/parent in this more complex age, but Joseph's life shows that some things never change. Though silent, he continues to teach by example. It was from Joseph that Jesus learned that comfortable intimacy that enabled him to relate to God as '*Abba*' ('Daddy'), and to approach life with openness, wonder and courage. Modern fathers can learn from Joseph to be a 'man of dreams who knows how to accompany others' in quietness, and without judgement.[17] It was in his dreams that Joseph learned to discern and make sound decisions, and the Child he helped bring up went on to change the course of history. When we think of the dreams we have for our own children and grandchildren, we look to Joseph, and remember the words of Pope Francis, 'To dream is to open the door to the future'.[18]

---

16. Boff, *St Joseph*, 84.
17. Pope Francis, homily, 18 December, 2018 at <https://www.vaticannews.va/en/pope-francis/mass-casa-santa-marta/2018-12/pope-francis-mass-saint-joseph-teaches-silence.html>. Accessed 6 March 2021.
18. Pope Francis, homily, the 18th of December 2018.

St Joseph the Worker

Jo Brady rsj

The Year of Saint Joseph declared by Pope Francis is a fitting time to reflect on Saint Joseph, who was declared a Patron of the Church by Blessed Pius IX in 1870 and further declared Patron Saint of Workers by Pius XII in 1955. It is this aspect of Saint Joseph that will be considered and what the implications are for us in this time of pandemic when normally unobserved roles have been highlighted for their significance in this time of crisis.

Joseph the person

Joseph, described in the New Testament narratives as a shadowy and hidden figure, demonstrates for us the strength of those who hold hidden roles in family and society. Occupying a minor role in an obscure town in Galilee, he is shown as supporting and protecting the holy family; responding to the crises of his time, he became a refugee, fleeing to Egypt in order to save the child Jesus from certain death (Matt 2:13-23).

The purpose of Matthew's story is one of faith rather than history. Elizabeth Johnson explains:

> Even if not historically factual, the narrative of infant massacres and escape to Egypt reflects the historical situation that prevailed in Jewish Palestine under Roman and Herodian rule. Using death and destruction as a means of intimidating people, the imperial occupiers

> and their client-kings created thousands of refugees. When military action commenced, people were forced to flee from their homes if they wanted to avoid being killed.[1]

Therefore, with the time spent in Egypt not described and indeterminate, we can certainly imagine Joseph as a refugee with a family to support. He would have had to rely on his ability to ply his trade to support them or suffer the fate of those in a foreign land unable to find work. The time in Egypt would have been a time of deep insecurity, as is the case for many refugees who are forced to flee their home lands and seek employment in a foreign land. For this reason Pope Francis considers St Joseph as 'the special patron of all those forced to leave their native lands because of war, hatred, persecution and poverty'.[2]

St Joseph would have worked as a normal person; he was carpenter, a working man who freely accepted responsibility for Mary and Jesus. But what was the context of Joseph's work? To really appreciate Joseph we must move beyond the holy pictures and statues of an often elderly man to truly grasp what was the essence of the man Joseph, who was presumably a vigorous young man capable of supporting and protecting his family.

For the most part Joseph would have lived his life in the isolated village of Nazareth. It was situated in a basin but within walking distance of both Cana, three to four kilometres to the north, and Tzippori (Sepphoris), five kilometres to the west. This was the capital of Galilee in the time of Jesus. Nazareth was not a village which was readily accessible and not one through which anyone would pass on the way to anywhere else. It was a backwater with no particular social significance as evidenced by Nathaniel asking Philip, 'Can any good come out of Nazareth?' (Jn 1:46).

According to recent archaeological excavations, Nazareth at the time of Joseph would have been made up of few families with an estimated population of 300 to 400 people. A small community

---

1. Elizabeth Johnson, *Truly Our Sister: A Theology of Mary in the Communion of Saints* (New York: Continuum, 2003), 244.
2. Pope Francis, *Patris Corde*, (8 December 2020), 5, at <https://www.bing.com/search?q=%2C +patris+corde& form=EDGEAR&qs=PF&cvid=a660c20802964b23a91c8c6f409ed914&cc=AU&setlang=en-US&PC=HCTS>. Accessed 20 December 2020.

of peasants where people lived in small groupings, it was a world of subsistence farming where the farms were small and terraced.[3] People worked either as farmers who tilled their own land or as tenant farmers. They were supported in this world by craft persons who supplied the necessary tools and household furnishings. These people occupied the lower rungs in Jewish society.

The houses were simple, consisting of small rooms around a courtyard to form a compound. Houses had a cistern and access to a water source, the one in Nazareth known today as Mary's well. The courtyard housed the domestic animals and it was here that the grain was ground with a millstone. Sheep provided wool for clothing. The poverty was real with high taxes demanded by the Roman rulers. Joseph was required to meet the demands of his society in terms of obligations as a citizen, as a devout Jew and the head of a family.

As an accepting father of Jesus, Joseph set aside his own ideas and responded to the course of events to make them a part of his history. In the stories of the journey to Bethlehem, and then on to Egypt in response to a dream and the return to Nazareth, he is portrayed as yielding himself while escaping the sadistic ruler who pervaded Jesus' infancy. Paul VI sees a concrete expression of Joseph's fatherhood in this self-sacrifice. Although he had legal authority, he turned it away from himself 'to make a total gift of self, of his life and work; in having turned his human vocation to domestic love into superhuman oblation of self, an oblation of his heart and all his abilities into love placed at the service of the Messiah growing up in his house.'[4]

As portrayed by Luke, apart from Jesus' three-day temple disappearance in Jerusalem when he was twelve years old, family life appears to have unfolded in an ordinary way for the Holy Family. The years that followed finding Jesus in the temple were hidden. We are told that Jesus 'went down with them and came to Nazareth and was obedient to them' (Lk 2:41–52). His growth 'in wisdom and in

3. Amanda Borschel-Dan, 'What do we Know about Nazareth in Jesus' Time? An Archaeologist Explains' at <https://www.timesofisrael.com/listen-what-do-we-know-about-nazareth-in-jesus-time-an-archaeologist-explains/>. Accessed 8 February 2021.
4. Pope Paul VI, Discourse, (19 March 1966) *Insegnamenti* IV, 110 in *Redemptoris Custos* at <https://www. bing.com/ search?q=redemptoris+custos.&form=EDGEAR&qs=PF&cvid=3b35ce04339e4e84978d6535 e19e7f39 &cc=AU&setlang=en-US&PC=HCTS>. Accessed 4 February 2021.

stature, and in favour with God and man' would have occurred within the family of Nazareth under the supervision of Joseph, who had the duty to instruct Jesus in the Law and the trade and to ensure that he was fed and clothed. These were the normal duties of a father in the Jewish tradition and within the context of Nazareth. These duties also included travelling 150 kilometres three times a year to Jerusalem for the feasts of Passover, Shavuot and Sukkot. This alone would imply that Joseph was not an old man, since he was able undertake these walks.

We can surmise Joseph provided a model for Jesus in his commitment to work, demonstrating to his son that participating in work is participating in the work of the creator. Jesus himself proclaimed the 'gospel of work' as, like his father, he was a man of work, a craftsman like Joseph of Nazareth (Matt15:55).

Researchers inform us that the role of a carpenter in biblical times was not merely a lowly occupation. In the New Testament the word *tekton* is used only to describe the profession of Joseph (Matt 13:55) as well as Jesus (Mk 6:3). This word was also used to describe carpenters who worked on David's house (2 Sam 5:11) and the Temple (2 Kgs 12:11). More generally the word *tekton* was used to describe artisans or masters in any art. Our interpretation of carpenter is somewhat restrictive, as in biblical times a carpenter also fulfilled the role of stone mason. The Greek *tekton* is similar to the Hebrew *kharash* or *naggara*. Some scholars argue that the use of the Aramaic term *naggara* (craftsman) and its use in the Talmud to signify a learned man, could mean that this word was not merely the application of work terminology but rather the identification of Joseph as wise and well versed in the Torah.[5]

If Joseph were a stonemason, it is probable that he may have been a hired as a labourer in nearby Sepphoris and engaged in the rebuilding of that city. Working for 'invader' overseers and engineers from Rome would have been onerous indeed. In addition to his work as a craftsman, Joseph would also have been engaged in cultivating produce for his family such as wheat, olives for oil and grapes for wine for his family. There would have been a communal garden which supplied a variety of vegetables for the community. The agricultural

5. Jeza Vermes, *Jesus the Jew: A Historian's Reading of the Gospels* (Minneapolis: Fortress Press, 1983), 21–22.

images used by Jesus in the gospel accounts show a familiarity with countryside and less of an insight into the skills of a carpenter.[6]

From what archaeology tells us must have been the life of Joseph as a worker, we now honour him earning an honest living to provide for his family. The boy Jesus would have learnt from him the value, the dignity and the joy of what it means to eat bread that is the fruit of one's labour.[7] For Joseph, work would have been the daily expression of his love. He would have plied his trade as a carpenter with Jesus at his side. His obscurity in the gospel accounts does not diminish his model of life, which demonstrates for us that to be true to one's state in life and accomplish what is required of us will draw us to holiness. St Joseph remains for us one of the humble ones who through commitment and a genuine life shows us that all that is required is to be a genuine follower of Christ. There is no need to accomplish great things but it is sufficient to have common, simple and human virtues. However, they need to be true and authentic.[8]

Church Teaching on the Dignity of Work

The dignity of work has been expounded in church teachings through the centuries, drawing from the biblical accounts in the Book of Genesis that work is a fundamental dimension of human existence. The account of creation is interpreted by John Paul II as the first 'gospel of work'. We ought to imitate the Creator both in working and also resting, as God presented his own creative activity under the form of work and rest.[9] We are co-creators with God in the development of creation, as humans should 'be fruitful and multiply, fill the earth and subdue it' (Gen 1:28). Pope Francis expands on this in *Laudato Si'*: more than 'subduing' or 'having dominion' over creation; we should rather work in collaboration with the Creator. We are capable of developing the created world in a prudent manner and thus can

6. Mary Cresp, *In the Spirit of Joseph* (North Sydney: Sisters of St Joseph, 2005), 95.
7. Pope Francis, *Patris Corde*, 6.
8. Pope Paul VI, Homily of Mass, 19 March 1969 at https://blessedjoseph.blogspot.com/2014/10/blessed-pope-paul-vi-st-joseph.html. Accessed 18 February 2021.
9. Pope John Paul II, Encyclical Letter *Laborem Exercens* (14 September 1981), 25 at <http://www.vatican.va/content/john-paul-ii/en/encyciclicals/documents/hf_jp-ii_enc_14091981_laborem-exercens.html>. Accessed 4 February 2021.

become the 'the instrument used by God to bring out the potential which he himself inscribed in things'.[10]

From the Middle Ages, guilds of craftsmen emerged to both protect the worker, maintain standards within the particular trade, support the families of the members and ensure that members maintained their religious practice.[11] The guilds were the forerunners of the unions. Given the religious context of medieval Europe, each guild had a particular patron saint. One could expect that St Joseph would have been an obvious patron; however, this was not the always the case. While devotion to St Joseph as patron of the dying was readily adopted in response to the Black Death in the fourteenth century, his patronage of workers has only been promulgated in the last 150 years perhaps in reaction to the rise of socialism and communism. In contemporary times at least twenty-two trades or professions have St Joseph listed as patron, along with many countries and cities.[12] Recognition of St Joseph within the Eucharistic Liturgy did not occur until Vatican Council II in 1962 when his name was added to the list of saints in the Eucharistic Prayer I. As recently as 2013 St Joseph was added to Eucharistic Prayers II, III and IV.

The first encyclical on St Joseph, *Quamquam Pluries*, was issued in 1889 by Leo XIII, in which he developed a theology of St Joseph as guardian, spouse and protector. The encyclical promoted the Holy Family as the model of the dignity of labour. Joseph 'set himself to protect with a mighty love and a daily solicitude his spouse and the Divine Infant; regularly by his work he earned what was necessary for the one and the other for nourishment and clothing; he guarded from death the Child threatened by a monarch's jealousy'.[13]

In *Laborum Exercens,* Pope Saint John Paul II highlighted the value of labour and the right to work. Labourers and craftsmen and

---

10. Pope Francis, *Laudato Si'*, 124.at <https://www.bing.com/search?q=laudato+si%2C&form=EDGEAR&qs=PF&cvid=9d5a3f92425c46a898b5998eda0157fd&cc=AU&setlang=en-US&PC=HCTS>. Accessed 4 February 2021.
11. Gary Richardson, 'Craft Guilds and Christianity in Late-Medieval England. A rational-choice analysis', in *Rationality and Society* 17/2 (2005):141–152.
12. Patron Saints at <https://catholicreadings.org/what-is-st-joseph-the-patron-saint-of/>. Accessed 3 March 2021.
13. Pope Leo XIII *Quamqaum Pluries,* (15 August 1889) at <http://www.vatican.va/content/leo-xiii/en/encyclicals/documents/hf_l-xiii_enc_15081889_quamquam-pluries.html>. Accessed 17 February 2021.

women maintain 'the stable fabric of the world, and their prayer is in the practice of their trade'.[14] Everyone has the right to the work because it is 'part of the meaning of life on this earth, a path to growth, human development and personal fulfillment'. It is a vocation whereby one contributes to the welfare of the family and ultimately to society.[15] Through Saint Joseph's example we can recognise work is a participation in God's activity even through the most ordinary everyday actions. All can consider that by their labour they are unfolding the Creator's work, 'contributing by their personal industry to the realisation in history of the divine plan'.[16]

Human beings were created with a vocation to work. Work is a necessity, part of the meaning of life on this earth, a path to growth, human development and personal fulfillment. It is within this framework of humanity engaging in the creation as a co-worker with the Creator and the premise that all work has dignity that we come to an appreciation of St Joseph the Worker.

Highlighting St Joseph the Worker

Leo XIII's encyclical *Rerum Novarum,* launched in May 1891, outlined the duties and rights of workers in response to the challenges facing the world with the rise of capitalism and industrialisation. *Rerum Novarum* was a reaction against the degradation of human beings as the subject of work with accompanying exploitation of the worker through poor wages, poor working conditions and lack of security. The subsequent spread of communism and the ideologies of socialism likewise devalued the labourer and continued to be a challenge for the church in the first half of the twentieth century.

Of primary concern to the Church was communism's opposition to Christian principles regarding the common good and just treatment of workers. In 1920 Benedict XV promoted St Joseph as a 'special guide' and 'heavenly patron' of labourers to protect them from

14. *Laborum Exercens,* 124. Sir.38:34.
15. Pope Francis, *Patris Corde,* 6.
16. *Gaudium et Spes* ('Pastoral Constitution on the Church in the Modern World') in *Vatican Council II: The Conciliar and Post Conciliar Documents,* edited by Austin Flannery (Collegeville: Liturgical Press, 2014), 34.

the infection of socialism.[17] The socialism he reacted to denies the dignity of the human person, considering the person purely in terms of an individual element within society and subordinated within the functioning of the socio-economic mechanism. This form of socialism does not acknowledge the individual's free choice and promotes the advancement of the state at the expense of the individual. Humans exist for the flourishing of the state rather than the state existing for the flourishing of humanity. Socialism denies the principle of subsidiarity whereby the lowest level of society, whether individual, family or government, should be able to determine for itself.

In 1937 Pius XI continued to promote Joseph as a patron in the fight against communism, recognising Joseph as belonging to the working class and sharing the burdens of poverty for both himself and the Holy Family. Joseph's work as a carpenter and in his role of mentoring Jesus gives labour significant dignity. Pius XI speaks of Jesus not only being the son of a carpenter but also a carpenter himself, raising manual labour to a dignity of its own. Throughout the ages labour had been devalued and communism at this time had sought to dehumanise the worker.[18] Pius XI warned that communism 'strips man of his liberty, robs human personality of all its dignity, and removes all the moral restraints that check the eruptions of blind impulse'.[19]

To counteract this movement, Pius XI presented Joseph the just man as a model for all the faithful, so promoting a just and equitable society where the dignity of all is safeguarded and protected: 'To hasten the advent of that "peace of Christ in the kingdom of Christ" so ardently desired by all, we place the vast campaign of the Church against world Communism under the standard of St Joseph, her mighty Protector.'[20] St Joseph, through the performance of his everyday tasks, was an example for all who needed to toil by the work of their hands. Joseph was the example par excellence of the just man and a model for all wishing to advance a just society.

17. Pope Benedict XV, 25 July 1920 *Bonum Sane* at <http://www.vatican.va/content/benedict-xv/it/motu_proprio/documents/hf_ben-xv_motu-proprio_19200725_bonum-sane.htm>. Accessed 17 February 2021.
18. Pope Pius XI, *Divini Redemptoris*, 19 March 1937, 6 at <http://www.vatican.va/content/pius-xi/en/ encyclicals/ documents/hf_p-xi_enc_19370319_divini-redemptoris.html>. Accessed 17 February 2021.
19. Pope Pius XI, *Divini Redemptoris*, 10.
20. Pope Pius XI, *Divini Redemptoris*, 81.

From the 1920s the lay apostolate under the term Catholic Action was prevalent in many countries. Similar to the guilds, the movement saw the world from the perspective of the spiritual realm and sought to take Christian principles into the workplace. The Catholic Action movement attempted to counteract the secular organisations which captured the workers' allegiance. Belgium priest Joseph Cardijn developed the *Jeunesse Ouvrière Chrétienne* (JOC) which set about transformation in the workplace on the premise that workers would be more effective evangelisers with workers. It was putting faith into action.

In 1931 Pius XI had included and promoted the Jocist principles in his encyclical *Quadragesimo Ano.* Several movements followed the Cardijn model, such as Catholic Action, Catholic Workers Movement, National Catholic Girls Movement, and, in more modern times, Young Christian Workers and the Young Christian Students. These groups examined their life experience from the 'see judge and act' Jocist principles. After reflection on their experience in the light of Christian teaching and values the members took a variety of actions to address the situation to make their reality more aligned to standards of the gospel. These actions included, for example, the development of trade unions and political agitation as well as the more traditional faith practices.[21]

With similar concerns about the growth of communism and its impact on the faithful, particularly the workers, Pius XII declared the Feast of St Joseph the Worker in May 1955 as a reaction to the post World War II surge of atheistic communism. The May Day celebrations in communist countries were militarist shows of power in the achievements of communism for the worker. Thus the Feast of St Joseph the Worker celebrated on May 1 was designed to counteract the communist May Day celebrations, providing a Christian alternative which honoured the dignity of the worker. It highlighted for the faithful the true dignity of work and the role of labour in sanctifying the faithful, with Joseph as the model.

The church has upheld the dignity of work and the dignity of each person collaborating in God's work of creation. From the first social encyclical, *Rerum Novarum*, the dignity and rights of the workers

21. Katherine Massam, *Lay Catholic Spirituality: Adelaide and Perth*, Unpublished Thesis, University of Western Australia, 1962, 341.

have been upheld; prominence has been given to the idea of each person being made in the image of God, not merely as a cog in a machine or an instrument in a society emphasising productivity over human dignity. Pius XII called the faithful to 'Go to Joseph' (*Ite ad Joseph*), in order to be close to Christ.

In our times, Francis reminds us:

> Joseph was a carpenter who earned an honest living to provide for his family. From him, Jesus learnt from the value, the dignity and the joy of what it means to eat bread that is the fruit of one's labour.[22]

The sanctity of work and its fruits are acknowledged in a striking manner in the Offertory of the Eucharistic Liturgy where, in offering the bread and wine, the celebrant reminds us that, through the goodness of God, we have received bread that is 'fruit of the earth and work of human hands' and that 'it will become for us the bread of life'.[23] Our work, our labour is thereby transformed into the sacrament of Christ's self-giving. Joseph embodies this same self-giving, actively participating in the divine plan and so totally immersed in the incarnation story, thereby advancing the Kingdom of God.

The Hidden Worker

Joseph the Worker, the obscure and hidden guardian of the child Jesus presents us with a model for those whose work is often hidden but essential. In Australia, where there is high unemployment, it is difficult to understand the failure of famers to attract labour for the essential agricultural work of harvesting crops. During this time of pandemic, work has become struggle for those who have become unemployed because of the downturn in the economy, through tensions created through lockdown and enforced distance from the normal rituals of work. Working from home has imposed its own burdens on the worker and the family, while enforced lockdowns have caused significant disruptions to the education of the young.

22. Pope Francis, *Patris Corde*, 6.
23. *The Roman Missal*, English Translation, 2010.

Without work there is a sense of loss of dignity. Families without a regular income are more likely to suffer great insecurity and this can result in family disintegration. In St Joseph we have an example of one who continually sacrificed himself for his family. He demonstrates an incredible capacity to not only hear the word of God but to truly listen and respond. According to Matthew's narrative, he was challenged in his time to look beyond the normal social mores in order to accept the reality of Mary's pregnancy. He was prompted to widen his response, from one which would have always been honourable to one that required significant heroism. He allowed his reality to be shaped by God and altered his life accordingly, whether it was facing up to Mary's pregnancy, the plot to murder the infant Jesus and the decision to flee to a safe environment that would protect the child Jesus and to return to Nazareth. Joseph is portrayed as always doing the honourable thing; the virtuous thing. Similarly, those whose situation forces them today to go beyond what they have been used to in order to survive difficult times can find courage in Joseph's example.

Many are at last learning to appreciate the value of all work, as demonstrated by thousands turning out each night in Britain to clap for the healthcare workers and the valiant image of ninety-nine-year-old Captain Tom Moore raising millions for British National Health. There is now a greater appreciation of the more mundane work in our society such as those cleaning our buses, trains, supermarkets, and those in the supply chain who, in the ordinary work of their lives, daily respond in the way Joseph did in caring for the community at large.

Those who have lost employment, their income or a sense of purpose can, with confidence, go to Joseph and ask for his aid in this difficult time. Teresa of Avila, who promoted devotion to Saint Joseph teaches us, 'I have never known anyone who . . . honoured him by particular services who did not advance greatly in virtue, for he helps in a special way those souls who recommend themselves to him.'[24] Inspired by the writings of this great saint, Dorothy Day chose Saint Joseph as patron of her foundation, the Catholic Worker Movement.[25] Whenever she found herself in financial difficulty (as she often was), she would place any unpaid bills before his statue, presuming that

24. Teresa of Avila, *Autobiography* (London: Burns & Oates, 1962) VI, 11.
25. Dorothy Day (1897–1980) was a journalist and social activist in USA who joined the Communist Party but was converted to Catholicism and worked tirelessly to spread Catholic social teaching and promote justice for workers.

through his intercession the money to pay them would somehow be found. This practice of turning to Joseph has continued in many religious houses in times of austerity.

Saint Joseph was an inspiration for many in the appreciation of work during the times of the depression and leading to the rise of the Catholic Workers Movement and for the Young Christian Workers

This time of pandemic offers us renewed opportunity to be inspired by St Joseph the Worker and to appreciate the nobility of all work. May we value work in its different forms, and recognise that there is dignity in the most hidden of roles; that the most distasteful and arduous work is perhaps the most noble. In the words of Pope Francis, 'Let us implore Saint Joseph the Worker to help us find ways to express our firm conviction that no young person, no person at all, no family, should be without work!'[26]

A Prayer for Workers (Saint Pope Pius X)

O Glorious Saint Joseph, model of all those who are devoted to labour,
obtain for me the grace to work in a spirit of penance for the
expiation of my many sins;
to work conscientiously, putting the call of duty above my natural
inclinations;
to work with thankfulness and joy, considering it an honour
to employ and develop by means of labour the gifts received from God;
to work with order, peace, moderation and patience,
never shrinking from weariness and trials;
to work above all with purity of intention and detachment from self,
keeping unceasingly before my eyes death and the account that
I must give of time lost, talents unused, good omitted, and vain
complacency in success, so fatal to the work of God.

All for Jesus,
all through Mary,
all after thy example, O Patriarch, Saint Joseph.
Such shall be my watch-word in life and in death. Amen.[27]

26. Pope Francis, *Patris Corde*, 6.
27. Pope Pius X, 'Prayer for Work to Saint Joseph' at <https://www.columban.org.au/media-and-publications/ articles/ prayers/2019/prayer-for-work-to-st-joseph-by-pope-st-pius-x>. Accessed 21 February 2021.

Joseph and Justice

Susan Connelly rsj

The Gospel describes Joseph as a 'man of honour', a 'just man' (Matt 1:19). How does Joseph, the earthly father of Jesus, demonstrate the virtue and practice of 'justice'? Can we say that Joseph embodies the wonderful phrase that Gerard Manley Hopkins uses to describe the core, the inner nature of someone becoming visible in outer life: '*the just man justices*'?[1] This chapter reflects on the core and practice of justice in Joseph's life in the context of the old saying 'like father, like son'.

Some religious people baulk at the word 'justice', fearing that it points more to political realities than to the concerns of God. Albert Nolan describes how, unfortunately, the English word 'justice' is too often equated with judgement and punitive actions against wrongdoers.[2] Modern concepts of justice are strongly influenced by notions from Greek philosophy, some strands of theology, and modern ideas of rights. However, the richness of the biblical concept of justice contains and broadens these aspects. Biblical justice covers the whole of morality, both personal and communal. It means working towards situations that are good, right and true, so that people flourish. Justice is 'right relationships', the interdependence of people based on moral values.

Scripture and tradition have clearly tied the concept of right relationship, or justice, to Joseph. Matthew's description of Joseph as a just man is in relation to the conception of Jesus. Joseph, 'wanting

1. Gerard Manley Hopkins, 'As Kingfishers Catch Fire' in *Gerard Manley Hopkins Poems and Prose*, edited by WH Gardner (Harmondsworth: Penguin Books, 1953), 51.
2. Albert Nolan, *Hope in an Age of Despair* (Maryknoll, Orbis Books, 2009), 130–133.

to spare [Mary] publicity, decided to divorce her informally' (Matt 1:19). But he did not divorce her, convinced that God was at work. Here is the presentation of a man who so valued right relationships—not only with his betrothed but with God—that he did not hesitate to replace the strictures of the Mosaic Law with actions more in harmony with God's desires. The law was designed to ensure that social relationships and a community's relationship with God were right and good. Thus in a small closely-knit group such as the one Joseph lived in, where culture and religion were intertwined and both strongly governed the lives of individuals, any deviation from the norm had enormous consequences. The conception of a child out of wedlock was one such problem. Death was the punishment for adulterous liaisons (Lev 20:10) and illegitimacy resulted in exclusion from the community, even to the tenth generation (Deut 23:2). Yet according to the gospel, Joseph was convinced of God's involvement in Mary's situation and placed his trust in God above the literal requirements of the law. This response of Joseph to the conception of Jesus is presented in Matthew's Gospel as the action of a 'just' man.

We know that there is no word of Joseph, husband of Mary, recorded in the scriptures. Mary has a few statements attributed to her, but there is nothing that we can repeat with the prelude 'Joseph said . . .' Yet undoubtedly, many people listened to him as he undertook the tasks of husband, father, refugee, artisan, astute reader of the social situation, and receiver of dreams. However, the silence of Joseph in the scriptures and his few recorded actions should not lead us to think that we know little about him. We can deduce a great deal about Joseph. For example, Leonardo Boff writes of him providing the child Jesus with the image of 'father' so monumentally important to Jesus' understanding of God.[3] The father image that Joseph supplied was the personal, powerful and gracious presence that influenced Jesus for decades. Then there is Pope Francis' comment in his recent letter *Patris Corde*: 'I like to think that it was from Saint Joseph that Jesus drew inspiration for the parable of the prodigal son and the merciful father (*cf* Lk 15:11–32).'[4] That insight can be explored further by

3. Leonardo Boff, *St Joseph: The Father of Jesus in a Fatherless Society*, translated by Alex Guilherme (Eugene OR: Cascade Books, 2009).
4. Pope Francis, *Patris Corde: Apostolic Letter* (Vatican City, 2020) at < http://www.vatican.va/content/francesco/en/apost_letters/documents/papa-francesco-lettera-ap_20201208_patris-corde.html>. Accessed 16 March 2021.

reflecting on the idea that most of Jesus' inspiration necessarily came from his home—from his mother and father. We declare the divinity of Jesus, but the weight of scripture and tradition attest equally to the humanity of Jesus. The letter to the Hebrews maintains that he was 'tempted as we are, but without sin' (Heb 4:15). Therefore, like us in all things, he was shaped and influenced by his home, learning from his mother Mary, and from his father, Joseph.

Imitation is built into the core of human beings. Imitation is the backbone of education and without it creativity has little in the way of a launching pad from which to develop. Joseph's contribution to Jesus' image of 'father' was that of the man whom Jesus imitated more than any other. Thus to gain some understanding of Joseph, we need look no further than the values, decisions and actions of the one who imitated him, his son Jesus. As with so much of our human reality, it is a case of 'like father, like son'. This reflection on Joseph's fatherly influence on Jesus is in three parts: first, Jesus' proclamation of his mission as found in Chapter 4 of Luke's Gospel, second, Jesus' attitude to the political morass in which he found himself, and third, Jesus' attitude to women. In each of these aspects of Jesus' life, the hand of the just Joseph can be discerned.

The Mission

In Luke's version of the good news, Jesus enters Nazareth after his baptism in the Jordan and his wilderness experience.

> He went to Nazareth, where he had been brought up, and on the Sabbath day he went into the synagogue, as was his custom. He stood up to read, and the scroll of the prophet Isaiah was handed to him. Unrolling it, he found the place where it is written:
>
> > 'The Spirit of the Lord is on me, because he has anointed me to proclaim good news to the poor. He has sent me to proclaim freedom for the prisoners and recovery of sight for the blind, to set the oppressed free, to proclaim the year of the Lord's favour.'
>
> Then he rolled up the scroll, gave it back to the attendant and sat down. The eyes of everyone in the synagogue were fastened on him. He began by saying to them, 'Today this scripture is fulfilled in your hearing' (Lk 4:16–21).

Jesus reads the Prophet Isaiah almost word for word—but not quite (Is 61:2a). Proclaiming good news to the poor, freedom for prisoners, sight for the blind, freedom for the oppressed, and a year of the Lord's favour bursts from his heart and his lips. But his words did not include, as Isaiah wrote, the phrase 'the day of vengeance for our God' (Is 61:2b).[5] Jesus did not proclaim vengeance. He left out the part of the sentence that included that concept. Isaiah declares a year of favour and a day of vengeance, but Jesus only talks of the favour, omitting any talk of revenge, reprisal, retribution. And he rolls up the scroll—he shuts the book—he takes the sitting position of teacher and tells everyone that the words have been fulfilled that very day.

The people listening began to question his authority with the exclamation, 'This is Joseph's son, surely?' He surely was. Given into Joseph's care, he learned the scriptures, but learned them in a way that coloured his whole life. There have been centuries of disputation over how and what Jesus knew, but that is not the focus here. Instead, what we are sure of is that Jesus lived under the authority of Joseph and Mary for many years before his short public life. It was in a situation of small town life with his parents, cheek by jowl with extended family and the animals, that the Word made flesh lived among us—like us in all things but sin. Joseph—the *paterfamilias*—taught him, guided him, corrected him, nurtured him, was proud of him, enjoyed him, laughed with him, and prayed with him the only written material available—the scriptures. Keen minds were sharpened on the swathes of Hebrew memories and prayers which formed them both. But Jesus deviated from the scripture that day in the synagogue at Nazareth. How could he omit Isaiah's reference to a day of God's 'vengeance' when he proclaimed to his neighbours that the fulfillment of that prophecy resided in him? Surely, because for years in his home, under the tutelage of Joseph and of Mary, the attribution to God of revenge was agonised over, questioned, and rejected.

Vengeance was foreign to Jesus' way of life and teaching. Throughout his life he befriended sinners and outcasts rather than announcing

5. 'Jesus' nonviolence according to the Gospels' in *Catholic Nonviolence Initiative* #2 (2018) at <https:// nonviolencejustpeace.net/wp-content/uploads/2020/08/Jesus-nonviolence-according-to-the-Gospels.pdf>, accessed 6 March 2021. It is to be noted that some commentators consider the phrase to have been omitted because Isaiah was referring to the Jewish people held captive in Babylon and their deliverance had already happened by the time of Jesus.

divine reprisal. He consistently taught and demonstrated that God is merciful to the reproachable 'other'. His parables demonstrated that it was the humble sinner who found God's favour, not the paragon of virtue (Lk 18:9–14), and that the repentant, ingrate son was forgiven and loved as much as the dutiful son (Lk 15:11–32). In the parable of the lost sheep God as shepherd shows a willingness to leave the ninety-nine 'in the wilderness' in order to pursue and tend the one that had wandered (Lk 15:3–7). Will we accept that his actions were completely the result of 'infused knowledge'? Do we only believe that as Son of God Jesus knew the heart of the heavenly Father and could not betray the boundless mercy? Or is it that he was indeed like us in all things, having to learn, to question, and to dare to challenge the status quo? And that he learned it from Joseph?

In this regard there is a very great challenge to us in whatever part of God's mission we are involved in, whether it be in the family or in the wider society. How do we omit vengeance in any of its forms in our dealings with others? How do we seek for just outcomes without also seeking retribution? How do we resist those who practise evil without doing to them what they do to us? How do we reject the temptation to imitate those we oppose? How do we distinguish between true justice and disguised retaliation? There are no easy answers, but there is the example of Joseph and Jesus that we can imitate.

The Politics

The political problem of oppression is integral to almost the whole of the Bible.[6] It is tempting to some people to imagine that a citizen, religious or otherwise, can be non-political. However, staying out of discussions, agreeing with whatever power is in place, or considering that religion and politics don't mix are attitudes that are not non-political at all. They constitute the political stance of the fence-sitter. That stance favours those in power, as acquiescence means consent.

Both Joseph and Jesus were embroiled in the politics of their times. Both faced the political challenge of being at odds with the Herods, the Jewish rulers of the nation. Herod the Great, father of Archelaus and Antipas, was not actually a Jew, but was installed by the Roman senate. He became increasing cruel toward the end of his reign, and

6. Nolan, *Hope in an Age of Despair*, 52.

ordered the slaughter of the innocents at Bethlehem. Thinking that his own family was about to overthrow him he murdered one of his wives, her mother, two of her sons, and his own eldest son. Then Herod Archelaus succeeded his murderous father in Judea. He began his reign by slaughtering 3,000 prominent citizens, thus ensuring less opposition to his position and policies. Herod Antipas, (who also survived his father) reigned over Galilee when Jesus began his public ministry. He beheaded John the Baptist. It was he whom Jesus called a fox, and Jesus was brought before him to be tried at the request of Pontius Pilate.

Matthew's infancy accounts relate the dangers of dealing with the Herods and their oppressive regimes. Herod the Great, Matthew says, caused Joseph to become a refugee, with Mary and Jesus refugees beside him. They fled the danger of death, evading the authorities bent on destroying them. The family's eventual return to the homeland from Egypt, no doubt joyous, was also a time of careful calculation and evasion, a journey that necessitated further travel to relative safety in Galilee. These experiences stood Jesus in good stead later in life when dealing with those who wielded power: the political and religious leaders, and the crowds. He was threatened with being thrown off a cliff (Lk 4:30), with being stoned (Jn 8:59) and with being arrested (Jn 10:39), but he either slipped away, hid himself, or otherwise eluded those who were hunting him.

Today's tens of thousands of refugees are either repudiated at other nations' borders, locked up, or in notable cases especially in the case of poorer nations, allowed in and given some support. Some governments, such as Australia's, have detained refugees and asylum seekers for years, ignoring the international responsibility to honour the right of people to seek asylum.[7] The anguish of refugees and asylum seekers today differs little from that of Joseph, escaping to a foreign land to save himself and his family from his own people. The current global problem of refugees calls for personal decision. To what extent would we have assisted Joseph as he fled to Egypt? On what past action or present attitude do we base our claim?

7. UNHCR The UN Refugee Agency, *The 1951 Refugee Convention,* at <https://www.unhcr.org.en-au/1951-refugee-convention.html>. Accessed 16 March 2021.

The practical question of paying taxes and dealing with Temple currency was another political reality which dogged Joseph as it did his fellow countrymen. Taxes were to be paid to the Romans, while the Jewish religious leaders, repudiating the foreign coinage, demanded currency exchange in Temple transactions. Both Joseph and Jesus, in their small home improvement business, would have been adept at the intricacies of money management in their oppressed society, and were well aware of the degradation that financial policies brought to some people. Jesus denounced the contribution to the people's poverty of both the foreign and domestic financial dealings. All four Gospels record that he drove the sellers out of the Temple, condemning the thievery and abuse of the poor caused by the Temple tax and exchange rate. At another time, refusing to be drawn in to a discussion about whether to pay taxes or not to the Romans, Jesus gives the famous dictum 'Give to Caesar what is Caesar's and to God what is God's' (Matt 22:21). Joseph's hand can be seen again in the background, teaching the young Jesus not only a trade, but trading, and teaching him the weight to be given to the concerns of earthly power as opposed to those of God. We have the duty to question the use of public taxation money, especially in rich countries such as Australia. The crisis in aged care, the disgraceful level of foreign aid, and the tax loopholes seized by the rich are moral issues intimately connected to the taxation system. With Joseph's influence behind him, Jesus took a highly political stand when it came to those ground down by inordinate taxes.

The Women

The third focus in this reflection on Joseph as a just man concerns women. The place of women in each and every society and culture throughout history remains a matter of unease. Although there is growing recognition of the equality of women now, too often the concept of 'human dignity' is not accorded to women as much as to men. Questions about the global state of women's health, their lower access to education, the amount of the world's work they perform, and the levels of physical, sexual and mental violence they endure are realities with which many societies are grappling. 'Six women are killed every hour by men around the world, most by men in their own family or their partners.'[8] Such an astounding fact demonstrates women's place and plight today. Even nations with a long history of relative freedom and progress nonetheless have much ground to cover before women are treated as equal to men.

Christianity has brought to the world a focus on human dignity never enjoyed by people of antiquity. Nevertheless, the pace and spread of attitudes akin to those of Jesus have been slow and narrow. Regarding women, Christianity has often accommodated itself to the cultures in which it has blossomed. One of the most influential theologians in the history of Christianity was St Thomas Aquinas (1224–1274). He was a man of his times whose views on women were influenced by the Greek philosopher Aristotle. These perspectives expressed and generated questionable theories about the place and worth of women, and they continue to prejudice thought and action concerning women. Questions fielded by Aquinas included whether women should have been part of creation, in view of their imperfections. He cites Aristotle, apparently with approval, that women are misbegotten males. The created order was interpreted to mean that women are subordinate to males for their own good, being inferior in intellect and reason.[9] Such absurdities continued to colour theology for centuries and have not yet been completely overcome.

While these perspectives have infected Christianity, they are not the attitudes of Jesus as found in the Gospels. Jesus broke with custom in his acceptance of women among his close followers. Luke's Gospel records that not only did the twelve disciples accompany him on his travels, but some women with difficult backgrounds also—including, but not limited to Mary Magdalene, Joanna and Susanna (Lk 8:1–3). Jesus championed women against powerful authorities, as in the case of the woman taken in adultery (Jn 8:10–11). This dangerous episode found Jesus pitting himself against the might of the Mosaic Law as interpreted by the scribes and the Pharisees. It is a reminder of the very situation which his mother Mary may have found herself in had not Joseph placed obedience to God above the literal interpretation

8. Douglas Broom, 'As the UK publishes its first census of women killed by men, here's a global look at the problem', (World Economic Forum, 25 November 2020) at < https://www.weforum.org/agenda/2020/11/ violence-against-women-femicide-census/>. Accessed 16 March 2021.
9. 'Thomistic Philosophy' at <https://aquinasonline.com/women/>. Accessed 22 March 2021.

of the Law. Furthermore, Jesus actually spoke to women directly in public, an unusual action for a man to take. These included the Samaritan woman at the well (Jn 4:7–26), the widow in the town of Nain (Lk 7:12–13), the woman with the haemorrhage (Matt 9:22), a woman who called out to him (Lk 11:27–28), the woman bent double (Lk 13:12), the Syro-Phoenician woman who challenged him (Mk 7:24–30) and a group of women on the way to the cross (Lk 23:27–31). It was a mark of politeness to address a woman as 'woman', which Jesus did to his mother. He also spoke to women as 'daughter' or 'daughters of Abraham'. Breaking with custom, Jesus chose women as his companions, they were people he defended, and human beings he spoke to with respect. 'To what extent did Joseph influence Jesus regarding women?' we may well ask.

This counter-cultural treatment of women is evident in the genealogy recorded in Matthew's Gospel (Matt 1:1–16). The Hebrew people were fixated on their family trees, carrying them around in their heads. Matthew's family tree of Jesus is a curious mixture, as when it comes to the women who appear in it, it is something that could have been seen as a scandal. In this genealogy there appear the names of five women only. What is extraordinary is that each of the five was tied up in some situation which was against the religious and cultural demands of their times. The first mentioned is Tamar, who entered the bloodline of Jesus by disguising herself as a prostitute and seducing her father-in-law, Judah, so that he would make her pregnant (Gen 38). The second is Rahab, a non-Hebrew, King David's great, great grandmother who didn't have to disguise herself as a prostitute, as she actually was one (Josh 2 and 6). Ruth was also a Gentile, and was a product of the incest committed between Lot and his oldest daughter (Book of Ruth). Matthew then lists Bathsheba 'the wife of Uriah', who suffered King David's sexual abuse and murder of her husband (2 Sam 11:1–27). And then Mary, the mother of Jesus, whose pregnancy had the makings of a scandal of great proportions (Matt 1:18–25).

These women in Matthew's genealogy obviously do not fit with the religion and the culture. Perhaps Matthew's list was not known to Joseph at all, as the genealogies are the early church's theological statements, meant to teach about Jesus. But the inclusion of five women in highly irregular circumstances is a startling introduction to Jesus' attitudes, and they are comprehensively followed in the gospels by numerous examples of his regard, defence, and support for women, whatever their circumstances. What did Jesus learn about women in his home at Nazareth? He saw the example of Joseph, the main male influence on his early life. He heard how Joseph spoke about women, how he spoke to them, how he treated them in his business dealings. He saw how Joseph treated Mary, and how she responded. He also saw other ways women were treated by others in the town, by the religious leaders, by the Romans. As son of Joseph, subject to his authority, Jesus found a model to imitate, a model in whom he apprehended the person of his heavenly father. But Joseph was also the model whom Jesus imitated—like father, like son.

Conclusion

God's justice demanded of Jesus the spurning of cultural and religious norms that went against right relationships among people. Jesus' living of this justice included recognising the favoured place of the poor in God's eyes, partnering with women, and being willing to take on the political might of the systems of his time and place. Glimpses of Joseph are found in these gospel-based testimonies to Jesus, as Joseph was the father with whom he lived for so long, the man under whose authority he worked and prayed, the model he imitated, and the image of the God he loved.

St Joseph and Ecology

Trish Hindmarsh (Josephite Companion)

It was a surprise to me to learn recently that on Victoria's Mornington Peninsula, in a store that sells what were once termed, 'piety goods', statues and holy cards of St Joseph are 'flying off the shelf'. It was even more surprising to learn that buyers often rely on the saint as a booster for business.

Owner of Ark Religious Supplies in Victoria, Angela Langton, states on her website that Joseph is the most 'popular statuette' in the store. She says, 'Saint Joseph is the patron saint of homes, who vendors pray to when they want some divine intervention to sell their property. Burying his statue in the garden or slotting a prayer card into contract of sale, is, for those of faith, a necessary ritual in a sales campaign.'[1]

'Burying' and 'garden' are terms intimately connected to 'ecology', but I doubt if even St Joseph, at least as a plaster replica, would add much compostable enrichment to the soil by being buried in a shallow grave, his feet pointing in the direction of a house on the market! As for his influence in business, perhaps that is for others to say. In any case, the saint remains a universal favourite. He was the one chosen to be the legal father of Christ on earth, and to rear to young manhood the Incarnate Christ as the historical 'Jesus'. With Joseph's fathering, during his early years Jesus grew in 'wisdom, knowledge and grace' (Lk 2:52). Joseph deserves to be the Patron of 'Homes' and of 'Family', even if perhaps 'Real Estate' is a stretch. Joseph was the guardian of the 'Holy Family'.

1. Angela Langton, 'The original real estate agent Saint Joseph maintains his popularity' at <https://www.domain.com.au/news/the-original-real-estate-agent-saint-joseph-maintains-his-popularity-20150909-gjf92s>. Accessed 4 January 2021.

The Earth is our 'Home', the one we humans have in common. Our earth home needs to be a place of nurture, and we need the 'wisdom, knowledge and grace' Joseph fostered in Jesus, the ability to know how to live well as 'earthlings', as a human 'family', and as an integral part of the whole 'Earth Community'. Thomas Berry's work as an eco-philosopher places humans within the 'New Story' of the unfolding of creation during the billions of years of evolution that included the development of the beautiful blue and green planet Earth. Its integrated systems of air, water, soil and sunlight supported all evolving life, and finally human life. Human beings are endowed with consciousness that enables us to choose how to live and love within that "Earth Community'.[2]

There are some natural connections between St Joseph and the 'Care for our Common Home', as Pope Francis has chosen to subtitle his 2015 encyclical on ecology, *Laudato Si'*. What beautiful words they are—'care' and 'home'.

It is not such a great leap in this context to think of Mary MacKillop and Julian Tenison Woods and their regard for St Joseph. I find particularly relevant Mary's constant references in her letters to Joseph's 'hidden virtues'—humility, poverty and obedience', and her advice to the Sisters that these virtues needed to form the basis of their 'charity' towards one another.[3] Those virtues, so dear to Mary MacKillop in the nineteenth century, can be claimed as the very virtues, writ large, and adapted to the twenty-first century, that are needed to underpin ecological responsibility. They can point the way to 'holiness' and wholeness for our time.

In this essay I set out to explore, firstly the relevance for our ecological age of those three 'Joseph' virtues so dear to Mary MacKillop, and secondly, the shaping influence Joseph had on both Jesus' love for the natural world and his mission to bring Good News to the whole of creation.

The overarching bond of 'Charity' (Love) MacKillop urged the Sisters to exercise in their communities is needed universally to bring

---

2. *Thomas Berry and the New Cosmology*, edited by Anne Lonergan (USA: Twenty-Third Publications, 1990), 18. This term 'Earth Community' is introduced by Thomas Berry, and signifies the integral belonging of humans within the ecologies of the earth. We are 'earthlings'.
3. Paul Gardiner, *Mary MacKillop: An Extraordinary Australian* (Sydney: EJ Dwyer, 2011), 473.

all humanity together in unity with the Creator God, who 'is Love' (1 Jn:4). Pope John Paul II, in his World Day of Peace Message for 1990, spoke of 'Peace with the Creator, Peace with the Whole of Creation'.[4] Charity (Love) and its fruit, Peace, are the 'glue' that hold together an understanding of and respect for both our human relationships and our relationships with creation.

The three 'hidden' virtues of St Joseph that Mary MacKillop so valued—humility, poverty and obedience—are reinterpreted here, for our time, with deep application for ecological responsiveness and spirituality.

In considering the value of humility in this context, it is a first step towards positive change to humbly face up to the reality that we humans are turning our planet into what Pope Francis calls 'a pile of filth'.[5] As a species, humans have been operating on the assumption, at least since the Industrial Revolution, that we are 'lords' of creation, free to exploit, use up, discard and waste the precious gifts of the earth at will, in the interests of so-called 'progress'.[6] This has been a failure to humbly face the true nature of the precious gift our planet is, a gift from God. We have been blind to the necessity to be loving and responsible members of the 'Earth Community'. An attitude of domination and recklessness in dealing with the planet, taking its abundance for granted, is the antithesis of humility.

The word 'humility' has often been misunderstood as subservience, or self-deprecation. Its linguistic origin derives from 'humus', the Latin noun for 'earth', and the adjective 'humilis' can be interpreted to mean 'of the earth'. One of the qualities Australians have always admired about the Sisters of Saint Joseph is what is perceived as their 'down-to-earthness', their humility, inherited from Mary MacKillop as a hallmark of her congregation. There seemed to be a readiness to roll up the sleeves, literally if necessary, to respond to a presenting need, especially from the poor, without fanfare or self-congratulation.

This homely quality takes on a whole new dimension in these times of ecological awareness as we are called to respond to the needs of our suffering earth, deeply conscious of the poor who are, as Pope

4. Pope John Paul II, 'Peace with God the Creator, Peace with all of Creation' at <http://www.vatican.va/content/ john-paul-ii/en/messages/peace/documents/hf_jp-ii_mes_19891208_xxiii-world-day-for-peace.html>. Accessed 4 January 2021.
5. Pope Francis, *Laudato Si'* (Vatican City: Vatican Press, 2015), 21.
6. Pope Francis, *Laudato Si'*, 22.

Francis teaches so clearly in his great ecological encyclical, *Laudato Si'*, always the first to suffer through earth's devastation.

There is a deeper connection here with 'humility', as we face the truth that we humans are ourselves, biologically, and spiritually, members of the 'Earth Community', needing to humbly own our status as totally dependent on 'Mother Earth' for all our human needs. The very word 'human' once again makes this connection through its Latin origin. Moreover, humans, endowed by God with the dignity of consciousness and free will, have a particular truth to face as members of the Earth Community. We are called to be 'carers', custodians of, not 'lords over' 'Mother Earth' as St Francis of Assisi affectionately personified her. There is ultimate humility in realising these truths. An ecological humility will empower us to accept the gifts of creation with gratitude, and to also accept our responsibility, our sacred duty, to 'Care for our Common Home'.[7]

There is nothing false and simpering about this kind of humility. The Sisters of St Joseph have taken up the ecological challenge with intelligence, energy and commitment, not waiting for a 'green light' from political and church leadership who have mainly been reluctant to act with courage and conviction. Like Joseph, fleeing into Egypt with his family, as he faced the unrelenting reality of massacre and murder in his own culture, the Sisters have always taken up the urgent challenges our culture presents. The most urgent of all at this time is the state of our planet. In their Chapter documents of 2013, the Congregation honours new, more scientifically-based understandings of the evolution of the cosmos, including humans as an integral part of the evolution of Earth, endowed with the gifts of mind, heart and will, both to respond to and share responsibility for, God's creation.[8]

The Sisters have explored the truths and implications of the 'New Story' of the universe and its unfolding, truths spoken by prophetic voices like Teilhard de Chardin, Thomas Berry and Elia Delio, who have helped inform and inspire the search for truth. If we humbly accept the truths that science and theology are opening up for us, we cannot but act to respond in love to the greater realities and particularly to the distress of the Earth. This attitude of humility in the face of

7. *Laudato Si'* Introduction.
8. Acts of General Chapter 2013, St Joseph's Congregational Archives, North Sydney.

reality, calls us, like Mary, Joseph's spouse, to 'magnify the Lord', able to 'do great things' (Lk 1:46), and not to remain in bondage to fear and a failure to face the truth, but open to the expansive belief that, 'with God all things are possible' (Matt 17:20). Joseph simply placed his trust in God and God's messengers, and acted as circumstances demanded. He was able to remain a faithful lover in the face of Mary's predicament as an unmarried pregnant young woman, and to be a brave, wise husband in the face of Herod's megalomania. Trust in God was always a source of empowerment for both Mary MacKillop and Julian Tenison Woods, facing the harsh realities that life in colonial Australia and an Irish-dominated Catholicism, presented to their great founding projects.

The virtue of 'Poverty', which has lost much of its currency in the modern world, can be powerful when revisited, and has much to say to 'ecological conversion', as called for in *Laudato Si'* and other Papal teachings.[9] Individual and corporate greed prompts humans to want more and more material goods at the expense of the earth. This is the antithesis of the virtue of 'Poverty'. Pope Francis calls us to understand that 'Less is more', and to live frugally, realising that the fruits of the earth are to be shared by all.[10] He reminds us that many of God's children live in hunger and poverty, while a few, the richest small percentage of humanity, take to themselves the greater portion of earth's resources.

The vow of Poverty Mary MacKillop and her Sisters committed to live in the spirit of simplicity of St Joseph, did not mean that they should choose lives of destitution. Mary was solicitous for her Sisters, just as Joseph was for his wife and child. Mary was always practical in this regard, wanting to make sure they had a paper bag of sandwiches if travelling on a long train journey, or providing proper heating for them in winter. Living in tents on gold fields may sound romantic, but Mary worked hard to ensure that camping would be a temporary arrangement and a safe convent home would be provided. Joseph too, returned from Egypt and sought refuge in Galilee to make a home for his young family (Lk 2:23). He was a 'home-maker' and a provider. Similarly, we know that the Earth needs to be a home for all to live in harmony and dignity. Pope Francis tells us it is always the poor

9. Pope Francis, *Laudato Si'*, 219, 220.
10. Pope Francis, *Laudato Si'*, 222.

who suffer the most from environmental devastation.[11] Their vow of Poverty has called the Sisters of St Joseph to opt first for the poor and their needs. Aspiring to provide for all on the planet and being in solidarity with the poor is about 'Home-Making' on a global scale - inclusive, respectful of the need to share the fruits of the earth with all.

The vow and virtue of Poverty reminds us that humans can live peacefully and productively without needing to depend on individually acquired property and money, similar to the way the early Christians lived in the Acts of the Apostles, holding 'all things in common' (Acts 4:32). Increasingly, post-COVID, more people seem open to the notion of 'Less is more'. Our motives in making decisions towards a more minimalist lifestyle are nearly always mixed, but surely the realisation that we can manage well without constant flights, huge houses, several bathrooms and the latest gadgetry, has to be seen as progress in our cultural evolution. The traditional virtue of 'Poverty' in our time may be better explained as 'mindfulness, 'down-sizing', 'modest living', 'gratefulness' and a number of other buzz words that are in vogue. To 'Live simply so that all may simply live' remains a universally powerful adage.[12]

'Obedience' as a virtue has lost appeal in the affluent, liberal democracies of the twenty-first century, except perhaps in the armed forces. Most moderns do not like being told what to do and want to make up their own minds about how to act.

In Christian theology, obedience is seen as acting in fidelity to God's will, following the example of Christ who prayed in his great agony, 'not my will, but yours be done' (Lk 22:44), and also said 'I always do the will of my Father' (Jn 8:29).

The word 'obedience' needs to be understood in this context as an attentive response, associated with listening, hearing, and acting on God's will.[13] Understood in this way, our failure to 'hear' and act upon the 'will of God' for all Creation is the antithesis of the virtue of 'Obedience'.

11. Pope Francis, *Laudato Si'*, 48.
12. Some attribute the origin of this saying to Mahatma Ghandi; others to the American nun Elizabeth Seton.
13. The word derives from the Latin *obedire, oboedire* 'obey, be subject, serve, pay attention to, give ear', literally 'listen to', from *ob* 'to' + *audire* 'listen, hear': <https://www.etymonline.com/word/obey>. Accessed 20 January 2021.

Creation is a gift given in love, requiring human respect for and cooperation with its intrinsic ecological blueprint. St Joseph was totally obedient to and in touch with what God revealed to him, spiritually very attuned to receive divine guidance about what to do. He was clear in his mind that to take Mary to himself as his wife, despite the outward appearances of the situation, the social stigma, was the will of God. He is described as a 'just man' (Matt 1:19), a great compliment for a Jew, meaning one who was upright, righteous and obedient to God's Law and teaching. Likewise, to decide to leave summarily and go on a journey fraught with danger and hardship into Egypt as a refugee family was, in Joseph's mind, a divine summons, to be heard and obeyed. At the same time, it was a responsible common sensible response to a harsh, threatening reality, over which Joseph had no control. In his Apostolic Letter *Patris Corde,* Pope Francis extols St Joseph's obedience to the will of God:

> In every situation, Joseph declared his own 'fiat', like those of Mary at the Annunciation and Jesus in the Garden of Gethsemane. In his role as the head of a family, Joseph taught Jesus to be obedient to his parents (Lk 2:51), in accordance with God's command (Ex 20:12). During the hidden years in Nazareth, Jesus learned at the school of Joseph to do the will of the Father.[14]

The Sisters of St Joseph are called to exercise the virtue of obedience by responding to the will of God. They interpret how to make that response for themselves as individuals, and also collectively, as they engage in processes of discernment to identify the 'signs of the times' and how best to respond to those signs. These 'signs' are pointers towards how God's will is to be known in any particular time and place. The most compelling 'sign' of our own times is the destruction of earth's eco-systems through the influence of human-induced climate change and disrespect for the systems of the natural world. Mary MacKillop and Julian Tenison Woods responded to the 'signs' of 1860s Australia by founding a religious order devoted to the education and care of the neglected poor in the colonies. Today, the 'Rule' does not remain ossified in the past. The Sisters take seriously

14. Pope Francis, Apostolic Letter *Patris Corde,* 8 December 2020, 3 at <*www.vatican.va* › francesco › apost_letters › documents >. Accessed 20 January 2021.

the work of reinterpreting their mission in each new time, remaining faithful to the foundational virtues of St Joseph and the dream of their founders. Today that mission includes embracing the wonders of creation and 'Care for our Common Home'. This is inspiring for us all.

St Joseph played another very important part in the development of the ecological spirituality and theology that has emanated from the Gospels. Not only did Joseph model a virtuous life as a 'just man'- Joseph was a role model and formator for the 'Cosmic Christ', the Word made flesh', who was at 'the beginning', and was 'with God, and was God' (Jn 1:1). The Christ of the cosmos was incarnated into this world as the historical Jesus of Nazareth, birthed by Mary, conceived of the Holy Spirit, and legally fathered by Mary's husband, Joseph.

Joseph is described in the words of a traditional Josephite hymn as, 'Joseph holy, faithful guardian, loving teacher of God's Word'.[15] As legal father, Joseph would have been the major influence in introducing Jesus to the natural world. We can imagine that Joseph was the one who taught Jesus the toddler about the streams, meadows, 'lilies of the field' (Matt 6:25), the olive and fig trees, times of harvest, the plantings and the changing seasons, and how to notice when 'summer is nigh' (Matt 24:32). Jesus' parents would have introduced him to wheat as the source of 'daily bread' (Matt 6:11) and yeast as the missing ingredient in the ceremonial unleavened bread of Passover. His father Joseph was, we are told, a carpenter, as was Jesus, so there would have been so much to learn about the value of wood and stone as building materials, the grain within the timber cut from a fallen log, and the quality of rocks. The 'rock' of Peter Jesus referred to (Matt. 16:18) may well have been modelled on a local type of stone he knew well, with particular qualities of both friability and strength. Who knows? The later parables and stories of Jesus, the images, and figures of speech, so often reflect the natural world. Perhaps Joseph taught Jesus to fish in the Lake of Galilee; Jesus seemed very *au fait* with fish and fishing. He was equally at home with pasturing animals, choosing sheep and shepherds as images of God's Kingdom.

Joseph would have helped Jesus befriend and memorise the scriptures, and prayed the psalms with him, praising God and creation. They were faithful Jews, and knew that all creation was

15. Dom Moreno (1889–1953), a Benedictine monk from New Norcia, Western Australia, composed this hymn for the Sisters of St Joseph.

holy, the work of God's hands, to be stewarded and honoured. 'God saw that it was good' is the refrain, like a litany, in Genesis, as the writer imagines God rejoicing at the end of each of the seven 'days' of creation in the gifts of sun, moon, waters, fruits of earth, animals and humans, that emerged from God's creative 'work'. Joseph and Mary would have instilled a creation spirituality in the boy Jesus as part of their religious culture, and he would have imbibed it as naturally as breathing the Galilean air.

St Joseph can be seen as the custodian of the Incarnation, as he shaped the character of Jesus, the Son of God, who had 'stepped out of the Godhead' so to speak, to become a dependent human child, God enfleshed. In Jesus, God had become identified with all that was material, dignifying all creation, inextricably linked through Christ's humanity.

Fr Denis Edwards, Australian eco-theologian, wrote that Jesus was 'made from Stardust', as are we all. Our evolution as earthlings is traceable from the first atoms that birthed the ancient galaxies and the 'stardust' (material elements) from which all that exists has evolved.[16] The Incarnation, this process of God entering human history as a member of the human race, assumed new visibility with the birth of Jesus, and it was Joseph who was there with Mary, watching over and providing for her and the new baby. He continued this close involvement through the years of Jesus' growth to manhood. We could almost claim Joseph as the 'Shepherd' of the Incarnation, and the tutor of the Messiah. Edwards wrote, 'In Jesus of Nazareth, God becomes a vital part of an ecosystem and a part of the interconnected systems that support life on earth'.[17] In other words this was truly a flesh and blood man, part of the 'Earth Community', sanctifying it through becoming one of us, made of the same elements as we are, and part of the evolutionary process.

Joseph guided from babyhood to manhood the one who was 'the image of the invisible God, the firstborn of all creation; from him all things in heaven and earth were created, things visible and invisible' (Col 1:15). Joseph 'grew' the human Jesus into the fullness of his physical, intellectual, spiritual and emotional self, and in doing

16. Denis Edwards, *Made From Stardust: Exploring the Place of Human Beings Within Creation* (Melbourne: Collins Dove, 1992), 5.
17. Denis Edwards, *Ecology at the Heart of Faith* (New York: Orbis Books, 2006), 59.

so was unwittingly, the guardian of the One from whom 'all things' originated. This is an extraordinary link between Joseph the humble saint, and the unfolding of the cosmos.

During 2021, declared by Pope Francis as the Universal Year of St Joseph, we are presented with much to contemplate about this saint. In *Patris Corde*, Pope Francis reminds us that Joseph 'earned an honest living to provide for his family'.[18] The Pope goes on to make an important point about work. 'St Joseph also teaches us the value, the dignity and the joy of what it means to eat bread that is the fruit of one's own labour.' We all need to grasp the ecological point that the work providing food for the table can either respect or disrespect earth's eco-systems. The Pope writes, 'Those who work are cooperating with God himself, and in some way become creators of the world around us.'[19] St Joseph wears many 'hats' as a popular saint, one being 'Joseph the Worker'. We can now widen Joseph's brief to include guiding workers to grow in understanding that the earth and its resources are to be used wisely and sustainably in meeting human needs.

St Joseph has never been more relevant. It is entirely appropriate to honour him as a saint for ecology. In 2013 at his inaugural Mass on the Feast of St Joseph, Pope Francis honoured Joseph as the 'Protector', and extended the beloved Saint's 'protection' from the Holy Family, the Church and the human family, out to the whole of creation. The Pope pleaded:

> Please, I would like to ask . . . let us be 'protectors' (like Joseph) of creation, protectors of God's plan inscribed in nature, protectors of one another and of the environment.[20]

Joseph, who loved the creator God and lived in humility, simplicity and obedience to God's will, prepared Jesus well to become 'the light of the world' and to 'proclaim the Good News to the whole creation' (Mk 16:5). Joseph can credibly partner with St Francis of Assisi as a universal guide and exemplar in responding to the call to 'Care for our Common Home'.

---

18. Pope Francis, *Patris Corde*, 6.
19. Pope Francis, *Patris Corde*, 6.
20. *Pope Francis, Homily of Inaugural Mass as Pontiff. March 19, 2013, Solemnity of Saint Joseph at* <http://www.vatican.va/content/francesco/en/homilies/2013/documents/papa-francesco_20130319_omelia-inizio-pontificato.html>. Accessed *14 January, 2021.*

St Joseph: Model for Educational Leaders

Catherine Mead rsj

School communities under the patronage of St Joseph are imbued with a spirit that inspires an approach to education in more than four hundred schools across Australia in rural, urban, regional towns and cities. This patronage was afforded to schools by the leadership of St Mary of the Cross MacKillop and Fr Julian Tenison Woods with the founding of the Sisters of St Joseph of the Sacred Heart in Penola, South Australia in 1866. The Josephite spiritual tradition emanating from the founding tradition of the Sisters of St Joseph was dedicated to educating 'the most neglected in God's vineyard'.[1] The spiritual tradition devolved from the patronage of St Joseph provides school leaders with a rich source of wisdom and authority to draw upon in creating learning environments characterised by justice, equity, dignity, solidarity, the common good and humility. Schools identifying with St Joseph's patronage and guidance in educating in the Josephite tradition speak to the enduring and unassuming presence of this spiritual tradition.

The context in which Catholic education and specifically schools under the patronage of St Joseph now educate is in a liminal time in the Catholic Church and society. This liminal time is characterised by a de-traditionalising and pluralising culture, a loss of moral authority, and a crisis of meaning and purpose. Schools under the patronage of St Joseph have the opportunity to turn to the Josephite spiritual tradition, bequeathed from the life and example of St Joseph. When this tradition is appreciated in a new context it is a rich source of

1. Mary MacKillop, Letter to Sisters, 6 March 1900, St Joseph's Congregational Archives, North Sydney (SJCA).

wisdom and authority, intuition and vision that can bring meaning and purpose in re-contextualising the gospel in new unchartered times.[2] School leaders imbued with and formed in the context of the Josephite spiritual tradition have the opportunity to create a shared vision within their school community to transcend the ordinariness of each day and to form inclusive faith and learning communities.

However, in the current milieu, there is also the risk that such a spiritual tradition could dissipate or be diluted if there is a lack of theological understanding of the tradition, its spirituality, shared symbols and rituals.[3] This risk is increased particularly when implementing a holistic approach to education that reflects the Josephite tradition. It is important in this liminal time for all who are responsible for educating in the Josephite tradition to be cognisant with the responsibility to nurture the spiritual tradition in and through their role. In this way the integrity of purpose and vision will be evident in schools that claim St Joseph as their patron.

The gift of a spiritual tradition once re-claimed with critical appreciation will enable school communities to thrive on the energy and clarity of the vision, dreams, purpose, values and goals inherent in the tradition.[4] Moreover, leaders and staff members who are attuned to the Josephite spiritual tradition have the capacity over time to integrate the past and present with the future, lending continuity and new direction to their school community.[5] When tradition is understood as taking the essential values contained in the tradition and expressing them in a new place and time, school leaders are able to effectively reclaim the expression of the tradition in their present context.

The process of reclaiming the Josephite spiritual tradition necessitates the transmission and formation of the tradition over time. One of the most effective means of transmitting the Josephite tradition is through storytelling. 'Stories create identity through

2. Michael Green, *Now With Enthusiasm: Charism, God's Mission and Catholic Schools Today* (Mulgrave, Victoria: Vaughan Publishing, 2018).
3. Monica Dutton. and Meg Kahler, 'Formation in a Founding Charism Setting', in Jill Gowdie, *Stirring the Soul of Catholic Education: Formation for Mission* (Mulgrave, Victoria: Vaughan Publishing, 2017).
4. Thomas Groome, *Educating for Life; A Spiritual Vision for Every Teacher and Parent* (Thomas More Texas: Allen, 1998).
5. Groome, *Educating for life*, 122.

music, language, images and features so that a series of events provide meaning.'[6] While so little is recorded of St Joseph's life and work, the scriptures provide a brief insight into St Joseph as a courageous man undertaking discernment in the midst of considerable pressure in order to act in a manner that demonstrated a keen sense of his inner authority (Matt 1:18–25). Further references provide an insight into the quiet, humble and just man who, along with Mary, was the first teacher in the life of Jesus. While the written stories are limited, the artistic representations of St Joseph create images and evoke feelings and a way of relating to the Spirit of St Joseph. Artistic representations in oil paintings, statues, stained glass windows and sculptures provide those school communities who bear the name of St Joseph with a rich source of reflection. St Joseph is portrayed as the protector, nurturer, teacher, worker, discerning guide, a wise man of justice and humility. Such stories and artistic representations of St Joseph enable school communities to write and re-write their identities in particular contexts.[7]

The Josephite spiritual tradition provides school communities with the capacity to draw on its depth of justice inherent in the tradition. St Joseph was 'a just man' (Matt 1:19), these few simple words illustrating his actions for justice with extraordinary consequences that enabled human dignity to be upheld. St Joseph's actions enabled dignity to flourish in the life of Mary, the Mother of God and in the life of Jesus. Joseph's discerned action to listen to the voice of God and his own dreams illustrate to school leaders that powerful interventions can preserve and enhance the human dignity of all those in the community. 'Human persons flourish and find lasting happiness or joy, to the extent that their particular lives are lived according to their nature, increasingly conforming to and fulfilling their creation in the image and likeness of God.'[8] Like St Joseph, school leaders are charged with the responsibility to nurture environments conducive to human flourishing. In particular, leaders are called to respond to the lives of young people in the context of

6. Gerald Arbuckle, *Catholic Identity or Identities? Refounding Ministries in Chaotic Times* (Collegeville, Minnesota: Liturgical Press, 2013), 12.
7. Mary Jo Hatch, *Organizational Theory: Modern, Symbolic and Postmodern Perspectives* (New York: Oxford University, 2013).
8. Stephen McKinney and John Sullivan, *Educating in a Catholic Perspective* (Burlington UK: Routledge, 2016), 176.

western culture, where the commodity of consumerism threatens to impact on the dignity of children and young people and their self-understanding.[9] In the context of Catholic education the principle of human dignity is applied to all those who contribute, whereby 'human dignity is considered as the very core of the vocation of a Catholic educator.'[10] Just as St Joseph was attentive to the world around him and, through listening to God in his dreams, learnt his vocation,[11] school leaders and staff members are encouraged to deepen their call to enhance their vocation and the dignity of those they serve. In effect, human dignity is everybody's business and concern in a school community. In the midst of the threats and demands of consumerism and globalisation, it is more important than ever for education to be for human fulfilment. Therefore, school leaders need to have an awareness that when ambition, competition and self-advancement dominate, it leads to frustrating dehumanisation for all whose dignity they seek to enhance.

The Josephite spiritual tradition, as exemplified in the life of St Joseph, reflects the social justice principle of the common good. In particular, St Joseph's attentiveness to the word of God is seen in his commitment to the wellbeing and safety of his family, and the common good of his community (Matt 2:13–15). Through the words of Scripture and its interpretation by community leaders, Joseph would have remained in tune with the word of God, allowing it to influence his decisions and to give shape to the truth of God within him.[12] This provides a model for leaders who seek to enable all members of the school community to achieve their authentic human development more fully.[13] The common good exercised in schools in the Josephite tradition where relationships and family partnerships are emphasised, calls for a communal effort of both teachers and

9. Michael Holman, 'Father Pedro Arrupe and Jesuit Education: A Personal Reflection' in *International Studies in Catholic Education*, 6/2 (2014): 140–147.
10. Mark Storz and Karen Nestor, 'Insights into Meeting Standards from Listening to the Voices of Urban Students' in *Middle School Journal*, 34/4 (2008): 11–19.
11. Mary Cresp, *In the Spirit of Joseph* (Sydney: Sisters of St Joseph of the Sacred Heart 2005), 5.
12. Cresp, *In the Spirit of Joseph*, 5.
13. *Gaudium et Spes:* 'Pastoral Constitution on the Church in the Modern World', in *The Documents of Vatican II,* edited by Walter M Abbott (London: Geoffrey Chapman, 1967), 52.

students in building a community that values every individual. School leaders striving for the common good in the context of a society characterised by individualism and the complexities of the diverse and pluralised communities they lead, are called to 'bring to life in the students the communitarian dimension of the human person, as every human person is called to live in a community, as a social being, and a member of the people of God'.[14] The value placed on relationships ensures priority is given to educating those who are in the most marginalised of circumstances. The example of St Joseph accepting life's circumstances encourages leaders to create learning communities where religious pluralism and diversity can be indicative of the common good.[15] When leaders and teachers encourage open views on social questions and religious diversity in the context of the Catholic faith tradition, they enable dialogue so that the integration of faith, life, learning and culture are able to find a meeting place.[16] An openness to such dialogue creates connection with others and is an antidote to individualism within society.[17]

The inspiration of St Joseph as the 'just man' (Matt 1:19) is readily applied to school communities where there is an awareness of the gospel imperative to care for the most vulnerable within the community. Prior to contemporary Church social justice teaching on 'the preferential option for the poor', St Joseph embodied justice in the profound action of going beyond the expected norms of his day to ensure right relationships imbued with dignity and love (Matt 2:21). Francis notes 'Joseph did not hesitate to obey regardless of the hardship involved.'[18] The ordinary, practical daily routines and

---

14. Congregation for Catholic Education, 'The Catholic School on the Threshold of the Third Millennium', in *Journal of Catholic Education*, 2/1 (1998): 4–14.
15. Didier Pollefeyt and Jan Bouwens, 'Framing the Identity of Catholic Schools: Empirical Methodology for Quantitative Research on the Catholic Identity of an Education Institute', in *International Studies in Catholic Education*, 2/2 (2010): 193–211.
16. Pollefeyt & Bouwens, 'Framing the Identity'.
17. Toke Elsehof, 'Catholic Schools and the Embodiment of Religiosity: The Development of Catholicity Toward the Common Good', in *Religious Education*, 110/2 (2015): 150–161.
18. Pope Francis, *Patris Corde* (8 December 2020), at <https://www.bing.com/search?q=%2C+patris+corde&form=EDGEAR&qs=PF&cvid=a660c20802964b23a91c8c6f409ed914&cc=AU&setlang=en-US&PC=HCTS>, 3. Accessed 12 March 2021.

encounters experienced in schools are laced with opportunities for leaders and teachers, like St Joseph, to consciously show children and young people a way through crises, seeking hope and adjusting routines to grow in maturity.[19]

School leaders under the patronage of St Joseph are called to seek ways of fulfilling their double mandate to prevent students and families being excluded from and within the school. The crisis of exclusion from school through a lack of accessibility, affordability, truancy, and illness and the exclusion within schools because of the hidden costs of excursions, access to technology and participation in extra-curriculum activity needs to be guarded against by school leaders.[20] Like St Joseph, leaders seeking to act justly are challenged to 'disentangle themselves from serving those at the top of society and instead to come into solidarity with those at or near the bottom'.[21] Furthermore, leaders in schools guided by St Joseph's example are called to serve those experiencing the impact of disadvantage including children and young people segregated by race, faith, culture and low income.[22] School leaders can exemplify the example of St Joseph to ensure the human dignity of children and the vulnerable are at the forefront of their discernment and actions. Human dignity in the life of the child 'is a source of inspiration for educators to see that every child is held in God's infinite tenderness, and God is present in each of their lives'.[23] School leaders who draw on the inspiration of St Joseph in caring of those most vulnerable, exemplify educational philosophies and practices that honour the authentic image of the child.

St Matthew's description of St Joseph listening to God's word deep within provides another aspect of the Josephite tradition particularly applicable to education (Matt 1:20). The 'pedagogy of listening'

19. Pope Francis, *Patris Corde*, Introduction.
20. Stephen McKinney and Robert Hill, 'Gospel, Poverty and Catholic Schools', in *International Studies in Catholic Education*, 2/2 (2010): 163–175.
21. Daniel Groody and Gustavo Gutierrez, *The Preferential Option for the Poor Beyond Theology* (Indiana: University of Notre Dame Press, 2013), 99.
22. Jim Gleeson, 'Critical Challenges and Dilemmas for Catholic Education Leadership Internationally', in *International Studies in Catholic Education*, 7/2 (2015): 145–161.
23. Pope Francis, *Lumen fidei* (29 June 2013) at <http://www.vatican.va/content/francesco/en/encyclicals/documents/papa-francesco_20130629_enciclica-lumen-fidei.html>. Accessed 14 March 2021.

between adults, children and the environment becomes central to every educational relationship.[24] In caring and educating for the most vulnerable and proclaiming that human life is sacred and that the dignity of the human person is foundational, teachers enable a new vision of humanity that rejects intolerance.[25]

St Joseph models obedience (deep listening) to inspire school leaders and teachers to critique curriculum policy and practice as a means of responding to those in poor circumstances.[26] St Joseph as a patient listener, can remind school leaders to encourage students' voices to be heard in the teaching and learning process. Such elements as teacher quality, curriculum issues, pedagogical practices and a lack of resources all need to be considered to ensure inequalities are eliminated.[27] Listening to the circumstances and realities of students' lives and responding to the needs of those on the margins is core in schools under the patronage of St Joseph. This is further reinforced when considering that, 'in its ecclesial dimension the Catholic school has its root; it is school for all, with special attention to those who are weakest'.[28]

The spirit of Joseph as protector and carer encourages school leaders and teachers to be responsible to act in ways that are creative and courageous, in solidarity with their community. Having listened deeply, St Joseph acted, responding to God's word in his life: 'Joseph did what God commanded of him' (Matt 1:24; 2:14, 21). As a provider, Joseph models ethical care, mutual service, co-responsibility, hopefulness and charity, terms that are all synonymous with the concept of solidarity.[29] Leaders in schools under the patronage of St

24. Carla Rinaldi, 'Re-imagining Childhood', in *Every Child,* 23/1 (2017): 4–7.
25. Holman, 'Father Pedro Arrupe and Jesuit Education'.
26. Gerald Grace. *Faith, Mission and Challenge in Catholic Education: The Selected Works of Gerald Grace* (Abingdon, Oxon: Routledge, 2015).
27. Mark Storz, 'Educational Inequity from the Perspectives of Those Who Live It: Urban Middle School Students', Perspectives on the Quality of their Education', in *The Urban Review,* 40/3 (2008): 247–267.
28. Congregation for Catholic Education, 'The Catholic School on the Threshold of the Third Millennium', at <http://www.vatican.va/roman_curia/congregations/ccatheduc/documents/rc_con_ccatheduc_doc_27041998_school2000_en.html>, 15. Accessed 16 March 2021.
29. Angelina Gutierrez, 'The Preferential Option for the Poor in Catholic Education in the Philippines: A Report on the Progress and Problems', in *International Studies in Catholic Education,* 1/2 (2009): 135–151.

Joseph can rely on his example of acting in solidarity when discerning administrative policies and practices so that the implementation reflects shared aims in the care of students, their families and staff members. The long-term impact of solidarity or 'walking with' as witnessed in the life of St Joseph (Matt 2:13) is more than a vague feeling of compassion. Rather, 'solidarity encourages mutuality, the sharing of perspectives of those marginalised with those who seek to empower them'.[30] Leaders who are cognisant with their local context and who walk with their school communities have the opportunity to work towards human solidarity where no-one is excluded by culture, race, socio-economic status or religion.

St Joseph's status as 'the worker' points towards the creative endeavour and dignity experienced when meaningful participation is afforded to all. School leaders and teachers can draw on the example of St Joseph in creating spaces where students, families and the broader community experience the positive functions of subsidiarity, namely, empowerment and respect for differences.[31] The principle of subsidiarity affirms and safeguards the personal initiative and creativity of individuals, where local context is valued.[32] In many cases, schools under the patronage of St Joseph, located in rural and regional areas, require leaders to be courageous in claiming the local context and avoid their school communities from being marginalised by centralised decision-making. School leaders inspired by St Joseph, are called to be creative and courageous in finding ways of enabling full participation of smaller communities within the context of the broader Catholic community, government and educational bodies that often make decisions in spaces removed from the impact of their decisions.

St Joseph's practical example of serving with humility provides a bedrock for leaders as they seek to empower and serve those in their school community. Far from being of the 'doormat variety', humility is rather an expression of each person's truth; it maintains

---

30. Gerald Beyer, 'The Meaning of Solidarity in Catholic Social Teaching', in *Political Theology*, 15/1 (2014): 7–25.
31. Scot Kelley, 'Subsidiarity: Challenging the Top Down Bias', in *Journal of Religious and Business Ethics*, 1/2 (2009): 1–11.
32. Australian Catholic Bishops, Introduction Sandie Cornish, *Building Bridges: Social Justice Statements from Australia's Catholic Bishops 1988 to 2013* (Alexandria, NSW: Australian Catholic Social Justice Council, 2014).

a sense of one's own strengths and limitations.[33] Furthermore, the humility witnessed in the life of St Joseph dissipates the falsified and counterfeit notions of humility, so that humility can be experienced as inner authority.[34] School leaders can be inspired by this quality of humility exemplified in St Joseph to strengthen their leadership, making decisions imbued with integrity so that others experience coherency in action and words. St Joseph's practical example of serving with humility is a foundational concept for leaders as they seek to empower and serve those in their school community.

A spiritual tradition derived from the spirit of St Joseph provides leaders and staff members with a source of 'spiritual capital' to draw upon and to influence discernment and the decision-making process.[35] Such a reserve of 'spiritual capital' can be described as a transcendent impulse to guide judgement and actions, enabling professionals to act as witnesses'.[36] Hence, school leaders and staff members who embody St Joseph's spirit through prayer and reflection come to holiness experienced in critical thought inspiring action for justice, peace and sustainability.[37] Furthermore, leaders are able to draw upon this source of 'spiritual capital' as inspiration to integrate mission and vision in their school communities. St Joseph's practical example, exemplified in his status as St Joseph the Worker, encourages leaders to integrate vision into the daily experiences of the school community in the pattern of relationships that influence teaching and learning, decision making, and administration practices.

---

33. Catherine Clark, 'The Spiritual Tradition of the Australian Sisters of St Joseph in Education in South Australia', in *New Ways of Living the Gospel: Spiritual Traditions in Catholic Schools,* edited by Jim D'Orsa and Therese D'Orsa (Mulgrave, Victoria: Garratt Publishing, 2015), 81–91.
34. Dean Brackley, *The Call to Discernment in Troubled Times: New Perspective on the Transformative Wisdom of Ignatius of Loyola* (New York: Crossroads, 2004).
35. Timothy Cook. and Thomas Simonds, 'The Charism of 21st Century Catholic Schools: Building a Culture of Relationships', in *A Journal of Inquiry and Practice,* 14/ 93 (2011): 319–333.
36. Gerald Grace, 'Renewing Spiritual Capital: An urgent Propriety for the Future of Catholic Education Internationally', in *International Studies in Catholic Education,* 2/2 (2010): 117–128.
37. Michael Dallaire, 'Holy Mischief Within Institutions: Charism and Conscience', in *Crosscurrents,* 63/3 (2013): 350–361.

The presence of St Joseph, quiet, silent and 'in the shadows'[38] embodies an aspect many school leaders aspire to integrate in their leadership. A trusting presence, as was St Joseph in the life of Jesus, is a quality difficult to attain and yet critical for leaders to nurture. An evolving understanding of the power of this presence, otherwise described as the spiritual dimension of leadership, is characterised by a holistic, transcendent, intrinsic human capacity for meaning-making.[39] Leaders and teachers in schools inspired by St Joseph can follow his example in nurturing prayer, contemplation and meditation, which are increasingly seen as factors that positively impact on leadership behaviour.[40]

School leaders and teachers who attend to the spiritual dimension of their lives and vocation open up the opportunity to engage with others in a profound and authentic way, so that they can be the best leader and teacher they can be.[41] St Joseph transcending his ego-self for a higher purpose, offers leaders an example to become self- and other-aware and to question thought-patterns and belief systems.[42] St Joseph's humility, evident in his self-giving and 'patient silence as the prelude to concrete expression of trust', is a most desirable characteristic of spiritual leadership.[43] Leaders and teachers who lead with the heart, stimulating trust and understanding, have the opportunity to experience both strength and consolation in meeting challenges they face on a daily basis. Moreover, leaders who create a reflective paradigm where they can reflect on decision-making in light of the needs of the people they serve, are more readily able to advocate for justice and to create practices that empower teachers, students and their families.[44]

---

38. Pope Francis, *Patris Corde*, Introduction.
39. Gowdie, *Stirring the Soul of Catholic Education*, 155–157.
40. Gowdie, *Stirring the Soul of Catholic Education*.
41. Sen Sendjaya, James Sarros & Joseph Santora, 'Defining and Measuring Servant Leadership Behaviour in Organizations', in *Journal of Management Studies*, 45/2 (2008): 402–424.
42. Jay Barney, Judy Wicks, Otto Scharmer & Kathryn Pavlovich, 'Exploring Transcendental Leadership of Men and Women', in *Journal of Management, Spirituality and Religion*, 12/4 (2015): 209–304.
43. Pope Francis, *Patris Corde*, 7.
44. Ronald Rebore and Angela Walmsley, *Genuine School Leadership: Experience, Reflection and Beliefs*. (Strathfield, Australia: St Pauls Publications, 2009).

In conclusion, let us rejoice in the fact that St Joseph exemplifies the qualities that can be emulated by school leaders as a source of inspiration for those who strive to reclaim and re-imagine the Josephite spiritual tradition in a new time and place. The Josephite spiritual tradition is a source of spiritual wisdom and authority that can be drawn upon in creating learning environments characterised by justice, equity, dignity, solidarity, the common good and humility. This spiritual tradition is bequeathed to us by St Joseph as a man of justice, humility, acceptance, a worker who demonstrates creativity and courage, and shows us how to listen and love deeply. The example of instilling trust in others is indeed a rich source of encouragement for those who lead schools under his patronage. School leaders who draw on the Josephite spiritual tradition and re-imagine it in the context of contemporary education will ensure the tradition is timeless, is authentically expressed and authors the depth of dignity to flourish in the lives of all those who make up the school community.

Joseph and Refugees

Betty Brown rsj

This year, 2021 declared by Pope Francis to be dedicated to St Joseph has given me the opportunity of reflecting on St Joseph the refugee and the plight of refugees today. It has brought me new awareness in two ways. I have understood how my Josephite formation and experience has influenced my later work with refugees and how working with refugees has given me greater appreciation and love of St Joseph. As Pope Francis noted, 'our lives are woven together and sustained by ordinary people; people often overlooked'.[1] Refugees can lift us out of the known, safe parameters of our lives into the unknown, an experience that, according to the evangelist Matthew, Joseph knew.

The foundations of my final twenty years of formal ministry accompanying refugees were laid in my early years as I learnt hymns, stories, prayers and devotions in honour of St Joseph. Throughout childhood and into early adulthood, my love of St Joseph increased, culminating in the decision to become a Sister of St Joseph of Lochinvar. The example and inspiration of other Sisters solidified his spirit within so that it became an integral part of my approach to ministry. Let me reflect on that journey.

Early Formation

One could trace my earliest introduction into a 'Refugee-Joseph' mentality to childhood at schools run by Sisters of St Joseph. At an

1. Pope Francis, in *Patris Corde,* acknowledged from *Meditation in the Time of Pandemic* (27 March 2020): *L'Osservatore Romano* (29 March 2020), at <www.vatican.va/content/francesco/en/apost_letters/documents/papa-francesco-lettera-ap_20201208_patris-corde.>. Accessed 8 March 2021.

unconscious level, hymns nurtured a simple, direct approach to him. Each morning we would march into school singing with zest, *Hail Holy Joseph, Hail:*

> Hail holy Joseph, hail. Sweet spouse of Mary, hail.
> Pure as a lily flower in Eden's peaceful vale.
>
> Mother of Jesus bless, and bless you saints on high
> All true and peaceful souls that to St Joseph cry.[2]

I picked up from those words love for Joseph, affection between Mary and Joseph, a sense of peacefulness. It touched on grief in souls that cry. There was the owning of sorrow that helped us pray simply in the world of reality, not make-believe.

We brought flowers for the altar, sang and prayed with the Sisters for our families, especially our fathers, uncles and brothers who were signing up daily for the war. Even in Australia, almost remote from war, we were drawn into a sense that we were in a bigger world where huge sad things could and did happen.

In the final year at primary school, when our youngest sister was diagnosed with scarlet fever, I was quarantined from school. My teacher, Sister Magdalen, spent hours after school directing my study and correcting my work so that I would not get behind.[3] Her kindness changed my life. I won a bursary to college for five years. Her kindness also taught me Josephite care for those separated from others, about going the extra mile for someone 'on the outer'.

In my five years at St Joseph's College, Lochinvar I became more immersed in the life of the Sisters and their devotion to St Joseph, with daily Mass, choir, liturgical feasts, Sisters' funerals, diocesan events, processions, concerts, team sports with flags and banners urging our loyalties under the patronage of St Joseph and his heavenly friends. We knew ourselves as belonging to St Joseph. It was then that I felt the call to join the Sisters of St Joseph.

---

2. Frederick Faber, 'Hail Holy Joseph', 1849 at https://tosingistopraytwice.wordpress.com/ 2018/03/06/hail-holy-joseph-hail/. Accessed 8 March 2021. Children in Josephite schools sang the two verses above, a simplified version of the original.
3. Sr Magdalen Brimstone at <www.ssjl.org.au/news-events/anniversaries/sr-m-magdalen-brimstone/> accessed 6 March 2021.

Learning 'On the Road'—Early Mission Among Refugees

After entering the Novitiate I was given a mission as a postulant to work with refugees.[4] I was assigned to join our Sisters at Greta Camp where they ran a school for children of the families from Europe, displaced by war.[5] We began school with morning assembly, prayer and then choir together in the school-church.

Singing engaged the children. They could repeat words and learn English quickly. A Sister would accompany the singing on the piano. I taught in an army hut separate from the other buildings.[6] When the kookaburras laughed in the trees above, the children would run outside and laugh.[7] I laughed too, and we returned to class.

I learned a great deal at Greta. I learned that Sisters of St Joseph went to those in need, when they were needed. There was no time for long preparation. I learned to know St Joseph and his spirit by what we did. The migrant camp presented an urgent need and we responded. The children had no English and we had no German, Polish, Italian or any of their languages. There were no ESL lessons at that time.[8]

We had to use our initiative and energy and teach as best we could. It was challenging but we had our enthusiastic principal, Mother Barbara.[9] Her example imprinted in me and others the readiness to take on new tasks with unknown parameters. She was a Joseph person for us, taking us smiling into the task. That is what Fr Julian Woods and Mary MacKillop wanted us to be.

Later I was appointed to St Joseph's school at Charlestown, a Newcastle suburb with many post-war migrant families. Again, with no special help like ESL, we did our best and so did the children.

---

4. Postulancy was the first stage of formation on joining the Sisters. This usually lasted six months while the candidate considered if this was her calling and the Sisters in authority considered if the candidate was suitable. The candidate was then received into the community, as a novice and was given the habit.
5. Greta is 8 kilometres from Lochinvar. A short account is given at <www.ssjl.org.au/news-events/latest-news/memories-of-greta-migrant-camp/>. Accessed 6 March 2021.
6. Such 'huts' had been part of the former local military base.
7. When the school opened, the older children, remembering bomb attacks, would rush outside and run at the sound of a plane overhead. It was a challenge to help them adjust in their new world.
8. The acronym ESL stands for 'English as a Second Language'.
9. Mother Barbara O'Neill at <www.ssjl.org.au/news-events/anniversaries/sr-mary-barbara-oneill/>. Accessed 6 March 2021.

I remember grieving to find a lad weeping loudly as he didn't know anyone and didn't know English.[10] A demonstrative, distressed Polish lady called at the door one day, shocked that she found a loaf of bread in the gutter. She was horrified at the waste and spoke of, or rather cried over, the starvation they had known in the war.

I learned that being with refugees leaves one feeling unsure about how to move forward: they are on new ground and so are we. Trauma can be triggered by something we find simple and commonplace. I remember the time when a family in Newcastle spent the night huddled in terror, thinking that they were about to be attacked when it was simply crackers going off in the area.

In 1962–1963 I was appointed to Parkside in North Queensland.[11] This appointment gave a limited experience of what it is to be a refugee, of leaving all we knew for a foreign place. Our Sisters worked in our diocese or places adjoining our diocese. We did not usually travel interstate and had not travelled by air. We left Sydney on 1 May 1962, the feast of St Joseph the Worker. As the day neared, we prayed to St Joseph to help us since, as Matthew's Gospel tells us, he was also displaced. Saying farewell to everyone in Sydney was hard because going to Townsville was like going to another country.[12]

Though we were warmly welcomed and supported there, I learned more than ever how important welcome is to the stranger, that the stranger needs to feel welcomed and accepted. But as I settled in, I experienced the cultural richness of their communities through the many Italian and Spanish children whose parents were cane-farmers. Such diversity prepared me for my ministry to African refugees in the latter part of my life.

This part of my journey gave me the experience of knowing what it's like to be displaced and moving from place to place. Sometimes I had felt unwelcome and unaccepted, disappointed and vulnerable. I saw the trauma of those who had known danger and uncertainty and became more aware of Joseph the refugee, companioning Mary and Jesus.

---

10. I learned years later that he joined the police force.
11. This was an unusual mission for Lochinvar Sisters. Our superiors responded to a request by the Christ the Priest congregation founder, Fr Whiting, to staff a school. We also had our Sr Jude, whose health required her to be away from our local winter.
12. Requested to write my memories of Parkside, I included them in a reflection at. <St Joseph's Convent Parkside Ayr | Parkside Project (parkside-project.com)>. Accessed 5 March 2021.

Mission Among Refugees for Twenty Years

With St Vincent de Paul Society

A verse which we sang at school came into new focus in 1998, when I joined the St Vincent de Paul Society in Waratah, Newcastle:

> Dear St Joseph, pure and gentle
> Guardian of the Holy Child
> Treading with the Virgin Mother
> Egypt's deserts rough and wild.[13]

My time with Vinnies involved work with African refugees who were arriving in Newcastle at that time in large numbers through the International Organisational for Migration (IOM).[14]

In Australia, with migration immediately after World War II and at other times as in the 1970 when refugees fled violence in Vietnam, there was a political climate of magnanimity for those traumatised by war and violence. However, in and from the 1990s, politically-led sentiment has hardened, no matter how desperate the plight of the refugees.[15] The sense of welcome to the refugee changed with the closing of borders and setting up detention camps. Pope Francis says, 'Our lack of response to these tragedies involving our brothers and sisters points to the loss of that sense of responsibility for our fellow men and women upon which all civil society is founded.'[16]

In the midst of this, there have been breakthroughs allowing refugees to come here. When the United Nations saw Africa as priority among the world refugees at the turn of the century, Multicultural Resource Centres (MRCs) in New South Wales were contracted to settle refugees in rented housing suited to family need and to provide them with access to banking, Centrelink and Health Services.

Vinnies was subcontracted by the MRCs to furnish houses and supply essential household items. Vinnie members from different parishes in Newcastle volunteered to form a refugee working party to distribute goods locally. We set up houses, took people shopping

---

13. Traditional hymn sung by children in Josephite schools in former years.
14. In 2016 IOM was made a Related Organisation of the UN.
15. John Howard, the 2nd of November 2001 at <pmtranscripts.pmc.gov.au › release › transcript-12332>. Accessed 7 March 2021.
16. Pope Francis, *Laudato Si'* ('On Care for our Common Home'), (Strathfield, NSW: St Pauls Publications, 2015), 25.

for food and shared a meal. We answered questions as they arose and became a network of friendship and support. I sometimes invited refugees to join in my school visits. Great was the excitement when the children, teachers and refugees met. The refugees were from many countries—South Sudan, Liberia, Ethiopia, Sierra Leone, Mauritania and the Congo.

With the Josephite Refugee Support Network—JRSN

In 2005, Northern Settlement Services (NSS), the local MRC, lost the settlement contract in Newcastle. Our Vinnies group was not needed for contract supply, but our members wished to continue their support of the refugees as a more flexible organisation. They sought affiliation from Congregational Leaders at Lochinvar and became the Josephite Refugee Support Network (JRSN) under their auspices.

The JRSN was on call to support the refugees, addressing emergencies as they arose. It had credibility in the community and was able to draw media attention to the inadequacies of the new contractors and improve the situation.[17] It was a hands-on experience with many involved, including refugees, who collected and delivered resources that were made available from local institutions that were closing, such as the former Newcastle Hospital.[18]

The needs of the refugees and their eagerness to work with us spurred us on. Like the refugees we, the JRSN, had no resources to rent or buy a dwelling place, so we made do with what was available.

Our first base for meetings and storage was in the recently-closed Redemptorist Monastery, Mayfield. When the Monastery was sold, we looked for another venue. Hearing that the disused Hamilton Police Station was before the court as a land claim by the local Awabakal People, JRSN requested New South Wales Police that we use the venue till the claim was settled. The request was granted, with annual rent to be $1.00. We were ready to enter the premises in 2007 when Newcastle experienced an extraordinary storm.[19] Part of the police station roof was blown away leaving walls destroyed. New South Wales Police repaired the roof and the JRSN did what it could with the rest.

---

17. ABC News, the 14th of December 2011 at <www.abc.net.au/news/2011-12-14/greater-scrutiny-for-refugee-housing-contracts/3730574>. Accessed 7 March 2021.
18. John Hunter Hospital, built in an outer suburb, replaced Newcastle's former hospital.
19. The stranding of the Pasha Bulker carrier on Nobby's Beach, the 8th of June 2007 was international news.

To rephrase Noel Pearson's later words, those who have become bereft know the meaning of opportunity and make the best of it.[20] Something learned in our work with refugees was that one became part of the refugee experience of needing to keep moving.

Penola House, Hamilton

The JRSN named the Centre 'Penola House' in the spirit of Father Julian Tenison Woods and Mary MacKillop and their initiative at Penola, South Australia. We commenced services on St Joseph the Worker Day, 1 May 2008.

The venue was near Northern Settlement Services who supported us by giving sewing classes for the women, training in business for women and men, a Friday barbecue and op shop, play group for small children and educational services by Hunter New England Health. It was in the spirit of the practical, loving Joseph. Generous volunteers helped finance the operation.

There was a readiness in the community to welcome the refugees who were supported in the spirit of Joseph. Funds were needed to assist family reunions. Sometimes help came in unsought ways, as when a 'secret millionaire' made a large donation.[21] A popular fund-raiser was a mannequin parade with the beaming refugee women wearing the most lavish costumes we could find. The refugees worked happily with us and blossomed through the experience.

When we entered into this ministry, we tried always to approach refugees with an openness that invited friendship. We sought to companion the people with love and joy. In many conversations, refugees shared their stories of loss and separation from family members, and where we could, we helped fund the process to bring the lost member to Australia. In one situation, a mother whom we were helping found that her daughter was still alive in Africa. We

20. From Noel Pearson's eulogy for Gough Whitlam, 5 November 2014 at <www. smh.com.au/opinion/noel-pearsons-eulogy>. Accessed 6 March 2021. Pearson's words for his own indigenous people were 'Those who are born bereft truly know the power of opportunity'. Many refugees also are born bereft; many have been made bereft.

21. Donna Page, 'Secret millionaire comes to Hamilton', *Newcastle Herald*, the 21st of October 2009, at <www. newcastleherald.com.au/story/448187/secret>. Accessed 6 March 2021. A group of young local people organised 'The Pink Diamond Ball' with all funds for Penola Place.

were able to advise, and help with the costly processes of DNA and the application for the child to come to her mother.[22] Their reunion was unforgettable. Many times the generosity of donors enabled such possibilities.

Penola House Mayfield

In the year 2011 when the Aboriginal land claim on the former Police Station was successful, the Catholic Diocese of Maitland-Newcastle offered the unused presbytery at Mayfield West for our use. Once again, we moved. The story of St Joseph's transitory time in Egypt was the example before us.[23] The Diocese took over renovation, linked us into the Diocesan communication system and website, and provided us with a vehicle. Besides the educational and social activities which continued at Mayfield, efforts were made to get refugees into the workforce.

New initiatives were begun and some failed. The Burundi families who had spent many months near Cessnock then moved south out of our area to a location near Wagga. The owner of a new local enterprise let us know that he was building glass houses to grow vegetables. He needed trained workers. We spoke with administrators at TAFE and encouraged many otherwise unskilled local refugees to learn the intricacies of hydroponics. The majority of refugees in Newcastle attended the TAFE programs. There was great disappointment when the business failed after two or three years of the refugees' training. Many who now possessed skills left the area and went to other rural areas or to Sydney and Melbourne for work or the support of larger similar ethnic communities.

Time eventually necessitated change to our ministry with refugees. There were new refugees from Afghanistan and the refugee scene had

22. Gabriel Wingate Pearse, 'Survivor Lovette Walker begins high school', in *Newcastle Herald* (29 January 2014) at <https://www.newcastleherald.com.au/story/2054986/survivor-lovette-walker-begins-high-school/>. Accessed 7 March 2021.
23. While Christians in Egypt have endured great hostility especially in recent years, there has been a treasured tradition of the Holy Family's stay there: Egypt Today Staff, '*Egypt's tourism & antiquities min., various officials attends screening of "The Path of the Holy Family in Egypt" documentary*' (Egypt: Egyptian Ministry of Tourism, 8 November 2020) at <www.egypttoday.com/Article/4/94005/Egypt's-tourism-antiquities-min-various-officials-attends-screening-of-The>. Accessed 8 March 2021. The text was approved by the Coptic Pope Shenouda III.

changed.[24] In a restructure of diocesan ministries, Penola House at Mayfield underwent a name-change and became a diocesan ministry. Thus the formal connection between our Sisters and this ministry to refugees was concluded.[25]

Zara's House

Since then, a new initiative has been born. A group of refugees and many of our friends, inspired by Penola House and with support from Newcastle community, established Zara's House, Refugee Women and Children's Centre at Jesmond, Newcastle.[26] It is an ongoing response to refugee needs in a changing world. In Harmony Week 2021, the diocese has also launched a centre for refugees, the Refugee Hub.[27]

In repeated statements on refugees, Pope Francis gives strong encouragement to refugees and those working for and with them. He exhorts 'all countries to a generous openness'.[28] He says that 'love calls for growth in openness and the ability to accept others as part of a continuing adventure'.[29]

In conclusion, my reflection on St Joseph and refugees has led me to a deeper love of Joseph as a man with and for refugees. He has been a teacher for me along the entire journey. It is as though we have been partners in this enterprise. In our companioning of refugees, we have had the joy and honour of living out the Josephite maxim, 'Never see a need without doing something about it.'[30]

---

24. Catholic Diocese of Maitland and Newcastle, 'Penola House talks settlement with MPs' in News & Events at <www.mn.catholic.org.au/news-events/news/penola-house-talks-settlement-with-mps/>. Accessed 9 March 2021.
25. Helen Gregory, 'Refugee support service Penola House loses sisters' in *Newcastle Herald* at <Refugee support service Penola House loses sisters>. Accessed 9 March 2021.
26. Sr Diana Santleben OP, a volunteer of JRSN from its inception and a leading person at Penola House, continues to be so with Zara's House. whose programs are described at <www.zarashouse.org.au>. Accessed 7 March 2021. I, (Sr Betty), continue to offer a supportive role.
27. Sarah James in <https://mnnews.today/social-services/2021/53643-diversity-celebrated-at-church-street-hub-launch/?utm_medium=email&utm> accessed 13 April 2021.
28. Pope Francis, *Evangelii Gaudium, The Joy of the Gospel* (Strathfield, NSW: St Pauls Publications, 2013), 210.
29. Pope Francis, *Fratelli Tutti on Fraternity and Social Friendship* (Strathfield, NSW: St Pauls Publications, 2020), 95.
30. Paraphrase of Julian Woods, in Paragraph XIII, *Rules of the Institute of St Joseph for the Catholic Education of Poor Children*, December 1868, St Joseph's Archives, Lochinvar.

When story leaves a small bruise: Joseph as a Symbol and Challenge for Contemporary Women

Michele Fairbairn (Covenant Josephite)

> Writing, real writing, should leave a small sweet bruise somewhere on the writer . . . and on the reader.[1]

The Story . . .

I love storytelling. What story can do. How story can transform. How the stories we tell each other and ourselves can be an act of treason, an act of confirming, a call to revolution. What stories we choose to share, tell and keep alive have the power to forge and inhibit connections, unite or destroy. The power to confine, to liberate, to find truth or perpetuate lies. Story is a way to reclaim or repair. Story as medicine or poison—you choose. What stories we tell, reveals who we are. As Dr Clarissa Pinkola Estés writes, 'Storytelling is bringing up, hauling up; it is not an idle practice . . . and whatever is left behind is our bounty to work with, to use towards soul-making.'[2]

There are numerous examples of how story can be therapy. How a person telling and retelling their story over again is a kind of medicine, a balm, an act of liberating that which is wounded, by breathing life into that which is fractured.

For example, Augusto Boal, Brazilian dramatist and founder of The Theatre of the Oppressed, understood the power of story as that which can imprison or liberate. He recognised that making space for people to tell their story, to become involved in each other's stories in dynamic ways as protagonist rather than spectator was an act of

1. Clarissa Pinkola Estés, source unknown.
2. Clarissa Pinkola Estés, *Women Who Run with the Wolves: Myths and Stories of the Wild Woman Archetype* (New York: Ballantine Books, 1992), 463.

liberation and revolution for storyteller, actors and spectator alike. By encouraging the spectator, the one-who-story-has-happened-to, to 'both see and to see himself'[3] allows for stories shaped by the individual and collective past to be liberated by the choices and alternatives available in the present. It allows those who are calcified by a story they have lived, or a story they have been told, to deep dive into possibilities, meaning, and agency.

And it is story that leads me to this place. The story of a figure who would be familiar to most folks, Christian or otherwise: Saint Joseph. Husband of Mary, Earthly father of Jesus, Protector of both, Carpenter, Worker.

I began the net-casting for this essay by researching. To attempt to separate the facts from fiction, the actual from the symbolic. After five years of studying psychology, with a completed thesis recently under my belt, it felt like the safe and useful way forward. Those who are more theologically inclined and knowledgeable than I may be smiling sympathetically at my aforementioned lofty quest. Not surprisingly, I fell down more than a few rabbit holes. Months of rabbit holes, it turns out. Theology can give psychology a good run for its money when it comes to theories. And there is a multitude of theories about Saint Joseph. Some would sit comfortably with the line of women in my family stretching back four generations who had a beautiful and unquestioning devotion to Saint Joseph. And some would curl the hair on their heads. I am, however, a fan of critical thinking, so I went excavating.

In a nutshell, here are some of the theories I encountered on my research journey:

- 'Saint Joseph was the silent type. He did not leave us a word.' Some would consider that there is an invitation to mine this silence for a loaded message that needs to be decoded.[4]
- 'Saint Joseph was more artisan than rabbi', in that the magic he wove was through hands and actions rather than words.[5]
- Andries Van Aarde in another take, posits that referring to Joseph as the father of Jesus is problematic given that, 'It is clear that

3. Augusto Boal, *The Rainbow of Desire* (London: Routledge, 1995), 26.
4. Leonardo Boff, *Saint Joseph: The Father of Jesus in a Fatherless Society* (Eugene, OR: Cascade Books, 2009), 7.
5. Boff, *Saint Joseph: The Father of Jesus*, 7.

regarding the role which Joseph fulfills in the New Testament that there was an enormous distance between the historical Jesus tradition and the traditions in the gospels and post-New Testament documents.'[6]

Further, Van Aarde poses a possible explanation for the cancelling out of the role of the earthly father—unlikely in Mediterranean culture where a male without connection to his father is a person without an identity—as lining up with the historical Jesus material, whereby the father had abandoned the family resulting in the possibility that 'no known father played a role in the life of the historical Jesus'. This theory and others like it may be attributed to the circumstances surrounding the conception of Jesus, of which historically, nothing is known. Van Aarde concludes that the figure of Joseph may have been a symbolic adversary of Judah, and an ethical paradigm.

- Maren Niehoff writes of Joseph representing a certain *Idealtyp* for those who depicted him.[7] The Gospel of Mark (the first Gospel written) does not mention Joseph at all, potentially referring to Jesus as being illegitimate.[8]
- Biblical scholar, Jane Schaberg, in her article 'Feminist Interpretations of the Infancy Narrative of Matthew', challenges the powerful images that feed into social control of women's lives and bodies.[9] She explores the idea that the birth of Jesus (and the person of Mary) was legitimatised through the righting of wrongs, and the restoration of social order by the figure of Joseph. His patronage provided mother and child with an identity, drawing Mary under patriarchal protection, while accepting responsibility for a woman who has damaged the social order.
- Michael Fox notes that Joseph is recognised as a 'god-favored man', in that Joseph is noted as unwittingly serving to further

6. Andries van Aarde, 'Jesus' father: The quest for the historical Joseph', in *HTS Teologiese Studies/Theological Studies*, 54/1&2 (1998): 324.
7. Maren Niehoff, *The Figure of Joseph in Post-Biblical Jewish literature* (Netherlands: Brill, 1992).
8. John Shelby Spong, *Born of a Woman: A Bishop Rethinks the Virgin Birth and the Treatment of Women by a Male-Dominated Church* (San Francisco: Harper, 1992), 149.
9. Jane Schaberg, 'Feminist Interpretations of the Infancy Narrative of Matthew', in *Journal of Feminist Studies in Religion*, 13/1 (1997): 35–62.

> the goals of God and the Holy Spirit.[10] Fox also notes that, while there is wisdom in the story of the figure of Joseph, this wisdom is not a practical and ethical wisdom consistent with Wisdom literature in that it does not model how to foresee and surmount difficulties, achieve success, and find relationship with God in times when God may not feel accessible. Rather, it is an inspired and pietistic wisdom.

In archaeological terms, if we were to compare the offerings from this essay's research journey to a dig, this brief cataloguing of a sprinkling of theories is stage one of field investigation. We haven't moved from shovels to trowels yet, much less gotten through the process of marking with strings and stakes. In working out what lies beneath the surface of the Joseph story, peeling back and excavation of the layers hasn't remotely begun in earnest. No doubt, that would be a whole other veritable can of worms.

One thing that it seems that writers and scholars can agree upon, is that the story of Joseph is one that is convoluted, open-ended, and open to interpretation. They speak to everything from a legendary figure to a character constructed of multifarious Old Testament figures and stories to establish a particular narrative for the conception and birth of Jesus as a defence against the gossip and scandal surrounding his creation story.[11] Additionally, a man who was not merely a zealous provider and protector but also engaged in his family's mission, to a figure whose story has yielded diametrically opposed details leading biblical scholars to an overwhelming consensus that the story is unlikely to be 'historically accurate' according to present-day definition of the term.. Further, other scholars theorise that the figure of Joseph is as an ethical symbol employed to elevate Jesus from human to divine.

After diving in to a story that has so many intricate twists, turns, and motivations–sometimes with the purpose of achieving different ends–I found myself (and not for the first time(!)) swayed in the direction of Bishop John Shelby Spong's reflections around liberating ourselves from biblical literalism.[12] While this may be a foundation-

10. Michael V Fox, 'Wisdom in the Joseph Story', in *Vetus Testamentum*, 51/1 (2001): 26–41.
11. Spong, *Born of a Woman*, 59.
12. Spong, *Born of a Woman*, 1–15.

rocking challenge for some folks, it is worth spending a few moments at least in exploring the pros for doing so. Spong invites us into a space of contemplating what was written, why it was written, and what that means for us as readers/custodians of these stories. Perhaps more importantly, what it means for us to subscribe to stories without asking questions about why they were told and how/why we seek to keep these stories alive. It doesn't take much diving to appreciate Spongs' invitation to 'escape the stereotypes of the past that define gender, sexual orientation, and sexual morality in a way that has always violated women and now is seen increasingly to violate everyone'[13] and his challenge for the church to, 'surrender its defining prejudices of a personalistic, masculine, and patriarchal worldview'.[14] Again, not comfortable stuff to ponder but well worth the effort; especially after researching and seeking to reclaim the story of Joseph through a female lens. And, perhaps even more so, when contemplating the nativity narrative which defines many people's relationship with the figure of Joseph.

The Challenge . . .

The following was attributed to Aristotle, 'To avoid criticism, say nothing, do nothing, be nothing,' which is all well and good unless you recognise the price of avoiding criticism. Desmond Tutu did:

> If you are neutral in situations of injustice, you have chosen the side of the oppressor. If an elephant has its foot on the tail of a mouse and you say that you are neutral, the mouse will not appreciate your neutrality.[15]

So, let's begin this by having a little conversation about the elephant in the room—the elephant with its foot on the tail of this particular mouse.

When I shared with someone that I was writing this essay, I told them that it was proving trickier than I thought it would be. That, upon diving deeper, there were some places of genuine discomfort that

---

13. Spong, *Born of a Woman,* 12.
14. Spong, *Born of a Woman,* 13.
15. *Oxford Essential Quotations,* edited by Susan Radcliffe (Oxford: Oxford University Press, 2017).

spoke more to grappling with power, politics, toxic culture, and the patriarchal lens than aligning oneself in a relationship with divinity and the story of a figure that was empowering to women. In response, this friend wrote to me, 'Why can't St Joseph just have been a loving nice man and *if* he was not, you're not going to change anything now.' And I get it. I really do. I get why my friend wrote this. I get what they were trying to protect—in themselves and in their spiritual journey. It's pretty foundational stuff, that when rocked, threatens to fall out of the boat and drift without anchor into unsettling seas. I also get why this is *exactly* the reason that we need to know more. Why we need to challenge what has been and what is. It is an act of revolution—akin to the bricks and mortar the Christian faith and Josephite community is built upon—to do what we can, to ask what questions we can, to challenge what we can, in order to evolve and distill what we can of the heart of the stories we have been told.

Stripped back to the barest bones, we are custodians of stories that, at their heart, are about revolutionary acts. About figures subverting a dominant culture that no longer serves. And yet somehow, for the most part, we find ourselves choosing our own comfort over inconvenience, conformity over rocking the boat, and being passive receptacles of tradition rather than informed, critical thinking activists continuing the work of the revolutionaries who preceded us–historical or symbolic. Spong writes:

> The only way to keep symbols alive forever is to crack them open periodically so that they can be filled with new meanings. No symbol can ever remain as a timeless truth, inerrant or infallible.[16]

Something that has confused me—in myself and others—is the seeming disconnect that occurs between recognising contemporary issues around inequality, violence against women and the dominant patriarchal lens, and how telling and re-telling stories that perpetuate these issues happens with relative ease and regularity. When we grip tightly to a story—without diving deep and breathing new life into the narrative we are at risk of loosening our grip on how the stories we tell grow root systems and develop an ecosystem of their own. Story can perpetuate harmful stereotypes, outdated gender norms

16. Spong, *Born of a Woman*, 189.

and unhealthy (not to mention, unattainable) ideals around who and how women are, and how women are placed in relation to men. One cannot help but notice that thousands of years along the track, current affairs and social media newsfeeds are full of stories about the inequality of women in the workplace, the church, and the world. Marginalisation, 'othering', and violence towards individuals and groups by virtue of their gender, race, sexuality, and beliefs.

It seems counterintuitive to reflect on what the figure of Saint Joseph holds for women without reflecting on what it means to be a woman. Statistics on Personal Safety in Australia show that one in six women experienced partner violence. One in two women experienced sexual harassment, and one in six women experienced sexual abuse before the age of fifteen, with the incidence of assault more often than not being perpetrated by a partner or someone known to the woman.[17] These acts of violence were also most likely to occur in her home. Further, recent gender pay gap statistics show that women are earning thirteen to nineteen per cent less average weekly earnings across all occupations and industries than men.[18] Spong writes that, 'The low value of a woman was everywhere assigned in the Bible',[19] which begs the question, how far have we come? And, in celebrating the year of Saint Joseph, when we reflect upon how the story of Joseph inspires and shapes how we are in the world, what are the stories that we are upholding, sharing, and living that continue to perpetuate the 'low value' women have been assigned?

When the symbolism used in the bible is taken literally, and perhaps none more so than the implications of the nativity narrative for women, we are complicit in upholding patriarchal ideals—ideals nearly 2000 years old and culturally incongruent from our ways of being in the world and society. We are actively participating in undermining important work around reclaiming agency and equality for women–in society and in the church. While the status of contemporary women still leaves a lot to be desired, there is an

17. Australian Bureau of Statistics, 'Personal Safety, Australia' at <https://www.abs.gov.au/statistics/people/crime-and-justice/personal-safety-australia/latest-release>. Accessed 1 April 2021.
18. Australian Bureau of Statistics, 'Average Weekly Earnings, Australia' at <https://www.abs.gov.au/statistics/labour/earnings-and-work-hours/average-weekly-earnings-australia/nov-2020>. Accessed 1 April 2021.
19. Spong, *Born of a Woman*, 167.

important invitation being extended around how and where we place Joseph in the nativity narrative, and in relation to Mary. Sometimes the revolutionary way is the essential way when we understand the shape of what church is–a community built upon the visionary, the revolutionary, and the embodiment of divinity made human.

Opening up conversations and moving into a more activist-oriented space around this, advances us beyond the passive and the stagnant into a more life-giving, inclusive story.

The gift of spirituality, mythology, and faith is that it creates a space for story to guide–the stories of those who went before us. Stories that we (like with any good story passed down) are able to mold and shape into something that makes more sense of the time and place we are living in–in such a way that the heart of the story, the crux of its message, continues to beat through generations to come in ways that feel inclusive and dynamic. Dr Clarissa Pinkola Estés writes of encouraging people to, '. . . do their own mining of story, for the scraped knuckles, the sleeping on cold ground, the groping in the dark and the adventures on the way are worth everything.' She adds, 'There must be a little spilled blood on every story if it is to carry medicine.'[20]

What blood needs to be spilled on the story of Joseph for it to resonate in a way that makes more sense for women, and in a way that positions women beyond the shamed/disenfranchised figure who requires protection under a patriarchal-approved wing in order to be legitimised?

The Invitation . . .

Whether one takes the nativity narrative literarily or not, at the very least, Joseph is depicted as acknowledging Jesus as his own and bestowing upon him his heritage as a way of legitimising his place in a family, and ultimately, society. The nativity narrative is an invitation to challenge exclusionary norms that lead to the othering of women who are considered less than because they may be single mothers, women who have experienced violence and rape leading to childbirth, same sex parents, refugees, etc. There is also the invitation

20. Clarissa Pinkola Estés, *Women Who Run with the Wolves: Myths and Stories of the Wild Woman Archetype* (New York: Ballantine Books, 1992), 463.

to remedy this othering by making and holding space for those who are disenfranchised, without seeking to transform the shape of that-which-is-disenfranchised into something that conforms better to the status quo, to the norm, to the overarching patriarchal paradigm. A paradigm that deems women, unless without spot and sin, as requiring the redemptive taking in and protection of a male figure–as something, or someone, whom divinity cannot otherwise find a home and expression in. We are invited to embody the symbol and archetype of Joseph in healthier, more inclusive ways that reclaim and assert the agency, autonomy, and divinity of those who are 'othered'. To dive deeper into the stories we have been told, and the stories we tell. Because story is powerful.

For example, note the ramifications of the shift from the midrash tradition, in relation to Matthew's gospel, to a more literal interpretation of the nativity narrative whereby the word 'virgin' was used to form a foundation for the narrative of Jesus' conception and birth. This was about setting the scene for what was to come in the life of Jesus, and to legitimise where the divine intersected with the human. It was not about the literal. While birth tradition narratives are powerful ways of providing a foundational story for those, who in adulthood, go on to achieve great things, there are also significant ramifications for women's autonomy, status and agency if taken literally. The defending of Mary's character with miraculous and elaborate birth traditions–and taking this literally–also has ramifications and messages for vulnerable/'othered' girls and women around where their value lies and how their value is reliant upon certain constellations coming into alignment in their lives. The stories we value, the stories we tell, say everything to people about how we witness divinity, and the divinity embodied in them. To land on the divine and human embodied in the person of Jesus–and in ourselves–there is the necessity to pause and reflect on what we flow with, as well as what (and who), this disqualifies. We are not evolving as an individual, a community, or a church when we have a tendency towards confirmation bias.

During his inauguration speech, Pope Francis spoke of Joseph as protector. And of the role of protector as a vocation intricately woven into the fabric of what it is to not only a Christian but also a human. He went on to say, 'It means protecting all creation, the beauty of the created world . . . it means respecting each of God's creatures and respecting the environment in which we live.'[21] Pope Francis beautifully frames an invitation, and a challenge, to dive deeper into the Joseph story and symbolism. To liberate it into new ways of being in a society and planet that aches for wounds to be acknowledged, held space for, and healed. To be the gatekeepers of where the human and divine intersect; where time and eternity meet, and ensure the gate is always open.

Josephite spirituality is the embodiment of the symbol and story of Joseph. It is a spirituality that can hold space for the uncomfortable challenges posed in this essay, and beyond. Those who align with the charism of the Josephites have the sacred task of rejecting the elements of the narrative that don't serve us as women, as humans, and as custodians of a living earth and the sentient beings sharing this home with us. We are invited to question and challenge that which does not make sense in contemporary society: outdated notions of gender, sexuality, belongingness–a women's place, shame and power. We must liberate these parts of the story that were written for times and a culture that is not ours, and weave new stories about holding space for those at risk, those who are disenfranchised and 'othered'—even in their own church–without smoothing over the so-called unacceptable bits. This is a time to hold space, warts and all.

The (New) Beginning . . .

Perhaps the ultimate challenge is to not cloak the story of Joseph in piety, meekness, and mild-manneredness. Instead there is a challenge around attributing these qualities to the realm and role of the feminine and females, and their compliance to the cultural dominance of the patriarchy. Perhaps the figure of Saint Joseph is best 'freed from the straightjacket of literalism'[22] and distilled through our imagination into a more contemporary and culturally appropriate symbol—an invitation to the ongoing revolutionary act of love, equality, accessibility, place-making, and advocating for those who are marginalised. When all is said and done, as Marianne Williamson,

21. Pope Francis, 'Homily of Pope Francis' at <http://www.vatican.va/content/francesco/en/homilies/2013/documents/papa-francesco_20130319_omelia-inizio-pontificato.html>. Accessed 5 April 2021.
22. Spong, *Born of a Woman*, 192.

author and activist, observed, 'The revolution that will save the world is ultimately a personal one.'[23] We are all co-creators in story. As seeds who are planted by those who have told stories before us, not only are we responsible for keeping these stories alive, but understanding what it is that we are breathing life into every time we tell the story. We are invited to know what it is that we are passing on to others, and how these stories–and ours interwoven with them–create the world and reality that we live in.

> It's only a story, you say. So it is, and the rest of life with it–creation story, love story, horror, crime, the strange story of you and I. The alphabet of my DNA shapes certain words, but the story is not told. I have to tell it myself. What is it that I have to tell myself again and again? That there is always a new beginning, a different end. I can change the story. I am the story. Begin.[24]

23. Marianne Williamson, *Quotes*, at <https://www.brainyquote.com/quotes/marianne_williamson_401955#:~:text=Marianne%20Williamson%20Quotes&text=As%20we%20go%2C%20so%20goes.is%20ultimately%20a%20personal%20one.> Accessed 5 April 2021.
24. Jeanette Winterson, *The Powerbook* (New York: Vintage Publishing, 2001), 4–5.

Part 3

Joseph's Cultural Outreach

St Joseph, a Great Model for All—An Asian View

Rose Vu rsj

The year 2021 is a time of jubilee, the 'Year of St Joseph', announced by Pope Francis to commemorate 150 years since the proclamation of St Joseph as patron of the universal Church by Blessed Pius IX on the 8th of December 1870.[1] The recognition of St Joseph's relationship to the Church has been renewed on many occasions since then. For example, on the 15th of August 1889, Pope Leo XIII wrote an encyclical where he asserted: 'It is, then, natural and worthy that as the Blessed Joseph ministered to all the needs of the family at Nazareth and girt it about with his protection, he should now cover with the cloak of his heavenly patronage and defend the Church of Jesus Christ'.[2] Pope John XXIII inserted the name of St Joseph into the first Eucharistic prayer in 1962, and later Pope Benedict XVI and Pope Francis had his name included in the other Eucharist prayers.[3]

Joseph, Patron of Vietnam

1. Pope Francis, Apostolic Letter *Patris Corde*, 8 December 2020 at <www.vatican.va›francesco›apost_letters›documents>. Accessed 5 January 2021.
2. Pope Leo XIII, *Quamquam Pluries*, 15 August 1889 at <www.vatican.va›leo-xiii›encyclicals›documents>. Accessed 5 January 2021.
3. *Archbishop Secretary* Arthur Roche, *Paternas Vices at* <http://osjusa.org/st-josseph/magisterium/paternas-vices/>. Accessed 5 January 2021.

While the jubilee celebration is important for the whole Church, it holds particular significance for the Church in Asian countries. St Joseph is recognised as the patron of the whole of Asia, along with Jesus' mother Mary, and the missionary St Francis Xavier. For the individual countries of Asia, Joseph is the first-named patron of Vietnam and Cambodia, and he is listed among the patrons of China, Japan and Indonesia. Since I was born in Vietnam, I will concentrate my observations of St Joseph in that country.

With mention of St Joseph, my mind immediately reverts to a hymn I memorised a long time ago as a teenager, even though I did not know its significance. 'Joseph of the small village Nazareth' by Pham Dinh Nhu and Nguyen Khac Tuan, is a well-known traditional hymn for most Vietnamese Catholics, old and young.[4] The hymn is usually sung on the feast of St Joseph and on occasions of reflection and prayer to honour St Joseph, particularly during March, the month of St Joseph. The melody of the hymn is relatively easy for the whole community to sing. The lyrics are full of inspiration and praise of St Joseph as the special exemplar of a humble, hardworking, protecting, loving, and caring person whom all Christians should imitate.

It is no wonder many Vietnamese associations of Catholic men, schools, youth, and seniors are named 'St Joseph' and acknowledge him as their important patron. Moreover, 'Joseph' as the Baptismal name for boys is as common as 'Smith' is for a surname in England.

Joseph—The Significant Patron Saint of the Vietnamese Catholic Church.

When he launched the Apostolic Exhortation *Redemptoris Custos* ('Guardian of the *Redeemer*'), Pope John Paul II re-asserted St Joseph as a protector of the universal Church:

Inspired by the Gospel, the Fathers of the Church from the earliest centuries stressed that just as St Joseph took loving care of Mary and gladly dedicated himself to Jesus Christ's upbringing, he likewise watches over and protects Christ's Mystical Body, that is, the Church, of which the Virgin Mary is the exemplar and model.[5]

4. Giuse Xóm Nhỏ - Lm Phạm Đình Nhu và Nguyễn Khắc Tuấn <http://thanhcavietnam.net>. Accessed, 9 January 2021.
5. Pope John Paul II, *Redemptoris Custos*, 15 August 1989 at <www.vatican.va›apost_exhortations›documents›hf>. Accessed 10 January 2021.

This renewal of the 1870 dedication would have reminded people in Vietnam of their own relationship with St Joseph. On the 14th of February 1670, Bishop Lambert had called the First Constitutional Council of Bac Ha (Cochin-China) at the Palace of the Constitution (Pho Don) in Son Nam town.[6] Attending the Council were Father Deydier, two French supremacies De Bourges and Bouchard, and nine Vietnamese priests, Fr Benedictine Hien, Fr John Hue, and seven newly-ordained priests. The Council officially accepted St Joseph as the Patron of the Catholic Church in Vietnam. The 'Constitutional Public Service' was approved by Pope Clement X in the *Apostolatus Officium* on the 23rd of December 1673.[7]

Thanks to God's consistent grace and the protective patronage of St Joseph, the history of the church in Vietnam shows people's faith to have been resilient and strong. During the seventeenth to the nineteenth centuries when the practice of Christianity was forbidden and persecuted under the monarchic feudal stratocracy in Vietnam, believers were sustained by St Joseph's intercession. One hundred and seventy Vietnamese Martyrs became powerful witnesses to Christian faith at that time.

More recently, under Communist rule since 1975, the Vietnamese Catholic Church finds itself once again subject to a hostile regime. Yet the community remains steadfast in the faith. At their Annual Meeting in Hanoi from 6–11 October 1997, the Vietnamese Bishops' Conference unanimously re-affirmed St Joseph as the Patron of the Vietnamese Catholic Church and communicated this fact in their General Letter to Vietnamese Catholics. It should be noted that the Vietnamese Martyrs had also been chosen as patrons of the Vietnamese Catholic Church in 1990. Therefore, St Joseph is the first-named and the Vietnamese martyrs the second as patrons of the Vietnamese Catholic Church.[8] The Bishops especially urged us to pray with St Joseph for our Church in Vietnam and encouraged fathers in each family to imitate St Joseph in the care and protection

6. Pierre Lambert de la Motte at <https://en.wikipedia.org/wiki/Pierre_Lambert_de_la_Motte>. Accessed 10 January 2021. In fact, the Council met under a merchant ship parked on the Song River (Red River) next to the Palace.
7. Về Trang MụcLục at <http://www.simonhoadalat.com/DIAPHAN/MUCVU/2004/mv0204/04CongDongDinhHien.htm>. Accessed 10 January 2021.
8. *LM GiusePhạm Đình Ái, SSS* at <https://gxanphu.net/category/tu-lieu/thanh-giuse/>. Accessed 12 January 2021.

of their spouse and children. They reminded us that family has an important role in the life of the Church and society.[9]

Joseph's Identity

The four gospels do not record a single word of St Joseph. He is portrayed as a quiet, humble, and private man who was of poorer status as a 'carpenter' living in the small, insignificant village of Nazareth. If the evangelists have people mention him, it is only to belittle, dishonour, or lower the identity of Jesus: 'Is not this the carpenter's son? Is not his mother called Mary? . . . . And they took offence at him' (Matt 13:55, 57a; Jn 6:42). We would expect that Joseph, living in silence, would fade into oblivion.

Nevertheless, in God's plan of salvation, the greatness of Joseph is remarkable. Joseph was on a level with Mary, as both appeared together on the first page of the unfolding mystery of God, concealed for long ages and now made manifest (Matt 1:16, 18; Rm 16:25). Joseph was a son of Jacob in the line of King David, the beloved and trustful husband of Mary (Lk. 1:27), the kind-hearted and loving (foster) father of Jesus (Matt 1:1–16; Lk 2:48; Jn 1:45). He was a 'righteous man' (Matt 1:19) who played 'an incomparable role in the history of salvation'.[10]

This combination of lowliness and nobility appeals to all classes in Vietnamese society and so makes it possible for everyone to identify with Joseph.

Joseph: Walking in the Mysterious/Darkest Phenomena of Life with Genuine Love and Strong Faith

Throughout his whole life, Joseph demonstrated strong faith in dealing with many difficult and challenging situations. At the beginning of his married life, before their official marriage celebration allowing Mary and Joseph to live together as husband and wife, he was faced

9. Pope John Paul II, Compendium of the Social Doctrine of the Church at <https://www.vatican.va/roman_curia/pontifical_councils/justpeace/documents/rc_pc_justpeace_doc_20060526_compendio-dott-sos_en.html#Importance%20of%20the%20family%20for%20society>. Accessed 15 March 2021.

10. Pope Francis, *Patris Corde*, Introduction.

with a dilemma involving his beloved fiancée. He found out she was pregnant. Although he did not understand what had happened to her, it must have been his genuine love and trust of Mary that motivated him to make a 'decision to protect Mary's good name, her dignity and her life'.[11] From the deepest corner of his heart, Joseph's honest love of Mary prevailed. He courageously and silently chose a humble and generous solution that would provide no harm for his fiancée. A 'righteous man and unwilling to expose her to public disgrace, [he] planned to dismiss her quietly' (Matt 1:19), so avoiding her sentence of being stoned to death (Lev 20:10; Deut 22:22–24; Jn 8:3–4).

Joseph's inner righteousness coincides with authentic love that is always directed to others. He did not turn back into himself to dwell on feeling insulted and deceived, but was willing to self-sacrifice for the happiness of the person he really loved.

This line of Joseph's story relates very well with traditional Vietnamese customs. A Western style of dating and romance is considered inappropriate for young men and young women who are unmarried. Despite the fact that Vietnamese youth nowadays have greater freedom to choose a partner, to engage with each other and arrange their marriage, some elements of the culture remain intact. An example is that the chastity of young women is highly valued; therefore, women are often under stricter scrutiny. Pregnancy outside of marriage is uncommon, and it is seen as a serious disgrace to the family's reputation. Because Vietnamese people are very concerned about their dignity and how they are to be perceived by family, friends and colleagues, they avoid doing anything that would embarrass and diminish a person in public. Similarly, Joseph belonged to a society dominated by notions of honour and shame:

> As part of a wider family, [Joseph's] concern would have been to conform to the standards of honour which governed the roles each person was to fulfil. To break these would bring shame on the group.[12]

---

11. Pope Francis, Homily, 8 September 2017, Colombia at <http://www.vatican.va/content/francesco/en/homilies/2017/documents/papa-francesco_20170908_omelia-viaggioapostolico-colombiavillavicencio.html>. Accessed 20 January 2021.
12. Mary Cresp, *In the Spirit of Joseph* (Sydney: Sisters of St Joseph of the Sacred Heart, 2005), 92.

For all cultures, Joseph's example about how to love are obvious. For those whose traditions are sensitive to shame and saving face, such as is common in Vietnam, Joseph is therefore a powerful model.

Walking alongside the mysteries of God's plan is like walking in a night shrouded in darkness. Joseph did not understand what was happening in his family life, but he voluntarily accepted all with confidence, courage and serenity, choosing to walk forwards in love and hope and to live so that God's will was fulfilled (Rom 1:5; 16:26 and 2 Cor 10:5–6).

Flight into Egypt, Rembrandt Wikepedia.

Among the paintings of St Joseph that speak strongly to me is my favourite, the 'Flight into Egypt' by Rembrandt van Rijn (a draughtsman, painter, and printmaker of the Dutch Golden Age).[13] The painting is a reflection on the narrative of Mary and Joseph awakened at night to take a sudden, urgent journey to Egypt to flee from Herod's wrath (Matt 2:13–23). They were travelling on dangerous roads and with sorrowful hearts.

The contrast of dark and light used in the painting indicates the nightmare that Joseph and Mary experienced. The picture is not only beautiful in its inspirational drawing, but also evokes many feelings: the sky is so dark, reaching to the end of the horizon. Mary, sitting on the back of the donkey, holds her baby Jesus. Joseph leads the way. Together, they and the donkey seemed to merge into the dark, silent night. Joseph walks in the silence of his beloved Mary and Jesus. God is revealed in the human—the mystery of God's silence.

And . . . Joseph walks in his own silence.

The silence is most frightening, particularly when faced with danger, with doubt, with life's serious problems. It is a confusing silence that can undermine the strongest beliefs. Yet Joseph is simply 'a figure of a respectful and sensitive man . . . In his hesitation about how best to act, God helped him by enlightening his judgment.'[14]

13. Rembrandt, information and image at <https://en.wikipedia.org/wiki/Rembrandt>. Accessed 20 January 2021.

14. Pope Francis, Homily, the 8th of September 2017.

The painting powerfully presents an example for refugees, including many Vietnamese families, who have experienced the hardship of leaving their country to search for a better place to live, forced to do so for reasons of war, harsh living environments, poverty and persecution. They can identify with Joseph who did not hear God speaking directly, but merely through the language of dreams echoing in the middle of the night. Yet God's message, even if it is as light as a gentle breeze, can make the strings of music vibrate. Joseph read this word of God and quickly accomplished it without hesitation. The sense of urgency and quick action is what many refugees remember. The feeling is urgency—they cannot let this dreadful threat happen. Although the night is so dark, his legs weary and his heart troubled, Joseph still leads the way. His tender love, courage, and strong faith provide the light to guide his footsteps in bringing his family to a peaceful place in Egypt.

Joseph: An Affectionate Father Who Nurtured Jesus in Joy

Joseph was chosen as the father of the Saviour—a father 'not of blood or of the will of the flesh or of the will of man, but of God' (Jn 1:13). He is father by the power of the Holy Spirit—the dispenser of ministries and charisms (1 Cor 12:11). According to the customs and traditions in Jewish society at the time of Jesus, a father had the duty to raise his children in the Law and in a trade (Deut 6:7). A Jewish boy would be apprenticed or trained by his father in the father's trade, whether it was farming, carpentry or fishing. The aim was to enable the boy to be skilled enough to be independent at an early age. The father would also teach his boy practical aspects of everyday living and the basic truths of the Law of God (Deut 6:7–9; Lk 2:41–52). The son would have to understand and relate to God's word before being obligated to observe the commandments of the Torah as an adult in the community.

Therefore, it was the responsibility of Joseph to teach his son Jesus all these things. The requirements would sound very familiar especially to Vietnamese rural communities. There, passing on trade and religious traditions to the children is an expectation for both parents, with fathers teaching the boys and mothers the girls. We see Joseph, with a heart full of love, completely committed to nourishing and educating Jesus to observe the Jewish Law, customs, and traditions. The account of 'the boy Jesus in the temple' from Luke's Gospel illustrates a prime example of how Jesus was raised by his parents in these aspects of their culture (Lk 2:41–52):

> They found him in the temple, sitting among the teachers, listening to them and asking them questions. And all who heard him were amazed at his understanding and his answers (Lk 2:46–47).

We can presume from this description that Joseph fulfilled his sacred and noble task of fatherhood excellently, bringing Jesus to maturity as he 'increased in wisdom and in years, and in divine and human favour' (Lk 2:52).

According to the teaching of Vatican II, parents are the first educators of their children, constantly accompanying them on their human and faith journey: 'Since parents have given children their life, they are bound by the most serious obligation to educate their offspring and therefore must be recognised as the primary and principal educators.'[15] In this context, it is encouraging that Christian parents in the modern world can look up to Joseph's example in their role as parents, especially in a secular, challenging society. For Vietnamese Catholics in particular, who live in a country governed by philosophies that can be hostile to religion, the picture of Joseph teaching Jesus can bring comfort and strength.

In the patriarchal world of his time, Joseph was 'head' of the family. Yet when we consider what he passed on to Jesus, we realise Joseph must have been a gentle, truthful, respectful and sensitive father and husband. He must have taken on his responsibilities with great courage, loving care and understanding. For centuries in Vietnam, traditional families emphasised the role of the father or the eldest son as the family's financial provider, although, in a modern family this is less experienced by the younger generations. Since the highest status belongs to the 'head', he may be the final decision maker, although he may consult with his wife and children. Many fathers have misused or abused this privilege. Joseph offers a practical example for those who carry out their fatherly duties to their children in a loving

15. *Gravissimum Educationis* ('Declaration on Christian Education'), Vatican II, 1965, 3 at < http://www. vatican.va/archive/hist_councils/ii_vatican_council/ documents/vat-ii_decl_19651028_gravissimum- educationis _en.html >. Accessed 1 March 2021.

and sympathetic way rather than dominating or controlling them. Furthermore, Joseph provides a significant model for those who are the leaders of countries such as Vietnam, where children, women and the most vulnerable have often been suppressed and treated unfairly.

Joseph: A Role Model for the Worker

From the Gospels we learn that Joseph was a manual worker—a carpenter or builder (Matt 13:55), which was not an honourable occupation, even though respected, in the Jewish society of the time. We can surmise that Joseph worked diligently, discreetly, and honestly. He 'earned an honest living to provide for his family'[16] and taught Jesus the value of labour and thus the dignity of human work. Joseph's sweat, fatigue, sacrifice, and generosity brought joy and happiness to his family and made labour meaningful. In his parables and teaching, Jesus speaks, for example, of the hiring of labourers, of farmers sowing and harvesting crops, of shepherds tending their flocks, all being activities that he would have observed and taken part in with Joseph in Nazareth. He also refers to cooking, cleaning house, interacting with family and community members that required love and patience which were practised by Joseph, and especially Mary as she carried out her humble household chores. Joseph and Mary expressed the dignity of work as they raised Jesus to maturity.

When mentioning labour, it is essential that we look at the creation story in the book of Genesis. After creating the universe, God created humankind in God's image and likeness and empowered them to look after the universe: 'The Lord God took the man and put him in the Garden of Eden to till it and keep it' (Gen 2:15). Thus, humans were made in the image of God, not only in thought and love, but also in their ability to create.

It is no wonder, then, that people suffer when they are unable to find work and earn a living. The lack of a safety-net for those who cannot obtain work, as happens in Vietnam, causes loss of dignity and distress to many. Inadequate wages force some people, men and women, to work night and day to the detriment of their health. Even worse, many people take the option of nefarious practices like corruption or theft and so respond to the inborn urge to be employed in some way, even if it is in dishonesty that causes harm.

16. Pope Francis, *Patris Corde*, 6.

It must be affirmed that working is part of God's plan of love; humans are called to cultivate and preserve the beneficial effects of creation, and thus to participate in creation. Labour is the cornerstone of human dignity. It helps us to resemble God, who worked and is always working (Jn 5:17). Labour gives us the ability to feed ourselves, our families, contribute to the development of the nation and promote humanity. Consequently, we are, as Christians, called to uphold labour, whether manual or intellectual. We are called to imitate the family of Nazareth and Joseph who is the exemplary patron of labourers in all societies. In 1955, Pope Pius XII established the feast of St Joseph the Worker on the 1st of May in the Catholic liturgical calendar to counter anti-religious May Day celebrations in communist countries. It is obvious, then, why this feast day is important to Catholics in Vietnam.[17]

Conclusion

As Christians, we honour the discreet but essential part Joseph played in Jesus' journey of salvation. We like to think of him as an enthusiastic, dynamic, silent, and humble husband and father. A true model for fathers, he carried on his shoulders, with strong faith and courage, the uncertainties that life brought his family. His spirituality will always be alive in the Catholic Church.

Joseph is forever an example for all of us to follow, a man always sensitive to the real-life situation. When listening to God's call, he was quick to respond to it without questioning, even at the cost of his life. He offers us the example of a man who steadfastly obeyed God's will. The Church invites us to honour an exemplary father and patriarch and urges us to imitate him.

The more I contemplate the great contribution of St Joseph to the plan of salvation the more I realise that the scriptures, in a distinctive way, reveal him as a treasure. The little we know of his life has produced precious, educative resources. It is as if he is a school to which everyone can come to learn how to live one's daily life.

---

17. Derek Rotty, 'Saint Joseph the Worker, Ora Pro Nobis' at <https://www.crisismagazine.com/2020/saint-joseph-the-worker-ora-pro-nobis>. Accessed 14 February 2021.

For the Vietnamese Church, Joseph is not only an important Patron, but also a dearly loved father who feels with us in the many difficulties and challenges of our lives. He is held up as the exemplary patron of Vietnamese fathers, especially for those who are struggling to find a decent job to provide finance for their children and wider family. He is also honoured as the great protector and guardian for widows, and for children whose lives are affected by broken relationships, parents' divorce, or by domestic violence.

May the fathers of today learn to follow the example of St Joseph to become a strong support for their family. May fathers generously give themselves for their family and children. May fathers generously forgive their children's mistakes and be patient in guiding them on their journey of life.

Come to Joseph!
Pray with Him!
Learn from Him!
Trust and hope in Him!

Amen!

Joseph a Man of Tradition

Nola M Goodwin rsj

In one of the more modern songs about Joseph, *A Strange way to save the world*, Mark Harris sings of Joseph:

> And standing at the manger he saw with his own eyes,
> The message from the angel come to life.
> And Joseph said, Why me I'm just a simple man of trade?
> Why Him With all the rulers in the world?
> Why here Inside this stable filled with hay?
> Why her She's just an ordinary girl?
> Now I'm not one to second guess what angels have to say,
> But this is such a strange way to save the world.[1]

Why Joseph? Why this simple man of trade? What did Joseph have to offer? What does Joseph have to offer us today? These are pondering questions that take us on a journey of learning anew who this man was and what his life has to offer to us today.

Tradition

In *Patris Corde* Pope Francis describes Saint Joseph as 'a beloved father, a tender and loving father, an obedient father, an accepting father; a creatively courageous father, a working father, a father in the shadows'.[2] However, Joseph was also a man of tradition, a man

---

1. Mark Higgins, *A Strange Way to Save the World* <https://www.youtube.com/watch?v=yGsarig0V2c>. Accessed 20 December 2020.
2. Pope Francis, *Patris Corde*. <http://www.vatican.va/content/francesco/en/apost_letters/documents/papa-francesco-lettera-ap_20201208_patris-corde.html>. Accessed 20 December 2020.

steeped in the Jewish culture, a 'righteous' man, or in another translation, 'faithful to the law', who knew the law and traditions and how they played out in Jewish life (Matt 1:19). With regard to Joseph being 'righteous', Long says:

> It's more than saying he was a member of the chamber of commerce or a really good ole boy. In Jewish terms it's saying he is bar-mitzvahed. He knows the commandments. He knows right from wrong . . . If you asked him what to do if your fiancé turns up pregnant by somebody else, he knows how to act.[3]

Every culture has its traditions, stories, dances and knowledge that make them unique, that make them who they are, that shape and reflect their identity. Today we see a loss of culture and traditions as many first- nation people have lost their language, land, customs, and rights. At the same time, we also see people striving to rediscover their culture and traditions, and with them their self-identity. The Indigenous people of the Kimberley in Western Australia write of this link between traditions/beliefs/stories and a person's identity:

> All the old people know the meaning of the story for their own country. People believe in that story and follow that story from the time we call Narrangkarni. Kartiya [non-Aboriginal] people say Dreamtime. Narrangkarni is just like 'In the beginning'. Just like the gospel has the story of Adam and Eve, Aboriginal people have stories about the land and animals and people from the beginning when the world was soft. These stories teach you everything. How to live in the country and how to respect each other. Those stories are the Law. They tell you about important places we have to look after. They tell you: marry the right skin group. If you break the Law, you will get punished.[4]

These Indigenous people see the importance of Law and traditions and of their impact on who you are and how you act. They know

3. Thomas Long, 'The Crisis, Wilderness, Blessing and Decision', Lecture at *The Festival of Homiletics, Washington DC* (May 2004).
4. 'Yirra: Land, Law and Language', *Strong and Alive,* 3 (Kimberley Aboriginal Law and Cultural Centre/Traditional Owners).

the importance of having elders to pass this knowledge on through the ages. Joseph, I suggest, was such a person for Jesus regarding the Jewish law, traditions, and lifestyle. In doing so, he would have provided Jesus with all the supports, knowledge, and skills he needed to become a Jewish man, sure in his self-identity and at home within his people and their traditions and beliefs.

Power of Law

Joseph was a Jew, depicted by Matthew as a descendant of David (Matt 1:1–16). With such a history and rich ancestry he would have been well-versed and raised in the Jewish traditions, history and culture. Tradition/law/culture are very important in giving a young person identity, in helping them know where and to whom they belong, and in knowing what sort of actions and beliefs are expected of them. Tradition is not just actions, but stories and knowledge and connections. At times tradition can have powerful effects not just to those taking part in the learning, or traditional event, but to others within the community who may not necessarily be part of that event or tradition. Traditional events and ways of life give others a view of this culture and what it might mean, as well as providing identity for the people.

Having lived many years in various Aboriginal communities in the Western Australia Kimberley and in the Northern Territory, I know that the power of tradition or Law is very strong. In one Northern Territory Indigenous community a men's Law ceremony meant that all girls and women, Indigenous or otherwise, wore skirts past their knees and shirts with sleeves for the length of the ceremonies, be it four to six weeks or however long it took. They did not leave home early in case they passed any Law business. They shopped at designated times and then went home early and stayed in the house. Some women had the role of cooking.

These restrictions make a powerful, emotional impression and statement. Each person knew their role within this time of Law. At the conclusion of the Law ceremony all women, girls and young children congregated together and sat with their heads bowed in silence and respect while the men and newly initiated youths returned and finalised their time of Law. In another community in the Kimberley when women came back from Law, all the community, men, children and other women, sat in silence with heads bowed as the women returned. Traditions, laws, culture can be extremely powerful and have lasting effects on many. Jesus would have learnt his role, his place and the role and place of others when Joseph made certain that Jesus took part in the Jewish cultural events.

Balance of Law and Compassion

Even though Joseph was a man of tradition, Matthew's gospel account shows him balancing tradition with compassion and with a respect for the person. After the angel's visit to Mary and her 'yes' to be the mother of God, Joseph had a decision to make. The scripture says,

> This is how the birth of Jesus the Messiah came about: His mother Mary was pledged to be married to Joseph, but before they came together, she was found to be pregnant through the Holy Spirit. Because Joseph her husband was faithful to the law, and yet did not want to expose her to public disgrace, he had in mind to divorce her quietly (Matt 1:18–25).

So Joseph 'was faithful' to the law. He knew his rights, and the rights of the woman within the law. The punishment for women found to be unfaithful or pregnant by someone else while betrothed could be stoning to death (Lev. 20:10). It depended on if they were in the city or the country, and sometimes the offending male could also be stoned. In the year of betrothal, the woman still lived at her childhood home but often the bride-price had already been paid. Joseph knew these laws but even before the angel appeared to him in a dream, he 'did not want to expose her to public disgrace' and so was thinking of a quiet divorce. He was showing compassion for Mary. Mary should have been stoned according to a literal interpretation of the law, but Joseph was going to act compassionately within the law. Once his dream revealed that Mary was not unfaithful, Joseph was prepared to take on the responsibility of the coming baby. The angel says, 'you are to give him the name Jesus' (Matt 1:23). This tradition of the father naming the child especially the first-born son, was an acceptance of responsibility of fatherhood.

It is interesting to speculate the effect that Joseph had on Jesus, growing him up as a young boy. The story of the woman caught in adultery told by the evangelist John is relevant:

> The teachers of religious law and the Pharisees brought a woman who had been caught in the act of adultery. 'Teacher', they said to Jesus, 'this woman was caught in the act of adultery. The law of Moses says to stone her. What do you say?' (Jn 8:4–5).

In many ways Jesus' compassionate reaction parallels that of Joseph finding out about the pregnancy of Mary:

> But Jesus bent down and started to write on the ground with his finger. When they kept on questioning him, he straightened up and said to them, 'Let anyone who is without sin be the first to throw the stone at her.' Again, he stooped down and wrote on the ground. At this, those who heard began to go away one at a time, the older ones first, until only Jesus was left, with the woman standing there. Jesus straightened up and asked her, 'Woman, where are they? Has no one condemned you?' 'No one, sir,' she said. 'Then neither do I condemn you,' Jesus declared. 'Go and leave your life of sin' (Jn 8:6–11).

Jesus also knew the law and what it meant for this woman, but he, too, showed the compassion that Joseph showed when Mary's 'May your word to me be fulfilled,' could have had drastic consequences for herself (Lk.1:38). We could say that Jesus' knowledge of the law gloved by compassion was a lesson well learnt from his father Joseph. This combination of sound knowledge of traditions and law, and the ability to pass these on with the wisdom to be compassionate and aware of the dignity of the person is a tremendous model to offer men and women today. Joseph is a man who displayed this capacity, and this provides a sound answer to the question in the song, 'Why me?'[5]

Within this event in the life of Joseph it is also notable that Matthew's portrayal shows him able to listen to his dreams, to think about them and to let his dreams influence his actions and decisions. It takes a risk-taking, intuitive, and trusting man to be able to do this. This side of Joseph's character would counterbalance any rigidity about keeping the law.

5. Higgins, *A Strange May to Save the World.*

Rites of Passage

In Aboriginal communities, traditions, ceremonies and Law have prescribed celebrations enabling the transition from boyhood to young manhood. So, too, Jewish tradition specifies certain occasions and ceremonies that they follow and that are intrinsic to the Jewish way of life. For example, male children were circumcised. At the period of Jesus's birth, the actual Jewish practice was for the operation to be performed at home, usually by the father. Some writers suggest that the responsibility for circumcision would have belonged to Joseph but that someone trained would have been part of the ceremony to carry out the actual circumcision taking place eight days after birth.[6] Again we see Joseph would have carried out his role as family carer and bearer of Jewish tradition being handed on to Jesus.

Another Jewish tradition was the presentation of mother and child at the temple. As the gospel of Luke says, 'When the time came for the purification rites required by the Law of Moses, Joseph and Mary took him to Jerusalem to present him to the Lord (as it is written in the Law of the Lord, "Every firstborn male is to be consecrated to the Lord"), and to offer a sacrifice in keeping with what is said in the Law of the Lord: "a pair of doves or two young pigeons"' (Lk 2:1–3). Luke introduces into his account of the ceremony two unexpected presences, that of Simeon and Anna. At this ceremony Joseph, with the words from Simeon, had vindication of his choice of taking Mary as his wife, and also confirmation of the importance of Jesus. Simeon's words also indicated the hardships those responsibilities would entail not only for Mary but for himself. Simeon speaks of the joys and sorrows of Jesus and then refers to Jesus as being 'destined to cause the falling and rising of many in Israel, and to be a sign that will be spoken against so that the thoughts of many hearts will be revealed'. He also refers to the sorrow Mary will suffer. 'And a sword will pierce your own soul too' (Lk 2:34–35).

Part of Joseph's responsibility was to protect Jesus and Mary from harm. Perhaps Simeon's words showed him that he could only do so much, but that sorrow would come, no matter how hard he tried. Matthew's gospel takes up other aspects of the difficulties of

6. Wikipedia, the Free Encyclopaedia in Schiller and Penny at <http://en.wilipedia.org/wiki/Circumcision_of_Jesus#cite_note-Schiller._89._Penny._116-7>. Accessed 10 January, 2021.

discipleship, most markedly portraying Joseph having to seek shelter from the massacre instigated by Herod. I often think that while Joseph may have fled to Egypt with his family as refugees, he was not able to save or protect those baby boys who would have been killed in Herod's efforts to rid his world of this new king. That would have been a heavy burden to carry, knowing that while saving and protecting one child he could not protect the many killed. This man of tradition would have had to come to terms with his limitations and with learning to live with the remorse of not being able to do more. He is shown spending time away from his country, his friends and family as a refugee in Egypt. Many refugees and first-nation peoples must somehow find a way to pass on their traditions to their sons and daughters while they are divorced from their country, their homeland, their place of birth. To the question in the hymn, 'Why me, I'm such a simple man of trade?',[7] the answer again is clear in that Joseph had so much to offer the boy Jesus in building up his identity as a Jewish man, even amid the trauma of the family fleeing from their home country.

Living Traditions

A religious Sister in an Australian Aboriginal community once shared that when one of the Indigenous men came to talk with her about the Christmas story, what struck him as right and normal, and more important than the rest of the story, was that Joseph took Mary and the soon-to-be-born Jesus to his home country to share the country with his son:

> In those days Caesar Augustus issued a decree that a census should be taken of the entire Roman world. (This was the first census that took place while Quirinius was governor of Syria.) And everyone went to their own town to register (Lk 2:1–2).

For this man it was important for Joseph to share his country with Jesus, to show him where Joseph grew up and the places that were important, to share the holy places, the holy traditions, to tell him the stories of these places and what they meant for his tradition—Joseph's tradition, Jesus' tradition. This Indigenous man saw that it was natural and imperative to share land with your son.

---

7. Higgins, *A Strange Way to Save the World.*

In local funerals at Wadeye, an isolated Aboriginal community in Northern Territory, Australia, the dead person's country is painted on sheets of material, with one being placed on the table under the coffin and one being brought in at the beginning of the ceremony by some of the close family members to place on the coffin. Some of the painting is of the father's land and some of the mother's land. This symbol is a very important part of the ceremony and shows the strong link between country and identity even unto death. For this Aboriginal man the 'census' enabled this transition, this sharing of culture, of identity, symbols and signs from Joseph to Jesus his son. Joseph was sharing his tradition, his culture. Even though Joseph had to flee into Egypt he still upheld his tradition.

Role Model

In a special way, we can recognise in the gospel stories of Joseph a role model for those instructing the next generation and for being able to do this amidst hardship, uncertainty, loss of country, refugee status, and danger. Moreover, he is shown to have done so while balancing the ability to hold and honour the dignity of the person within these traditions. Joseph is, then, an inspiring role model for those trying to bring up their sons and daughters according to their cultural tradition. Equally, he is a role model for those people involved in the formation of priesthood or religious life in the passing on of the charism and its spirit and traditions to those who have been called to 'Come and see' (Jn 1:39).

Joseph's life, the little we know of it, demonstrates that not only must he have guided Jesus in the many things that enabled him to develop a strong, confident self-identity within his tradition, but he enabled him to venture beyond their confines. This is the very thing needed today to ensure that our youth and our religious and priestly candidates are confident, strong people steeped in their traditions but able to critique them and go beyond, as Jesus did.

Holding

In his thesis based on male health in the Indigenous community at Wirrimanu (Balgo), Western Australia, Brian McCoy speaks of the 'Kanyirninpa-holding' as a way for young boys to grow into men, to know their identity, to make the transition from a boy looked after by the women to a young man learning greater independence. He says, '*Kanyirninpa* applies not just to men at the time of Law but to everyone. It includes people of all ages and both genders'.[8]

Regarding any young boy, 'holding' begins when he is born and cared for by his mother. Later, it is done by men—uncles, fathers, and other male relations—and handed on by the many big events such as Law but also by many other smaller events along the life span of the young male. If done properly, then the boy has the chance to know his identity, to become a responsible adult and to meet the duties of being a young adult.

Similarly, in Jewish law the father has such a responsibility. The idea of 'holding' can be understood in the way that Joseph is depicted as taking on the role of 'holding' Jesus into adulthood. When Joseph takes Mary and the child Jesus into Egypt, he shows he is taking his responsibility of *holding* seriously, not just for the child Jesus but also for Mary. Joseph was providing the tradition in which Jesus would grow. Waxman refers to the Talmund, which gives a brief statement of the responsibilities and duties of a traditional Jewish father: 'The father is required to circumcise his son; to redeem him (referring to the first-born son, as per the Biblical passages in Numbers 18:15–16); to teach him *Torah;* to assure that he marries; and to teach him a trade.'[9] Ed Kessler also writes, 'Jesus and his family would have been observant of Torah, paid tithes, kept the Sabbath, circumcised their males, attended synagogue, observed purity laws in relation to childbirth and menstruation, kept the dietary code—one could go on.'[10]

Even knowing that the lived reality of fatherhood is sometimes a long way from the written law, we can still say that when Joseph agreed to name the unborn baby Jesus and to take on the responsibility of a father and to be the husband of Mary, he agreed to all these things. He obviously never got the chance to choose a wife for Jesus, but he would have carried out his other responsibilities. Joseph then would have spent many years in the 'holding' of Jesus so that he grew into his manhood, knew who he was and knew his tradition.

---

8. Brian McCoy, *Holding Men—Kanyirninpa and the Health of Aboriginal Men* (Canberra: Aboriginal Studies Press, 2008), 21.
9. Chaim Waxman, *The Jewish Father: Past and Present* (NY, American Jewish Communities, Institute of Human Relations. 1984), 60.
10. Ed Kessler, 'Jesus the Jew', <http://www.bbc.co.uk/thepassion/articles/jesus_the_jew.shtml>. Accessed 10 January 2021.

Throughout the years of family life Joseph would have been teaching Jesus a trade and also the Torah. Teaching can be done in many ways, telling, discussing, modelling, reading. When you watch the young Aboriginal boys learning to dance, they always have an eye on the elder or adult who is doing the leading. Many times, the adult leader dances and the children follow, but at times he will call out what to do, or men singing the songs will call out what to do. Much of the learning is done by imitation. The dancers do not appear to sit down beforehand and go through in detail what will be done. The painting and dressing up beforehand is very much part of the whole dance and learning. Learning seems more by modelling than by telling. In formation for religious and priests, learning also occurs in many ways, discussing, reading, listening, observing, living the life, meditating, praying. Candidates imbue the spirit, the life which they want to join.

Over the years of his childhood Jesus would have learnt much of his trade and knowledge of the Torah by watching Joseph as well as listening to him, learning how to argue a point and give his own view while respecting others. He would have imbued his Jewishness from Joseph.

There is a wonderful little song, 'Tradition', from the musical *Fiddler on the Roof*, where Tevye, the father, refers to tradition and what it means to his Jewish family in Anatevka. He sings:

> Because of our tradition, we've kept our balance for many, many years.
> Here in Anatevka we have traditions for everything . . .
> how to eat, how to sleep, even, how to wear clothes . . .
> This shows our constant devotion to God . . .
> Because of our traditions, everyone knows who he is
> and what God expects him to do.[11]

Joseph, then, was 'holding Jesus' and sharing with him all these traditions, the skills, knowledge, stories, beliefs, understanding, and support so that the young Jesus would eventually be able to become a fully responsible Jewish adult man. Instructed by Joseph, Jesus would

11. Broadway cast, 'Tradition: Fiddler on the Roof' <http://www.themusicallyrics.com/f/371-fiddler-on-the-roof-the-musical-lyrics/4062-tradition-lyrics-fiddler-on-the-roof.html>. Accessed 20 January 2021.

know the law and live the Jewish life but would also be able to do so with compassion, understanding and respect for the individuals living within that life. This would enable Jesus to be confident enough to be able to live and critique that Jewish life under the light of love.

In Luke's New Testament story of finding the child Jesus in the temple, where we last hear of Joseph, we imagine that Joseph would have had a real shock hearing Jesus' words, 'Why were you searching for me? Didn't you know I had to be in my Father's house?' (Lk 2:49). Yes, Joseph was supporting Jesus to come to responsibility and adulthood. Yes, Joseph was teaching Jesus the Torah. Yes, Joseph was teaching Jesus the Jewish traditions and more. But Joseph was not expecting Jesus to be an expert at these things yet. Jesus was still a young boy. Joseph and Mary must have trusted Jesus and seen him as a reasonably responsible twelve-year-old, otherwise they would have kept a lot tighter hold on the reins when they went to Jerusalem. When they found him with the teachers in the temple court he was listening and answering questions. Luke's gospel says that 'everyone who heard him was amazed at his understanding and his answers' (Lk 2:47). This was obviously a well taught, deep thinking young boy used to discussing the Torah, steeped in tradition, at ease with his beliefs. This is the big dilemma, the big adjustment for any father, any parent, and any formator to make. When is it time to let the reins go and let the seeds you have planted come to fruition? When is it time to know that this person is ready to branch out on their own?

Brian McCoy's thesis points out,

> People continue to experience being *held* (*kanyirninpa*) until adults recognise they are no longer in need of being *held,* or as young adults they recognise that they are ready to take responsibility for their own lives and begin to *hold* others. As one adult described it, this stage occurs when a young man recognises that he is ready to 'put his foot down'. He believes he is ready to step out as an adult. In some cases, the person will announce that they are no longer in need of being *held*. In other cases, it will be apparent.[12]

12. McCoy, *Holding Men*, 31.

In this gospel story it is evident that Jesus is very close to being ready to step out as an adult but there is still a way to go. It says much for the relationship between Jesus and his parents and to Joseph's 'holding' of Jesus when we hear the following verses in Luke:

> Then he [Jesus] went down to Nazareth with them and was obedient to them. And Jesus grew in wisdom and stature, and in divine and human favour (Lk 2:51–52).

The relationship between Jesus and Joseph and between Jesus and Mary, was enough for Jesus to settle back into the process of the give and take of adolescence, the gradual release of adolescence and a growing confidence and comfort with young adulthood. He was learning to take responsibility for his own life. Although we hear no more of Joseph in the gospels, we gather he was very much a key player in this part of his son's life. He enabled Jesus to be the amazing, challenging person we see in the Scriptures.

'Why me? I'm such a simple man of trade?[13] For all his simplicity, his lack of celebrity status in the bible, his scant survival in only the first two chapters of Matthew and Luke, Joseph's life had a lasting impact. We learn Joseph to have been a man of tradition, a man who passed that tradition on to the boy for whom he took responsibility, a man who not only 'held' Jesus into becoming a Jewish adult, but who taught him to act compassionately within that tradition, to always respect the individual and their feelings. We know Joseph as a man who was willing to listen and act on his dreams, was willing to take responsibility, was willing to live with the things he could do and deal with the hardships of the things over which he had no control.

Why not him? Joseph stands as a model, an inspiration, an advocate for us today, for the communities passing on their traditions, for the formators trying to pass on the spirit of their founders. 'This is such a strange way to save the world', says Harris.[14] But perhaps it is not so strange. Joseph, a man of tradition, supplied all that the boy Jesus needed to become the man we see in the gospels. Joseph's 'holding' of the boy Jesus enabled him to become the man who could and would carry out his mission.

13. Higgins, *A Strange Way to Save the World.*
14. Higgins, *A Strange Way to Save the World.*

Joseph Within the Context of Māori Culture

Makareta Tawaroa rsj

May I introduce Joseph in a Māori way.
Te Whakapapa o Hohepa
Tēnā koutou katoa.
Ko Hohepa tōku ingoa
Ko ahau te tama a Hākopa
Ko te iwi o Hura
Ko te whare of Rāwiri;
No te rohe o Parihitini;
He maha ngā whakatupuranga o taku tūpuna, mai ia Aperahama, tae atu ki a Rāwiri ki te Karaiti;
Tōku whaea tūpuna, he Tamar, Rahab, Ruth me Bathsheba;
Tōku maunga, Nāhareta ngā maunga;
Tōku roto, ko Karirī te ingoa;
Ko tāku moana, te Mediterranean;
Ko tāku awa, ko Hōrano;
Ko tāku pā tapu, ko Hiruhārama;
Ko tāku tāone tūpuna, ko Peterehema;
Ko tāku kainga, ko Nāhareta;
Ko ahau te hoa tāne a Mere, whaea o Hehu;
Ko ahau te papa tangata te ture o Hehu;
He tohunga mahi ahau i te rākau;
He mea whiriwhiri ahau nā te Atua.
Tihei mauriora!

Hato Hohepa
Statue of St Joseph
St Joseph's Convent, Whanganui

Joseph's Ancestry

Greetings.
This is my Family Tree.
My name is Joseph.
I am the son of Jacob.
I belong to the Tribe of Judah
and the House of David;
I belong to the region of Palestine,
My ancestry spans many generations; from Abraham to King David,
to the coming of the Messiah.
Tamar, Rahab, Ruth and Bathsheba are my female forebears;
My mountains are the Nazareth Mountains;
My lake is Galilee;
My sea is the Mediterranean;
My River is the Jordan;
My holy city is Jerusalem;
My ancestral city is Bethlehem;
My home village is Nazareth in Galilee;
I am the husband of Mary, the mother of Jesus;
I am the earthly and legal father of Jesus;
I am a craftsman, a worker in wood;
I am Chosen of God;
This is who I am.

Whakapapa (Family Tree)

Joseph has always been one of my favourite people in the Gospels for lots of reasons but mainly because he was a tribal person. He belonged to the tribe of Judah, one of the twelve tribes of Israel, which was ruled by the House of King David in Jerusalem. The tribe of Judah prophesied that the Messiah would come from among its members. Matthew's gospel calls Jesus, the Son of David, indicating his royal origins, and the Son of Abraham, indicating that he was an Israelite.

I come from the tribe or *iwi* of Ngā Paerangi, one of the many tribes that live along *Te Awa Tupua* (Whanganui River) in central North Island of New Zealand. Tribal people have a common ancestor with similar customs and traditions and generally, they have a sense of communal unity among themselves. When I lived in the city, I didn't really know my neighbours. But at home in my own *marae*, (village) I am related to everyone. Knowing my *whakapapa* is important because it gives me an identity and a place to put my feet, expressed in the word *tūrangawaewae*.

Tūpuna Noa (Common Ancestor)

In some parts of the world, tribal people are considered backward with customs that are frozen in time and out of touch with the *real* world. Even the word 'tribe' is considered an insult for some tribal people. In this case, it is always good for tribal people to use their own words to describe themselves. In New Zealand, Māori tribalness was described as 'beastly communism' by European officials. But despite our differences, all people have common hopes and aspirations such as living a long, peaceful and happy life. We all come from a common ancestor.

Tūpuna Paerangi

We all have ancestors. Paerangi is one of my favourite ones. He lived on the southern side of Te Kāhui Maunga, a cluster of mountains on the central plateau of Te Ika a Māui (North Island) of New Zealand. Many other tribes in the area also link to him. Paerangi named many places around my *iwi rohe* (tribal boundary) and along *Te Awa Tupua*, the Whanganui River.

Ngā Mōhiotanga (Knowledge and Skills)

Joseph is mentioned only a few times in the gospels but they are important, because they give us a glimpse of how he and Mary responded to the circumstances surrounding the early childhood of Jesus and some of the responsibilities of a Jewish father. Joseph lived in the village of Nazareth in Galilee where he belonged to a family of carpenters and craftsmen. He would have completed his apprenticeship under the tutelage of his father Jacob who would have been taught by his father. Skills were passed on from father to son and from mother to daughters from generation to generation.

Whakapakari (Building Capacity)

Today most *marae* (villages) are upskilling their people, their building capacity and their capability, as so much damage has been done since the arrival of foreign powers. For a long time, Mātauranga Māori (Māori Knowledge) was considered inferior, discouraged and suppressed. There was a general belief among educationalists and crown agencies that Māori had to reject their own culture and spiritual beliefs and accept proper knowledge if they wanted to be part of the modern world. The book, *A Civilising Mission?*, looks at the role that European-run schools played as one of the main agents of colonisation.[1] An ongoing result was loss of both identity and sense of self-worth that we are still coping with today.

While the past has happened, our people have decided to be victims no more and so have taken positive steps to enable future flourishing. The biggest change in education for Māori people has been at tertiary level with the setting up of *Whare Wānanga* (House of Learning). The first, Te Wānanga o Raukawa was established in 1981 by three main tribes in and around the Otaki/Wellington area, Te Atiawa, Ngāti Raukawa and Ngāti Toa. This was in response to the decline of *te reo* Māori speakers within their *rohe* (tribal areas). Te Whare Wānanga o Aotearoa was established in Te Awamutu in 1984 and is one of the largest tertiary educational providers in New Zealand. Then in 1992 Te Whare Wānanga o Awanuiārangi opened in Whakatane, the first indigenous tertiary education institution accredited to teach courses to PhD level.

Success in Māori education is slowly rising. At all ages, participation in higher level study has increased: At Auckland University 28% of Māori students were studying at bachelor level and above in 2012, up from 21% in 2007 (an increase from 17,500 to 21,900 students). And the rate at which Māori complete qualifications has also increased: of Māori who started full-time study at level 4 or above in 2007, 62% had completed a qualification within five years, compared with a rate of 53% for those who started in 2004.

1. Judith Simon and Linda Smith, *A Civilising Mission?: Perceptions and Representations of the Native Schools System* (Auckland: Auckland University Press, 2001).

Utu Moni (Taxes)

People in Joseph's time, were heavily taxed, sometimes as much as 50% of what they earned. There was a tax for everything—customs, imports, exports, bridges, crops, sales, properties and even a wartime tax for fighting campaigns. It was very hard for struggling families to make ends meet. Local men were hired as tax collectors to collect taxes. They often charged over and above the legal taxes to make a living for themselves as they were not paid. The well-known story of Jesus and Zacchaeus, the tax-collector, reminds us of the situation Joseph would have had to face (Lk 19:1-10). The result was that relationships between the rich and poor were often tense and confrontational.

Whakatika (How Just?)

New Zealand is one of the most heavily-taxed countries in the Asia-Pacific region. According to last year's Treasury findings, the lowest paid workers pay more tax than millionaires who only pay 10% of their total income, which is less than the 10.5% rate paid by the lowest income earners. The wealthiest people in New Zealand have their wealth in parts of the economy which are not taxed at all or are taxed lightly either in housing or trusts. For example $263 billion dollars are held in trusts by five percent of the wealthiest people in New Zealand.

Putanga Rereke (Different versions)

The early chapters of Matthew and Luke give us different versions of the circumstances surrounding the birth of Jesus; they differ around time, events and people. But both gospels record the challenges that Joseph faced once he accepted his role as *hoa tane* (husband) and *matua whāngai* (earthly father) of Jesus.

In Matthew 13:55 Joseph is not mentioned by name, rather in a disparaging way, describing him by what he does, rather than who he is; '*Is not this the carpenter's son?*' Nazareth too, the place where Joseph nurtured Jesus, was also scorned; 'Can any good come out of Nazareth?' (Jn 1:46). These are subtle racist references that Māori, like Nazarenes, are aware of.

The 22 March 2021 report, '*Whakatika*', was conducted from February 2019 to February 2020 and describes Māori experiences of racism. The two thousand and seventy-three Māori who completed the survey came from across the country and were of all genders and ages, with rural and city backgrounds. Seventy nine percent (79%) pointed out that non-Māori media negatively portray Māori all of the time or often.

One survey respondent, a twenty-nine year old *wāhine* (woman), remarked, 'It would be fine if they treated everyone equally; however, they push an agenda to ensure we look at Māori negatively.' Ninety three percent of Māori felt racism impacted on them on a daily basis. Ninety six percent said it was a problem for their wider *whanau* (family), at least to some extent.

Hoa Tāne (Joseph as Husband)

Joseph's story is a love story. He was looking forward to bringing the girl of dreams, Mary, home, but got the news that she was *hapu*, pregnant. He knew he was not the father of the child, but following his heart, decided to end their relationship quietly out of respect for Mary.

Te Whare Tangata (House of Humanity)

In speeches by Māori men, it is common to hear them refer to women as *te whare tangata*, (the house of humanity). This description recognises the vital roles that *ūkaipō* (mothers) play in providing life and nurturing the future generations. Women are respected for their ability to create life, so deserve to be treated with the same consideration as Papatūānuku (earth mother) the creator of all life.

During the Covid 19 lockdown last year, some Māori groups closed the roads around their areas to tourists or anyone from outside their region—'We must protect our *whakapapa*' (family tree) said one of our *kaumātua*, elders.

Rerenga (Refugees in Egypt)

Every day in the newspapers and on our TV screens we see thousands of families forced to leave their homelands because of war, persecution or the collapse of their country's infrastructure or environment.

We are reminded of the command given to Joseph: 'Arise and take the child and his mother and flee into Egypt' (Matt 2:3). Egypt was the traditional place of refuge for Jews both in biblical and in Maccabean times. Instructed through his dreams, Joseph took the *whanau* to Egypt to keep safe. It would have been a struggle for the family to live if they didn't know anyone who could help. Being a refugee in a strange land can't be easy.

Whakatika Rūri (Survey of Māori Experiences of Racism, 22 March 2021)

Many Māori people feel that they too are refugees in their own country. Many do not have a safe place to live, many live in their cars, on the beach in a tent; others are constantly on the move.

The Whakatika Survey confirms this. One respondent said: If I'm trying to get a motel room, I get my *Pākehā* (European) missus to do it. So there is no hassle.[2]

During the last three or four decades, many Māori people have migrated to Australia for work and lifestyle. In three out of the four most populous states, construction and manufacturing figures were the top two industries of employment for Māori in Australia, ranging from 25.3 per cent in New South Wales to 29.7 per cent in Queensland. Western Australia was distinctive in that mining ranked as the second most popular sector, employing 13.7 per cent of all Māori living within the state. It would seem the picture of Israelite slaves in Egypt building the pyramids in the days of yore are repeated in these days of 'economic refugees'.

Te Wero (The Challenge)

One of the toughest challenges Joseph would have faced as a father was when Jesus, at the age of twelve, went off on his own without letting his parents know: 'Your father and I have been looking for you.' Jesus had made a decision to look more deeply into the teachings of his ancestors, and the temple elders thought he had the knowledge and intelligence to do so. Jesus answered his mother: 'Did you not know that I must be busy with my Father's affairs?' (Lk 2:48–50).

2. Survey respondent, 51 *tāne* (male).

This must have been a shock for Joseph. Who was this other Father? And what were his affairs? What sort of fathering approach would Joseph use in this new situation? We can draw the conclusion that Joseph did well from what Luke tells us—that Jesus 'grew in wisdom and stature and in favour with God and men' (Lk 2:52).

Rangatahi Māori (Young Māori)

Māori elders are convinced that, given good guidance and opportunity, their young people can likewise 'grow in favour' with God and today's society. Like Joseph, we have to believe that younger off-spring will respond to their God-given potential. Sir Mason Durie, professor of Māori Studies and research academic at Massey University, points out the following:

> Twenty five years ago it would have been hard to imagine a generation of young Māori who were fluent Māori speakers, or to think that thousands of Māori learners would be as comfortable online as offline. So imagining the future on the basis of today's problems, is not a good predictor of tomorrow. Despite adversity and inequity, there are strong signals that Māori futures will be both rewarding and productive . . . Māori have the knowledge, skills and foresight to create a future where younger generations and generations yet to come, can prosper in the world, and at the same time live as Māori.[3]

Whakapono Māori (Religious Observance)

Māori people identify with those who join with ancestors and the present community in religious observance. Again, Joseph speaks to us. Luke tells us in his first chapter that Joseph took his family to the temple in Jerusalem to dedicate Jesus to God, in accordance with the law of Moses. They were greeted with great joy by a devout *kaumātua* (elder) a *urie* called Simeon who took the child in his arms and said: 'My eyes have seen the salvation . . . the glory of your people Israel . . . ' (Lk 2: 30–31).

---

3. Mason Durie, *Ngā Tini Whetū: Navigating Māori Futures* (Welllington: Huia, 2011).

Tikanga Māori (Customary Values)

Today, *kaumātua* (elders) play an active role in giving guidance and assistance to the younger generations, especially those in leadership roles. The practice of *tikanga Māori* around *tangihanga* (burial ceremony) for example, has been a challenge in Covid 19 times with reduced attendance. Understanding *kohinga* Māori (Māori cosmology) is an important part of how Māori people understand the world, and the role that Ranginui (skyfather) and Papatūānuku (earth mother) play.

In the picture of the Jewish elder, Simeon, taking the child Jesus in his arms and Mary and Joseph standing by him we have a wish for the future of our culture—that our parents and children will integrate the divine and human (sky father and earth mother), which is provided by the stability of knowing where they come from, and how they are supported and held as they go through life.

Te Awa Tupua Whakatauki

Māori spirituality played a big part in helping Parliament recognise that the Whanganui people and the River are inextricably linked, as expressed in the words: '*Ko au te awa, ko te awa ko au*' ('I am the River and the River is Me'). After 150 years of battling through the courts, the Whanganui River Claims Settlement Act was passed in 2017, acknowledging the River as a *Tūpuna*, an ancestor, with Māori having a greater voice in its care, protection and management.

It is good that Pope Francis is catching up with the indigenous peoples' understanding of ecology through his marvellous reflection *Laudato Si'*, where he recognises the links between human identity and welfare and creation. Knowing one's rightful place in the wider scheme of things is one of the gifts of indigenous consciousness as expressed by Chief Seattle: '*Korero taiao–Titiro me te whakarongo*' ('Nature speaks—look and listen').[4]

---

4. Chief Seattle Speech at <https://suquamish.nsn.us/home/about-us/chief-seattle-speech/>. Accessed 4 April 2021.

Whakaingoa—(Naming)

Names are a huge issue for Māori, whether it be for people or places. Sometimes, a name comes naturally and bears significance. For example at Pakaitore in the reclaiming of Moutoa Gardens in 1995, a baby born to one *ūkaipo* (mother) in residence, named her *pēpi* (baby) Pakaitore. In Matthew's first chapter, Joseph is told in his first dream to name Mary's child as Jesus 'for he will save his people from their sins' (Matt 1:21). Many examples in the gospels show how the name of Jesus drives out demons, performs miracles and provides protection from evil. He is what his name says—'saviour'.

There are thousands of places all over New Zealand where Māori names have been replaced with new names. At the end of 2020, an *Iwi* called Ngāti Maika petitioned the Whanganui District Council to rename the small rural township of Maxwell back to its original name Pakaraka (where Karaka trees grow). George Maxwell was a volunteer of the Kai Iwi Yeoman Cavalry in the mid 1800's and shot a small group of *tamariki* (children) from Ngāti Maika who were out pig hunting. Many petitions have been received on both sides of the debate. The issue is under still under consultation. Joseph, I am sure, would understand the emotions of the Māori people being constantly reminded of this tragedy: his distress at Herod's killing of innocent children at Bethlehem must have accompanied him as he fled with his family for safety.

Whanaungatanga (Family relationships)

The word *mātua* means parent and the word *whāngai* means to feed. Joseph as *Mātua Whāngai* (earthly father) and legal father was responsible for the health and wellbeing of his family. He had a craft so he was able to provide for their basic necessities through work. As a faithful Jew he would have participated in Sabbath worship in the local synagogue, learnt the scriptures, ensured that the commandments of God were kept and kept faithfulness to God as the focus of family life. Jesus would have grown through the stages of his manhood under the gentle guiding hand of Joseph.

In his being, then, Joseph offers a model for Māori fathers. Many Māoris are of the opinion that Western culture changed the image of father for their people. Journalist Michelle Duff puts these facts to us:

> For hundreds of years, Māori men have been gentle, kind and involved fathers. They have wiped away tears and sung to their babies, as little hands cling to their necks. How and why have these stories been lost?[5]

We need to reclaim this former cultural model, and Joseph can help us do that.

Hauora Māori—Wholistic Health

Many acts of parliament, particularly the Land Act of the mid 1860s, were devastating. Whole families and villages were displaced. For example, 1500 troops invaded Parihaka, destroyed much of the village, raped the women, dispersed the people even to the South Island where many died in appalling conditions, and detained Tohu Kākahi and Te Whiti o Rongomai without trial for six months.

Intergenerational trauma is a very real but hidden sickness that flows through many Māori people today. Finding a cure for the illness of the soul, is often more difficult than diagnosing an illness of the body.

An approach to 'wholistic health' is making some headway as the diagnosis of the whole person is considered; *Hinengaro* refers to the mental and emotional aspects of a person; *tinana* refers to nutrition, exercise and other bodily aspects of a person; *wairua* includes the beliefs, spiritual and religious aspects of a person; and *whānau* includes the people's life together in community. The medical model normally looks at only the sick part of the body.

While we do not look to Joseph's life for examples of how to deal with the ongoing effects of displacement and trauma, perhaps we can be encouraged to search for a balanced life as his was. Matthew describes him as a 'just man'—that is, one who is in right relationships with God and others (Matt 1:19). Joseph could listen to his inner and outer voice. This is the description of 'wholistic health'.

Tangata Moemoea (Joseph, Man of Dreams)

Joseph had many dreams, all of them were pointing in one direction—being the provider and protector of Mary and Jesus. He was told to

5. Michelle Duff at <https://interactives.stuff.co.nz/2021/03/maori-dads/>. Accessed 4 April, 2021.

take a pregnant Mary as his wife even though he knew he was not the father. Then he was told to go to Egypt and find a safe place there, and then to go back to Nazareth. Dreams dictated his life.

Moemoea Ngātahi (Māori Dreaming together)

Māori People continue to work toward the self-determination and autonomy which they enjoyed in pre-colonial days. Accepting defeat at the hands of a colonial power is not easy, even for a small nation such as Māori. With borders open, sailing ships bursting with passengers, eager to start a new life but accompanied by the Bible and the gun, the consequences were inevitable. The extent to which regaining *rangatiratanga* (self-determination) within the context of the continual ongoing colonisation of today, is not a subject that any New Zealand government will talk about. The courts have maintained what is for many years.

But God living in us has given us a dream. Like Joseph, we have to believe in it and find solutions that can be put into action. With our actions we are creating a future that is 'de-colonised'—that is, free of attitudes that would treat first peoples as inferior or without power. We can only do this in partnership with all those who make up our country.

Whakamutunga (Conclusion)

Joseph stood at the crossroads of the old and new testaments, fulfilling the obligations of the past while responding to the challenge of the present. Who will be the new interpreter of dreams in the Māori world today? There is a Māori proverb that says: '*Kia whakatōmuri te haere whakamua*' ('I walk backward into the future with my eyes fixed on the past').

A few weeks ago I watched Elon Musk's Starlink train of satellites travel cross the night sky from the Kaiwhaiki hinterlands, surrounded by the resting place of long gone ancestors, in a humble village surrounded by those with whom I share DNA.

My thoughts took me back through time, past the countless generations before my ancestors sailed the great ocean of Kiwa, back to the time when they crossed the continents, back to their primate ancestors, back to the single cell and other early life forms, into the molten planet and the forming of the solar system, back to exploding stars, giving birth to carbon, oxygen and iron, far across the galaxy, to the amazing creation that humankind is today.

While I am conscious that I am so much more than my ancestral background, it takes time for a conquered people to heal. It takes time to learn how to live many worlds in one moment.

The life of Joseph teaches us a lot. He followed his dreams and changed our lives forever.

Treasured Father: Joseph

Lusiana Matai sjc and Carmel Pilcher rsj

Introduction

It was interesting to note, that in the Apostolic Letter declaring this the Year of Joseph, Pope Francis chose to dwell on the fatherhood of Joseph. He could have chosen another attribute, Joseph the just man, the dreamer, the man of faith, the hidden silent one. But instead we are invited to reflect on '*Patris Corde*', 'With a father's heart'. Maybe those who know Pope Francis best might not have been surprised by this choice. Perhaps the pontiff had his own father in mind as he shared his thoughts on Joseph the father. Indeed, one could appropriate this title not just to Joseph, but equally to Francis himself, who, many would believe, has shepherded his flock 'with a father's heart'. Joseph the father resonated with the two of us who have wonderful memories of our own fathers. We write as two religious sisters who also have Joseph as our father and patron. We are a Fijian Sister, and an Australian Sister, who each currently live and serve the Archdiocese of Suva.

Lusi shares her own experience of family life in Fiji: 'The liturgical Year of St Joseph deepens my gratitude to God for the gift of my father who played a major role in my happy and treasured childhood memories. Together with my mother they modelled values and showed me how to relate within the family, within my village community and beyond. I treasured deeply the life-giving aspect of fatherhood shown by my father when tilling the land to provide food for the family, selling yaqona and copra to send us children to school, fulfilling responsibilities to the '*vanua*'[1] and to the church, leading family and

1. *Vanua* is a word meaning land, home or village and the dynamics of relationships therein.

community prayers, taking us to Mass to neighbouring Catholic villages when Mass was available, acknowledging family paternal and maternal links, sharing Jesus and the faith with us, respecting our freedom and giving us a sense of security and 'at homeness' by his presence.

Imperfect as he was, my father gave his best as a brother, husband, father, grandfather, uncle, grand uncle and cousin. He was a provider for our family and he protected the family, the village and the faith community from any form of harm. He upheld universal values of love, compassion, service and honesty by his own example. My siblings and I often sit and reminisce with great humour, laughter, affection and gratitude about our personal and family experience with our loving father.

Losing my father at the age of twenty-three, I realise that I have lost someone who brought me joy, beauty, light, meaning and security. While I accepted his death, I acknowledge that I deeply grieved his loss. I then wrote a poem titled 'Treasured Fatherhood' as a way of dealing with my grief. Through God's grace, I understood that the love my siblings and I had for our father and his love for us his children is only a shadow of God's love for us all, and yet it is also how I understand God as Father, and indeed Joseph as father of Jesus.'

This paper will argue that the church's invitation to dwell on the fatherhood of Joseph this year is timely for the people who live in the Fiji Islands. Family life has traditionally been highly valued amongst the people of this nation. In the past families have always been strong and supportive. There is a strong network in the village that centres around family life. This was sustained by rituals to mark significant moments in the life of the community. The family that we call 'holy', the family of Joseph, husband of Mary and their son, Jesus, also lived in a village, Nazareth, in Galilee. We note that there are many similarities between Fijian family life lived in villages, and that of the holy family of Nazareth. We also recognise that many of the concerns and worries Joseph experienced resonate with contemporary times. Here in Fiji the pressure of COVID and harsh weather experiences is straining family life in a worrying way that is fracturing the very fabric of the society. This shows itself in many ways including the rate of domestic violence that in this country has become disproportionately high. It is our opinion that reflecting on Joseph as father, through the eyes of Pope Francis, may well provide a source of inspiration to families and restore harmony. We take our picture of Joseph from the Infancy narratives of the gospels of Matthew and Luke. While the evangelists' focus in these narratives is the person of Jesus, it is our hope that their portrayal of Joseph the father may become a model for all Christian fathers here in Fiji.

The Family—At the Heart of Traditional Fijian Culture

Fiji continues to recognise and experience the family as amongst its most important traditional values. One aspect of Fiji life that has always attracted visitors is the great sense of generous hospitality. 'Come and eat' is a spontaneous reaction that will be an invitation as much to a stranger as to a member of the family or village. It is not so much the food that is important, but the sharing of food, and the *talanoa* (conversation) that is always part of the sharing. Seated on the mat around the food will be the family. The father has a very significant role in the family. Here in the Pacific the father who gives life, the biological father, may not be the father who raises the sons or daughters. This role might belong to a grandfather, an uncle or perhaps a cousin, but always there will be a father figure at home or at least in the village.

Although geographically far from villages on the Islands of Fiji, the family that was eventually to settle in the village of Nazareth would also have lived a traditional way, where the homes would have been close together, and everyone probably knew every other family. Family, for Western society, usually means a 'nuclear' family; that is, one or two parents and siblings, or a 'blend' of parents and new parents, and 'half' brothers and sisters. But in the Nazareth of old, and the Fiji of today, a family is much less clearly defined. Parents, aunts, uncles, cousins and grandparents all come under the term 'family'. Indeed, it is difficult for a foreigner to understand familial relationships in Fiji and the interrelatedness that is experienced extending well beyond a 'Western' understanding.

We know that Joseph supported his family by working as a carpenter, as scripture scholars remind us, working probably not just with wood, but as a general builder. Much of Fiji is rural. Those who work in the villages here are often farmers who work the land, or fishermen. Usually those who work sustain not only their own family but all the families in the village. Social historians tell us that Joseph would have done the same.

Joseph Names Jesus

Pope Francis reminds us that while they tell us little about Joseph, the scriptures tell us something of the kind of father he was. When Joseph learnt that Mary was pregnant and the child was not his own, he was left with a serious dilemma. In her own small village if he disclosed this information, he would have made Mary an outcast amongst her own family and the entire village. He decided instead to quietly call off the betrothal. But before he could do this he was advised in a dream: 'Do not be afraid to take Mary as your wife, for the child conceived in her is from the Holy Spirit. She will bear a son, and you are to name him Jesus' (Matt 1:20).

While the first part of this message might initially have confused Joseph the second is very clear. To name a person gives the person a particular ownership and responsibility for that person. This is true in the ancient Jewish culture and continues today in traditional Fijian culture.

A newborn Fijian child is usually named after an elder relative of both the father and mother. The first born is usually named by the father and the second born child named by the mother. It is considered an honour to have someone named after you. It is a sign of love and affection that people have for their elder relatives. Occasionally, some older people can ask the couple expecting a child to have the newborn named after them or some other deceased relatives, so that the name continues in the family lineage. Naming a newborn in Fijian culture also strengthens the relationship among immediate and extended families. To name a person or to have a person named after you gives you a connection, a bond that is unique.

That Joseph was asked by God's messenger to name Jesus inferred that Joseph's relationship to Jesus was that of his legal father. Joseph was to treat the yet to be born Jesus as his own son, his own flesh and blood. Matthew goes on to tell us that Joseph obeyed without question or hesitation. His trust in his God was absolute. Joseph was now the protector not only of his wife Mary, but also of her/their son whom he was to name Jesus.

Joseph Trusted Amid Uncertainty

In Mary's humble village of Nazareth, from the moment Joseph agreed to marry Mary and become the legal father of Jesus, his life became clouded in uncertainty. Before Jesus was born, Joseph was required to leave Nazareth with Mary for Bethlehem, to register in the census ordered by the emperor (Lk 2:1–4). There must have been much anxiety for them both, as Mary's time to give birth was imminent. When they made the arduous journey, they discovered there was nowhere for them to stay in Bethlehem. It is hard to imagine the worry and fear as they faced this trial together.

Perhaps the uncertainty of Joseph's time might be compared to today. We currently experience times of great uncertainty. In much of the world the pandemic continues to spread unabated, despite the fact that a vaccine is becoming available. Here in Fiji COVID 19 has been contained, but we live with its adverse effects.

When the pandemic first struck an early casualty here in Fiji was widespread unemployment, especially when the borders closed and the travel industry, such a significant source of income for the nation, all but collapsed. Those laid off did what their forebears have always done. They returned to planting, both to provide themselves with food to eat, but also produce to sell. This proved successful. Within a few months whole villages had begun to grow healthy crops, soon ready for harvesting. And then the cyclones came. Cyclone Harrold, then Yasi, then Ana, destroyed crops and flooded the land. Many found themselves not only without food, but houses were also destroyed. Parents were left wondering not only where the next meal would come from because they had no money, but how to put a roof over their heads.

This has resulted in tension that has threatened traditional family life and brought great stress and strain on parents, and especially fathers, who struggle to put food on the table. In too many cases we know that fathers and husbands who should be trusted protectors and love their wives and children with a 'father's heart' have instead brought serious physical and emotional harm to those in their care.

Again, after the birth of Jesus, Joseph had to flee the relative security of Bethlehem, to take himself and Mary and the newborn and go to a foreign land where he had not only to find food and shelter but also work, providing for his young family. While he was clearly directed where to go, nothing else was certain. Joseph had no idea how long he was to stay in Egypt. He could only trust, one day at a time. Joseph and Mary experienced the life of the refugee.

Like the holy family, many people in Fiji suffer the plight of the refugee. Because of natural disasters or political or management misfortune, some families and villages have lost whole livelihoods and all their belongings. In some ways they have become refugees in their own land. Some fathers have resorted to finding employment overseas to provide for their families. They sometimes need to take employment in another country such as Australia or New Zealand, or a nearby island. Some may go to sea and work on a cargo ship to provide for their families, being away for months or even years at a time. They suffer loneliness and separation, and sometimes this drives them to unfaithfulness to their wives and families back home.

Although he didn't understand fully, Joseph's faith motivated him to trust in his God. He, no doubt like others of his time, believed that his dreams were significant. As a man of great faith, he believed that it was God who was speaking to him in his dreams. And his response was always the same: prompt obedience, trust and action, no matter what the cost. Just like Mary and Joseph, Fijian parents needed the reassurance of the angel: 'Son of David, do not be afraid!' (Matt 1:20).

Joseph, a Father in the Shadows

While the Infancy Narratives of the gospels do not touch on the daily lives of Jesus, Mary and Joseph, we can glean from studies in archaeology and social history what they may well have been. After the family returned from Egypt, Jesus would have spent many years of his life growing up with his family in the small village of Nazareth. Pope Francis reminds us that: 'fathers are not born but made'.[2] Joseph needed to learn how to be a father just like any first-time father. In Nazareth Jesus would have learnt his father's craft, carpentry and building. Jesus also would have accompanied his father to the synagogue and learnt from his father the Jewish Torah. While Mary would have led the domestic prayers, it was Joseph who led Jesus to the liturgical prayer of the synagogue and temple. In Joseph, Jesus would have experienced the relationship of a father and son, and while we are not given any details, one could assume this was a stable nurturing time. Jesus would also have enjoyed the security and companionship of an extended family, as in any small village.

2. Pope Francis, *Patris Corde*, 7.

We do have one story told by Luke (2:39–52), about the young Jesus. The twelve-year-old boy was left behind after the family travelled from Nazareth to Jerusalem for the festival. Luke tells us his parents spent three days looking for him. One could imagine the anxiety of Mary and Joseph during that time. To lose your only son, not knowing if he has come to harm or even if they would ever find him, must have been a devastating time of anxiety and worry. Again, in this very human story, we are reminded of the responsibility of parents towards their children. It is Mary who admonishes Jesus, while their son, Jesus, seems to wonder why they are worried at all. Joseph is there but remains in the shadows. This is the last we hear of Joseph in the scriptures. Like so many fathers his life appears to be lived in obscurity.

Pope Francis likens the role of Joseph in his family at Nazareth to those workers, serving on the frontline of the COVID pandemic. The Pope describes these as 'ordinary people' who, during the crisis, 'are surely shaping the decisive events in our history' through their care giving and responsible service.[3] Here in Fiji these caregivers have watched over and served those who have returned from overseas and been found to be COVID positive. This has meant four consecutive weeks away from their family, two weeks' caring for patients and two weeks in isolation themselves, before returning to the community. With this selfless dedication, always in the shadows and obscurity, Fiji has been largely spared community transmission. Like Joseph, who, quietly cared for his family without any fanfare or accolades, so many caregivers and security workers have done the same. Joseph can surely be their inspiration.

Joseph, a Beloved Father

Joseph was Jesus' earthly father. What we understand about fatherhood is formed, for good or ill, by our own experience of fatherhood. Pope Francis speaks of the tender love of Joseph, and he tells us that he likes to think that Jesus' references to fatherhood in the scriptures, for example the story of the prodigal son (Lk 15:11–32), are based on Jesus' experience of his own father Joseph.

3. Pope Francis, *Patris Corde*, Introduction.

Towards the end of *Patris Corde,* Pope Francis offers a powerful reflection on fatherhood. The Pontiff says:

> A man does not become a father simply by bringing a child into the world, but by taking up the responsibility to care for that child. Whenever a man accepts responsibility for the life of another, in some ways he becomes a father to that person.[4]

Francis speaks of the role a father has in introducing children to 'life and reality.' It is necessary to allow a child to be free, even to make mistakes: 'The logic of love is always the logic of freedom, and Joseph knew how to love with extraordinary freedom.'[5] The opposite of this is an overprotective and over possessive father. The child in this relationship becomes like a prisoner, made miserable by feeling constricted. As Francis reminds us: 'Every child is the bearer of a unique mystery that can only be brought to light with the help of a father who respects that child's freedom.'[6]

He then makes a profound statement. A father is one who realises that he is most a father and educator at the point when he becomes 'useless', when he sees that his child has become independent and can walk the paths of life unaccompanied. Then he becomes like Joseph, who always knew that his child was not his own but had merely been entrusted to his care. The Pope goes on to say that in the end, this is what Jesus would have us understand when he says: 'Call no man your father on earth, for you have one Father, who is in heaven' (Matt 23:9).

So many of us have been blessed to experience such loving care from our fathers. But the opposite is also the case, where some children are afraid of their fathers.

The Breakdown of Family Life in Fiji

Fiji fathers are very revered in the community. But there is also a very worrying trend where fathers do not always show love and care. Fiji has one of the highest rates of gender-based violence in the Pacific, and in the world. The statistics speak for themselves. In Fiji two out of

4. Pope Francis, *Patris Corde*, 6.
5. Pope Francis, *Patris Corde*, 7.
6. Pope Francis, *Patris Corde*, 7

every three women face violence at some stage of their lives. Women, young girls and children are the ones mostly affected by gender-based violence. Statistics show that eighty percent of perpetrators are known to the victim and they are either relatives or neighbours. In addition, fifty percent of perpetrators are either a spouse or an intimate partner. In 2019, ten women were killed by intimate partners. Recent reflections and sharing on the Year of St Joseph show that even devout men and fathers who experienced abuse and trauma in their childhood can easily repeat the cycle of violence in their own families and towards their wives and children. For some men, the only way of resolving conflict is through violence.

With the current rise in domestic violence, physical abuse, sexual abuse, and bullying in Fiji, some organisations are working with men and boys in communities, training them on how to live out their role as men and how to treat women and children, especially during this challenging time of COVID 19. There is a need to address the abuse of power and to shift the mindset of people's understanding of power.

Just as many Fijian men live with worry and concern for their families, Joseph was often afraid and troubled. When he discovered Mary to be pregnant, he could have divorced her and brought scandal and shame to the young girl, her family and the whole village. When repeatedly being asked to uproot his family and begin again, Joseph could have refused. Instead he trusted, even when it seemed foolish and even foolhardy. The quiet Joseph is there as a steady anchor in the storm.

Pope Francis offers encouragement:

> Today, in our world where psychological, verbal and physical violence towards women is so evident, Joseph appears as the figure of a respectful and sensitive man. Even though he does not understand the bigger picture, he makes a decision to protect Mary's good name, her dignity and her life. In his hesitation about how best to act, God helped him by enlightening his judgment.[7]

7. Pope Francis, *Patris Corde*, 18.

Joseph, a Model and Inspiration for all Fijians

Joseph did not look for shortcuts, but confronted reality with open eyes and accepted personal responsibility in each situation. Violence is never a solution. Trust, love and firm gentleness are the marks of a true father, a father who becomes 'useless', not because his children fear him, but because he has raised them with a 'fathers' heart' so that they have become independent and mature young women and men.

Could not Joseph become the model for fathers? Could not Joseph become the shining beacon that guides all fathers, both here in Fiji and beyond? Could not Joseph show another way to overcome conflict without violence? 'With a Father's heart, this is how Joseph loved Jesus', says Pope Francis.[8] In this year of Joseph, we pray that this quiet, humble, trusting man might become the father to be emulated. As the scriptures tell us: 'Go to Joseph' (Gen 41:55).

8. Pope Francis, *Patris Corde,* Introduction.

Saint Joseph in Perúvian Culture: A New Challenge to Notions of Manliness

Jenny Mori rsj

In the midst of this COVID 19 pandemic, Perú is going through a time of uncertainty and we need signs of hope to face it. This context provides a favourable setting to reflect on the figure of Saint Joseph, a man of deep faith who faithfully responded to what God asked of him, and who knew how to resist and face the adversities of life with hope, in unity with his family.

The pandemic has affected millions of people in the world, but especially the poorest; the most vulnerable populations are the most affected and they are suffering devastating consequences. In Perú and other countries of Latin America, we are experiencing the pain of loss of loved ones or neighbours not only because of the virus, but also because of another reality that has been aggravated by confinement—violence. Quarantine, hunger, unemployment and insecurity have caused violence to rage in all communities.

Entire families in Perú have been forced to leave their rented rooms and seek refuge in the streets or return to their towns and villages in the interior of the country, facing the fear of dying on the way. The majority of those who have carried the care of family and home, and have also suffered abuse and violence, are women. One of the main causes of this problem is *machismo*.[1]

Gender violence, caused by machismo, has been ignored for years in Perú, relegated to being considered a 'private matter'. In the last decade it has become obvious that it is a problem that affects every society in the world and has worsened during the pandemic.

1. The negative characteristics of *machismo* in Latin America typically result in physical and psychological dominance, with the male aggressively imposing his will upon women. The equivalent in English-speaking societies is *chauvinism*.

According to Dante Carhuavilca, head of the National Institute of Statistics and Informatics (INEI) in Perú, 66% of women over 18 years of age have suffered psychological or physical violence or both, and 58% of women between 15–49 years of age have suffered trauma at the hands of their partner.[2] From January to March 2020, 41,802 women suffered violence in Perú. According to the country's Women's Ministry, from January to September 2020, 91 female murders were registered and more than 3,000 women were reported missing, 2,100 of them being girls and adolescents.

Machismo is what gives support to the imaginary traditional sense of masculinity in Perú and violates women by casting them into certain subservient roles. At the same time, the notion casts men into other artificial roles as well. It is an urgent task that we work on social representations—that is, the image that has been built of what comprises masculinity and femininity.

In Perú, becoming a man has come to mean being physically strong and subordinating women by making them their property. On the other hand, when a couple marries, roles and tasks are not shared at home in an equitable and co-responsible manner. The man is the one who provides the material needs, and the woman is in charge of taking care of the house, husband and children.[3] Machismo configures the male by emphasising the body and physical strength, nullifying the expression of their emotions. On the other hand, it defines a woman and her ability to express emotions as fragile, affective and needing a man to care for and protect her.

---

2. 'La violencia contra las mujeres se ha convertido en 'La pandemia de la sombre' ['Violence against women has come into the "Pandemic shadow"'] in *Centro de investigación Económico y Social* (*CIES*), (*September 2020*) at <https://www.facebook.com/CIES.Lima.Peru/videos/328978941753727?_rdc=1&_rdr>. Accessed 28 February 2021. People who participated in that dialogue wereJorge Javier Portocarrero (moderator), Dante Carhuavilca, Daniela Viteri, Silvia A Rispeand Jennie Dador.
3. Kaarina Valer and Susana Zapata, 'Nuevas masculinidades para erradicar la violencia contra las mujeres e integrantes del grupo familiar'in *Observatorio Nacional de la Violencia contra las mujeres* (11 febrero 2019) at <https://observatorioviolencia.pe/nuevas-masculinidades-para-erradicar-la-violencia-contra-las-mujeres-e-integrantes-delgrupofamiliar/#:~:text=Bibliograf%C3%ADa,C%C3%B3mo%20se%20construye%20la%20masculinidad%20en%20el%20Per%C3%BA,el%20aguante%20en%20el%20trabajo.&text=en% 20suma%2C%20el%20trabajo%20se,masculinidad%20y%20el%20reconocimiento%20social>. Accessed 28 February 2021.

According to this reality, I want to address in this essay two features of the male figure of Saint Joseph. The traits that I am talking about are: his masculine authority sustained by deep faith, and his protective role in the home as a father. Both features come from the history of the devotion to Saint Joseph in Perú. To reflect on them, in this special year, can contribute to this task of building masculinities that allow for a harmonious, complementary and violence-free coexistence of male and female.

As Josephite women committed to building the kingdom, it is necessary to begin by saying that 'God's call at this time is to be audacious Josephite women raising our consciousness of love . . . [to] heal, include, untether, set right and serve.'[4] To heal, correct and serve requires reading reality with contemplative eyes. In this sense, reflecting on Saint Joseph can allow us to have a gospel look at what masculinity implies.

On the other hand, and coincidently, the Year of Saint Joseph joins the celebration of the bicentenary of the independence of Perú—two hundred years of republican history in which, even though there are important achievements, patriarchal colonial structures still remain. They are present in various areas of public and private life, and many systems sustain machismo and discrimination in our society. We have great challenges as a country, but overall we owe a great debt to those who have been violated and oppressed for centuries by practices which continue to these days.

To understand the context in which the devotion to Saint Joseph began and how Perúvian people perceive this male figure of holiness, we should go back to the arrival of the Spanish people and what it meant for Perú to be a Spanish colony. Part of the colonising mission was the introduction of the Catholic religion and with it, devotion to the saints. For this reason, devotion to Saint Joseph was promoted not only by the church, but even by the Spanish government and later by the Perúvian government. Bishop Dammert, in one of his writings which is part of ecclesiastical history, points out that in 1592, at the request of the Brotherhood of Saint Joseph (founded in 1560), the bishops of Perú declared that the feast of Saint Joseph was to be

---

4. Sisters of St Joseph, 'Bring Me What You Have', 27th General Chapter, October 2019.

celebrated on March 19.[5] At that time devotion to Saint Joseph had already spread to various sectors of the population who named him the patron of: parishes, chapels, monasteries, seminaries, schools, social works, ecclesiastical prefectures and other organisations. In 1828 the patriarch (Saint Joseph) was declared Patron of the Perúvian Republic and at the request of the Episcopal Assembly in 1957, Pope Pius XII ratified Saint Joseph as the patron of Perú.

Brotherhoods played an important role in promoting devotion to the saints. Many of them were made up, to a large extent, of groups of Spanish and indigenous elite. Although the aim was to introduce Christian culture, to achieve this, a network of relationships (economic, social, political and religious) was established among the members. Researchers such as Vega suggest that many of them were useful to keep a certain type of domination by the elite and the government.[6]

During this time, the Brotherhoods did not emphasize the doctrinal aspects to get more devotees, but rather promoted the religious festival. In these cultural festivals it was the emotions that they experienced in those celebrations that moved the faithful to become part of the brotherhoods. Celebrating festively as a community, giving offerings to the saint in gratitude for some miracle granted (which increased the faith of the devotee) and committing to the saint through promises to be fulfilled at the next festival, gave certain social prestige to the members of the brotherhoods.[7] It is necessary to take into account all these elements to understand religious devotion to the saints. It is from this perspective that the miracle, punishment, blessing, promise, festival and pilgrimage are understood since 'they are the key to popular religious experience in Perú.[8]

5. Bishop Dammert Bellido (1957) 'San José, patrono de la República del Perú', in *Historia de la Iglesia en el Perú*, (Lima: Pontifica Universidad Católica del Perú [PUCP], 1957): 158–159. The brotherhood of St Joseph was founded by the first archbishop of Lima, Fr Jeronimo de Loayza on 3 November 1560 at the urging of Bernardo Moreno who was a faithful devote of St Joseph.
6. Walter Vega, 'Cofradías en el Perú colonial: Una aproximación bibliográfica', in *Diálogos* 1 (1999):145.
7. Manuel Marzal, *Los santos y la transformación religiosa del Perú colonial.* (Lima: PUCP. 2005), 9.
8. Marzal, *Los santos y la transformación*, 12.

Currently, in Perú we celebrate 6,882 religious festivities during the year.[9] Sixty-three of them are in honour of Saint Joseph. The distribution of Saint Joseph festivities, per month, can be seen in the following table:

St Joseph's celebrations per month

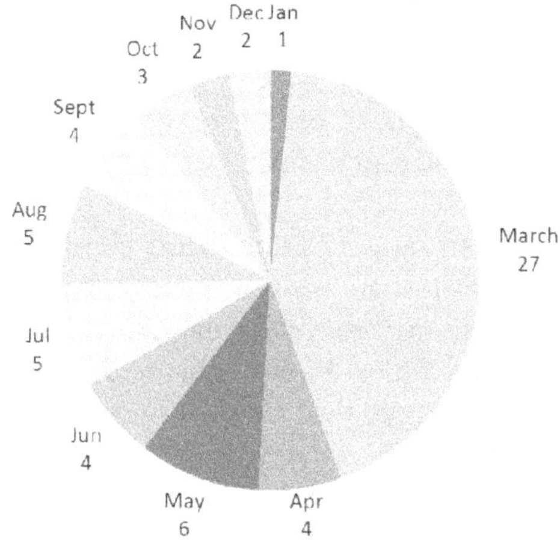

INEI (2013) Graphic created by Jenny Mori

Devotion to Saint Joseph must be read through this context to understand the imaginative impressions that people have about him.

Schenone, a famous historian of Spanish American baroque and colonial art, observes in his study about the iconography of Saint Joseph that is held in Perú, that the saint was portrayed in paintings of the time, in scenes that convey a catechetical discourse where the royal lineage, miracles, the supernatural and the divine are common themes, in addition to highlighting the European physical features of Saint Joseph.[10] The scenes are taken from the Gospel and the

9. Directorio Nacional de Festividades a Nivel Distrital elaborado por el Instituto Nacional de Estadística e Informática_INEI (2013).
10. Hector Schenone, *Iconografía del arte colonia, Los santos*, Volume 2 (Buenos Aires: Fundación Tarea, 1992). These paintings portray such scenes as: David's Family Tree; The Flowering of St Joseph's Staff; At the Inn with Mary; The Dream of St Joseph (all found in Cusco and Yucay). Two scenes worth the search are: St Joseph in conversation with Jesus, and a painting in the Parish of Accha-Cusco. In Lima, at the Church of St Joseph, there is also a painting in which Joseph takes a thorn from the finger of Baby Jesus (a reference to Jesus' passion) and Joseph being crowned with a wreath of flowers by the Boy Jesus. Paintings at the Church of the Third Order of St Francis in Arequipa depict The Burial of St Joseph and St Joseph being taken from Limbo.

apocryphal Gospels. Most of these paintings are anonymous and they are in churches, convents and museums in Cusco, Arequipa and Lima. The discourse of these pictures shows us how the authority of Saint Joseph comes from a divine royalty and his protective role comes from his sacred mission.

In an analysis of the investigation of the historian Irma Barriga about the cult of Saint Joseph, Monica Pulido points out that one of the aspects that we can see behind these paintings is the political weight of devotion to Saint Joseph, since it gave support to the discourse of authority, political power and protectorate of the viceroyalty over the colonies.[11]

Even though doctrinal and catechetical elements were not the basis of devotion to St Joseph, we can observe that what the faithful recognised in St Joseph was his intercessory, protective and comforting role in the face of difficulties. Pulido affirms that St Joseph was the person in whom Spanish people, Indians and castes found protection and consolation in the face of adversity and misfortunes of nature. St Joseph is, in this sense, the image of a man who protects and cares for his sons and daughters in life and even on their deathbed. He is the image of the father in charge of caring for the whole family. This is presented as a reality that must be accepted without question and that also has divine support.

Contained in this concept are the traits of traditional masculinity referred to previously. It helps construct an image of the sanctity and masculinity of St Joseph that responds to authoritative political and religious systems and devotees' need for protection and social recognition. In this representation, authority and power are exercised from the perspective of a protectorate that sees the other as subordinate, inferior and in need. While not detracting from faith nor from devotion to St Joseph, it is urgent that we reflect on the need to build a new discourse in our catechesis and celebrations with the people of Perú.

11. Mônica Pulido, 'Patrocinio, monarquía y poder: el glorioso patriarca señor san Joseph en el Perú virreinal' in *Anales del Instituto de Investigaciones Estéticas*, 33/99 (2009): 279–283. Historian Irma Barriga has worked extensively on the history of the cult of St Joseph in Perú. Her work focuses on the treatises of three statesmen—the Jesuits Juan de Alloza and Pedro de Torres, and the Dominica Joseph de Pastrana. Alloza highlights the paternal and docile relationship between father and child, elements that sustained political and social relations between hierarchies.

Two Gospel scenes contrast what has been developed in the previous paragraphs, and can give us an image of St Joseph that corresponds with an evangelical perspective. The first is taken from Matthew, Chapter 1. Joseph is a descendant of generations whose lineage comes from simple townspeople and from kings. In this family-line there are men and women who are noble, loyal, adulterers, infidels, foreigners and so on—saints and sinners. These are ancestors with something in common: their faith and their security in being sons and daughters of God, part of a people divinely chosen from ancient times.

Following this genealogical narrative, the evangelist closes the list with the figure of Joseph engaged to a young woman named Mary, who is also pregnant with a child not his own. Like any man of his time, his first reaction was to disown her, but secretly, so as not to put her in danger; a noble gesture for someone who is Jewish and whose social structure is patriarchal. If people found out about Mary's pregnancy and the unknown paternity of her child, it could result in her being stoned by the people of the town.

But the story continues with Joseph. In dreams he listens to an angel who speaks to him and explains the divine origin of the child's conception. Joseph, listens and obeys because he is a man of faith. He listens with an open heart to God and not with the denseness of prejudice and custom, or the role of a deceived man. He was not the owner of Mary; he was a man of faith who welcomed Mary as his wife because they were united by a sacred mission—to bring the expected messiah into the world.

Joseph is the man who lives his masculinity centered on his faith and not on prejudices or social and cultural customs. He respects and values Mary: even before listening to the angel he does not want to hurt her. His lineage, authority and role as husband and father are lived from his faith and obedience, from his respect for the dignity of the woman who was going to be his wife and from love for the child she carried in her womb, even when the baby was not his son.

This reading, contrasted with the image presented of Joseph in the colonial world of Perú, allows us to be open to faith and also to reflect on how Joseph experiences his masculinity from a more human and sensitive perspective. This is a masculinity that is not carried away by mental control or customs that cloud reason and close the heart to faith. Indeed, Joseph leads us to faith, to a just and obedient posture before a reality that he knows not only involves him, but also his people.

Dreams are the place where our deepest desires are processed and woven. The psychoanalysts Freud and Jung have extensively plumbed the depths of this topic by studying the subconscious. They have helped us realise that when men and women of faith are open to God, they instinctively stop to listen to, discern and order their affections so to do God's will. This interior movement then takes us towards the more, the something greater. We venture beyond our comfort-zone, able to take risks and make decisions. These decisions not only change our own lives, but also the lives of many other people who are part of our journey. This is Joseph's experience; he leaves his place of comfort and listens to God as his ancestors did. He takes Mary and accepts the risk. What is offered by Joseph, then, is the example of how to be a man of real courage, whose strength is to be tender and whose love is selfless.

The other scene is taken from Luke 2:41, depicting the loss of Jesus and his finding in the temple. Jesus stays in Jerusalem without his parents knowing. When Joseph and Mary realise the absence of Jesus, both return to Jerusalem. Jesus is found, and the one who speaks is Mary on behalf of both herself and Joseph: 'She said to Jesus: your father and I were anxious looking for you.' Jesus' response might seem disrespectful. A child who feels the call of God and wants to respond with fidelity, is learning along the way and does what he believes is right. Both Joseph and Mary allow Jesus the space to answer and receive what he says without further reproach, even though they do not understand what he means. According to the evangelist, Mary keeps everything in her heart. At the same time, there is nothing said about Joseph; he, too, is silent. In fact, Luke depicts him as silent throughout the whole chapter. We only know that Joseph acts, respecting his faith and his traditions, but not looking for the limelight. From him we learn how to accept the word in silence, sensitivity and kindness.

We are told that, after Jesus' reply, 'Did you not know that I must be in my Father's house?' he then 'went down with them and came to Nazareth, and was obedient to them' (Lk 2:49). Would it not be appropriate to say that Jesus learned attention to God's will from Joseph? We can surmise Joseph sees in Jesus's obedience what he himself has experienced: his desire to respond faithfully to God who calls. Just as he listened to God and obeyed in the case of taking Mary as his wife, Jesus listens to his parents, returns with them and continues to obey them. The three of them are united by love, respect, trust and listening as a family. God dwells in all three—in Mary physically in Jesus' conception, and in all three in the love that unites them as a family. Leonardo Boff, a Brazilian theologian wrote: 'In a similar way to the Son and the Holy Spirit, the Father also put his tent among us in the person of Joseph.'[12] For Boff, Joseph is the image of the Father on earth, Jesus of the Son and Mary of the Holy Spirit. This statement expresses in a simple way what unites the three, the mystery of the Trinity. They are two men, Joseph and Jesus, whose masculinity is complementary to the femininity of Mary, whose family unity is shown in the respect and love that nurtures all of them.[13] It can remind us also of the parable of the prodigal son where Jesus uses the concept of masculine compassion perhaps learnt from his parents, Joseph and Mary.

Contemplating these two passages, we can appreciate the communion that existed between the three. Joseph shows us a masculinity that is based on love, listening, trust and sensitivity. These characteristics give him authority as a male and as a father. His protective role is not unilateral but shared with his wife. It is in mutual listening, obedience and faith that they take care of each other.

The evangelic narratives of Matthew and Luke allow us to get a deeper sense of Joseph and reclaim the image of God that his life reflects to us. Masculinity and femininity lived in love and complementarity can sustain a family and a home. Made in God's image and likeness, we were created to live in communion with people and with all creation. St Joseph shows us that it is possible, through listening and discernment, to overcome customs or ways of conceiving reality that work against full life.

To be a male in Perú is not easy. Social pressure and sexist customs can suffocate the lives of both men and women. I believe that the figure of St Joseph can help us bring a different message. St Joseph

12. Leonardo Boff, *San José Padre de Jesús en una sociedad sin padre* (Santander, Spain: Sal Terrae, 2007), 119.
13. Many Perúvians would be familiar with the painting, *Double Trinity with Saint Augustine and Saint Catherine of Siena* by the Cuzco School, 1700–1730, and housed at the Museo do Arte de Lima, Lima, Perú. The painting of Bartolomé Murillo (1617–1682 from Seville, Spain,) also depicts *The Two Trinities*, the vertical image showing the Father, the Holy Spirit and Jesus flanked on each side by Mary and Joseph. This was a popular European devotion in the seventeenth century.

is the man who can help us exercise authority with love and in communion with others. His masculinity is the expression of a call to live in God from the acceptance of oneself, with one's limitations and one's virtues, and the acceptance of the people we love as part of one's life.

History may have built a skewed image regarding the experience of masculinity in Perú and which, unfortunately, has become quite traditional. However, this can be gradually transformed. This year, the Year of St Joseph, may be the gateway to reflect on masculinity from the point of view of faith and on the role of men in the family and society. This is a mission that everyone can act upon, even in very simple ways. We are not going to change the world, but we can contribute a grain of sand to this mission.

Double Trinity with St Augustine & St Catherine: Cuzco School, 1700–1730, Museo do Arte de Lima, Perú.

Why St Joseph is so Important to Timorese

Getrudes da Silva (Covenant Josephite)[1]

For at least two hundred years before anyone in Australia heard about Saint Joseph, the Timorese knew of him through the Gospel being preached by Portuguese missionaries. Many changes have taken place since the Dominican friars established their mission in the area around Lifau in the sixteenth century. In this 'Year of Saint Joseph' proclaimed by Pope Francis on 8 December 2020, I will consider how Saint Joseph relates to Timorese culture, his importance to us and how we celebrate his feastday and friendship.

How are the Timorese Related to Saint Joseph in our Culture?

In Timor-Leste we believe in both the Catholic Religion and Traditional Culture. Some of the old *mitos* (oral history) stories from our ancestors tell us that Saint Joseph, Jesus and the Virgin Mary are actually from Timor-Leste and live in a specific mountain area where Ramelau, Cablaque and Matebian stand, the three highest mountains in Timor-Leste. Our grandparents believe the story, and respect this place as holy. They do not even allow children and adults to play or disturb plants in this sacred place. Sometimes our old people gather here to celebrate by bringing traditional foods. First, they pray, asking for salvation, and then they start eating the food with the family in silence, making no noise. They believe that if they make noise or disturb the plants they will get bad luck for themselves and the next generation.

---

1. This essay is written in consultation with Josephite Companions Maria Dos Santos and Milka Pinhero.

St Joseph is usually associated with Jesus and Mary in Timorese thinking. For example, during the month of May every village organises for the community to do house to house prayer each night. We call it the month of the Virgin Mary. In the month of June we celebrate the Sacred Heart of Jesus, and the same thing happens. October is the month of the Holy Family, and of course St Joseph is part of that. Each household prepares themselves to welcome the holy statue as it travels around the village. They have to prepare a song of welcome and a poem, and they place a *tais* scarf on the statue—a sign of reverence.[2] After prayer, people gather together to have a cup of coffee or tea to celebrate together. The statue stays for a night with the family who receives it, and then on the next night another family will do the same thing until the statue is brought back to the church in procession.

While these are ceremonies to do with Christian faith, they have always been part of Timorese culture in other settings. Because the culture was oral, Timorese people have developed great skills in storytelling and poetry. Songs, stories and poems are a significant part of a ceremony to welcome important visitors, for weddings, births and deaths and for marking other significant events. When the statue of the Holy Family arrives at the house during October, we can expect that, besides the songs, the welcoming person will recite long verses about what this happening means.

The *Tais* scarf is another significant part of the cultural heritage of Timor Leste. For thousands of years *Tais* cloth has been woven by the women using techniques passed down through generations. It is used for personal clothing, and has been used in trade and for ceremonies. *Tais* scarves are given as a sign of respect and honour to guests, relatives and friends. Special messages can be woven into the pattern of the fabric to record notable happenings. An important part of enculturation by the Catholic Church is the use of *Tais* during our religious ceremonies.

The eating of food is also a traditional way of bonding. For example, when couples marry, the groom's relatives supply enough food for guests to last for days. Timorese people are well-known for being hospitable. When people unite around Jesus, Mary and Joseph, they spread peace and joy to everyone around them.

2. The *tais* scarf is hand-woven and dyed using plant products and bears local designs.

Traditional dances and music play a part in the processions leading the statue through the village and back to the church. These are vibrant and enjoyable. In times past, women would perform dances and beat small drums to welcome men home from wars. The drum is called a *babadok* and is still used when dancing in religious processions today.

By practices and celebrations, the figure of Saint Joseph has become part of Timorese way of life. He lives with us in a symbolic way. We honour him in ways that mean a lot in our culture. Jesus, Mary and Joseph are a family and our families relate to them like friends. But they are 'holy' friends, because they help us get in touch with God.

Why is Saint Joseph Important to us as Timorese?

In Timor-Leste, ninety-eight percent of the people belong to the Catholic religion. In the whole of Asia, only the Philippines have a greater percentage of Catholics. Most people, young and old, actively go to Mass and participate in church events. What is important for us is the Catholic way of life. God brings the living and the dead together in one family, so we believe in the Communion of Saints. All the saints, including Saint Joseph (patron of fathers) are in this family.

In the Gospel stories we hear about Saint Joseph living in a country that was invaded by the empire of Rome and other empires before that. People from Timor Leste have also had the experience of having another country rule us until the year 1999. First of all, Portugal had control from the sixteenth century until, with a short time of occupation by Japan during World War II, Independence was declared in November 1975. Then nine days later, in December 1975, Indonesia took over.

During the years of this last occupation, the Catholic Church played an important part in helping the people maintain their identity and in defending citizens against abuse. One important aspect of culture is language. The indigenous language of Timor Leste, *Tetun*, was in danger of being wiped out as its use was forbidden in the public forum. During a visit to Australia, Bishop Belo from Dili took a risk by asking the Sisters of St Joseph in Australia to create and support the printing of books in *Tetun* for use in schools and villages. Sisters got Timorese refugees in Australia and also priests in Timor who were experts in language to guide them in doing this. The Sisters followed up the production of the books on visits to our country where they got to know the people and helped to train teachers to use them. So in a way, Saint Joseph was active in making sure our culture survived in very dangerous years.[3]

Another reason for Saint Joseph's importance to us is that he suffered in ways that our people have suffered. Especially in 1999 and many times before that there were terrible massacres in Timor Leste. Some people had to flee to other countries for safety. It is good to think that Saint Joseph understands us because of what he went through. Saint Matthew tells the story of the massacre of innocent children in Bethlehem and of Saint Joseph taking refuge in Egypt. His faith was strong, and we remember his story as he prays with us to God to help us make our country strong now that we govern ourselves.

Since the year 2000 Timor Leste has been recovering from the many hardships it has suffered, and Saint Joseph is still helping us in a quiet way. Over sixty percent of our population is under twenty-five years of age, so education is what is needed most. When they left our country in 1999, Indonesian soldiers destroyed our schools, libraries and public buildings. They burnt any books they could find. Nearly all teachers had come from Indonesia because all education and business had used the Indonesian language. Now they had all gone back to their own country. So we were like Australia was when Mary MacKillop and Father Julian Woods began the Sisters of St Joseph. We had to start everything from the beginning.

At first, after 1999, the United Nations were here. In Timor Leste most people live below the poverty line. For hundreds of years poor people were helped by Portuguese Religious, and a number of Timorese men and women joined them to be Sisters, Brothers and Priests. Since the year 2000 many others have come to train local teachers and those serving in the medical profession. The Sisters of St Joseph started getting the books printed again. There were books for schools and also for medical clinics with instructions in basic hygiene and sanitation. All of these were needed especially in rural and remote villages. In the hungry months when there is very little food that grows,

3. At present this same ministry is undertaken by *Mary MacKillop Today*, an outreach arm of the Sisters of St Joseph.

there is much malnutrition. For example, the organisation, *Mary MacKillop Today* has found that 'approximately forty-seven percent of children under the age of five are chronically malnourished (stunted) and forty-three percent severely malnourished (underweight)—one of the highest rates in the world'.[4]

The Sisters of St Joseph got a house in Dili and asked a group of us to help them travel to far-distant villages to give basic instruction to schools and deliver food and other things that were needed for people to get back on their feet. We had a strong combie-van called 'Josie' and it was equipped with chains and everything to get through the rough, mountainous country-side.[5] Maria Dos Santos, Milka Pinheiro and Antonio de Padua were the first Timorese to work with the Sisters.[6] The aim of the program was for us to become trained and then to train others. People from Timor Leste are very musical, so music is an important part of education and training. Antonio is a pianist and he runs the musical side of the teacher program.

After a few years, the Sisters involved more young Timorese to train the teachers, so Saint Joseph's influence is growing here in Timor Leste through Mary MacKillop's legacy. Besides, the Sisters of Saint Joseph and young Timorese established the Josephite Associates (now known as Josephite Companions) in 2009. Since then many more have joined, and we hope the number of Josephite Covenants will also keep growing. We gather together every quarter and before the feast days of Saint Joseph and Saint Mary MacKillop. When we meet up we share information about the Josephite Companions and reflect on its motto (friendship, prayer and service). For service, we get a group from each parish to visit the prison and pray with them, and also visit the older people and share some food and clothing. Sometimes we are able to meet special needs. For example, we visited a widow whose shelter was dangerous when she lit the fire to cook because the covering was only loose leaves. So we built her a simple house that was much safer. Mary MacKillop said in 1899, 'Find happiness in making others happy', and that is what we did.

---

4. Mary MacKillop Today at <https://www.marymackilloptoday.org.au/what-we-do/where-we-work/timor-leste/>. Accessed 21 March 2021.
5. Editor's note: According to Sister Josephine Mitchell who pioneered the mission, the second-hand Toyota land-cruiser had been donated by the New South Wales Rural Fire Service who had refurbished the vehicle and set it up with everything needed to cope with unchartered terrain.
6. Maria and Milka became Associates and are now Covenant Josephite candidates.

In Timor Leste, some other groups who provide services to help the people of our country have also chosen Saint Joseph as their patron. Catholic schools, clinics and even suburbs and villages have been named after Saint Joseph. So we feel his presence with us in many places. Popular festivals often involve Saint Joseph. For example, in each diocese, processions are held in honour of the Virgin Mary, Saint Joseph and the Sacred Heart of Jesus. In the Dili diocese, the processions can sometimes last for four to five hours depending on where the original church is situated. The end-point is Our Lady of Lourdes shrine in the Lecidere Garden, Dili. In certain municipalities a local church may decide to have the procession in a different place.

Hundreds of adults and children participate in these processions. A typical procession is led by acolytes, a group who carry the statue (Saint Joseph, the Virgin Mary or Jesus), followed by priests, nuns, brothers and aspirants, then the choir, a church categorical group such as the Legion of Mary, Youth for Christ and Adults for Christ wearing red chasubles, and after that the rest of the community. The procession is guided by scouts in the church and there is prayer and singing during the procession. When we arrive at the designated end-point there could be a Final Mass before we go to home. For some, when the procession has taken place in the afternoon, this could be at 8 pm. But people are really happy that they can be involved in this activity, even though they might have to walk for five or six hours to get home, as there is no public transportation during the night.

I am sure Saint Joseph is honoured and happy that these Festivals provide a way of coming together and having a good time in his name and in the names of his wife, Mary, and his foster-son, Jesus. To build community is an important part of spreading the good news of God's love for us all. Saint Joseph who taught Jesus to be aware of God in ordinary life and occupations can be a teacher for everyone. I am especially happy that I have been able to play a part in the ministry of *Mary MacKillop Today* who continue to provide resources and training for teachers in Timor Leste in the name of Saint Joseph, the teacher of Jesus.

How do we Celebrate Saint Joseph's Feast Day?

We Catholics celebrate Saint Joseph's feast day on the nineteenth of March every year. Each place, school, clinic or person celebrates Saint Joseph's feast day in different ways.

Groups in suburbs or villages might organise a special Mass in their place and individuals who have Saint Joseph as their patron also go to Mass at their local church to celebrate and give thanks on this special day.

We have special songs for Saint Joseph in different languages (Tetun, English, Portuguese and Latin) which we sing at Mass and party celebrations. The celebration always starts with Mass and after that each group, school or village has a meal or party together.

For us in Timor-Leste, to prepare for a big celebration is no small thing. Sometimes we spend one or two thousand dollars to feed many people. For a Mass offering according to Timor-Leste custom we prepare a setting of goat, chicken, fruits, cassava, sweet potato, the Host, wine and flowers. To prepare for a party we have to procure a live buffalo or cow, a pig and a chicken to kill for the meal. There must be plenty of food to feed hundreds of people, so we serve rice, different kinds of meat, vegetables, fruits and drinks. All of this is accompanied by enough music and dancing to provide entertainment all night until morning.

However, during Covid-19 we have had to celebrate in different ways which has become the 'new normal'—attending Mass through television or online, and having a short prayer with our family in the house and having a celebratory meal together.

Our celebrations demonstrate the importance of community in Timor Leste. While some of these may foster competition or a sense of obligation, as long as good relationships are maintained, they can create a 'oneness' with each other and the saint whose example influences our daily lives. Pope Francis says that we can learn from Saint Joseph 'to accept and welcome others as they are, without exception'.[7] Our celebration of his feastday helps us do this.

How Have People Found Him to be a Good Friend?

When we were children, our parents taught us about the Saints, brought us to Mass every week, and encouraged us to participate in the important events of Catholic celebration in church and community. So we grew up with the Communion of Saints, and they became our heavenly friends.

7. Pope Francis, Apostolic Letter *Patris Corde,* 8 December 2020 at <*www.vatican.va* › francesco › apost_letters › documents>. Accessed 20 February 2021.

For families, Saint Joseph is a special friend, since on his feastday we celebrate Fathers' Day. If Saint Joseph's feastday falls during Lent, the celebration is quieter, and if it is during Holy Week it is moved to another date. As we greet our own fathers, and children present them with gifts they have made, we also pray for them through the intercession of Saint Joseph. We pray that, like Saint Joseph, our fathers will be humble, work hard, and be good men, fathers and servants to their wives and children. Our fathers feel so blessed and so important, standing in the company of Saint Joseph.

Pope Francis describes Saint Joseph as 'a tender and loving father'. He says,

> Joseph, then, teaches us that faith in God includes believing that he can work even through our fears, our frailties and our weaknesses, He also teaches is that amid the tempests of life, we must never be afraid to let the Lord steer our course.[8]

As a true friend and through his example, Saint Joseph will encourage our fathers and everyone in Timor Leste who have witnessed much violence to practise gentleness and peace and not be afraid when bad times come. We live in a country of great beauty. We pray that Saint Joseph will show himself 'a father, and guide us in the path of life.'[9]

8. Pope Francis, *Patris Corde*, 2.
9. Pope Francis, *Patris Corde*, final prayer.

Index of Names and Subjects

D

E

F

G

K

L

P

R

S

T

U

V

W

Y

Z

Index of Authors

F

G

H

J

K

L

M

N

O

P

R

S

T

V

W

Z

Index of Church Documents

CPSIA information can be obtained
at www.ICGtesting.com
Printed in the USA
BVHW042005291021
620152BV00002B/97

9 781922 582393